This volume grew out of the work of a
distinguished panel of U.S. and British
politicians, public officials, businessmen
and academics, who have been studying
the problems of the new political
economy in both countries. The research
findings deal with the issues of managing
America's intricate new system of
tapping private energies for public
purposes and are here published for the
first time – with each essay organized
around the theme of how to reconcile
democratic accountability with private
freedom. A number of problem areas are
identified, including the workings of the
sector of the economy dominated by the
governmentally-financed corporations,
the interaction of government and the
health care providers, the changing
nature of the university's compact with
society, the relation between 'federalism-
by-contract' and traditional federalism,
the future of the not-for-profit charitable
organizations working for governmental
agencies, and the special and growing
role of the audit function in assuring that
the new range of tasks assumed by the
government is efficiently managed in
the public interest. Separate essays
explore each topic within a common
analytical framework. Although few pat
answers emerge, the conclusions reached
by the authors will be of interest and
concern to the close observer of
governmental affairs.

Contributors to the book include:
Elmer B. Staats, Comptroller General of
the United States; Alan Pifer, President
of the Carnegie Corporation; Dael Wolfle,
former Executive Secretary of the
American Association for the
Advancement of Science and now
Professor of Public Affairs at the
University of Washington; Paul M. Densen,

ontinued on the back flap

Harvard University's Center
nity Health and Medical Care;
man of the University of
; Michael Reagan of the
f California; Ira Sharkansky
ersity of Wisconsin; Joseph
University of Pittsburgh;
onds of the University of
David C. Warner of Yale
and Harvey C. Mansfield of
niversity. Professor Bruce
of Columbia University has
olume and provided an
y essay.

Smith is Professor of Political
Columbia. University. He has
idely for government agencies
fit organizations. He is the
he Rand Corporation: Case
Von Profit Advisory
*(1966), co-edited (with
) The Dilemma of Account-
odern Government*, the
to the present volume, and
d (with G. R. La Nove) *The
Politics of School Decentralization* (1973).

The New Political Economy:
The Public Use of the Private Sector

Also by Bruce L. R. Smith

THE DILEMMA OF ACCOUNTABILITY IN MODERN GOVERNMENT
(*co-editor with D. C. Hague*)

THE POLITICS OF SCHOOL DECENTRALIZATION
(*with George R. La Noue*)

THE RAND CORPORATION

THE NEW POLITICAL ECONOMY:

THE PUBLIC USE OF THE PRIVATE SECTOR

Edited by
Bruce L. R. Smith

A HALSTED PRESS BOOK

JOHN WILEY & SONS
New York

First published in the United Kingdom 1975 by
The Macmillan Press Ltd

Published in the U.S.A.
by Halsted Press, a Division
of John Wiley & Sons, Inc.
New York.

Printed in Great Britain

Library of Congress Cataloging in Publication Data

Smith, Bruce L   R
  The new political economy.

"A Halsted Press book."
  1.   Public interest—Addresses, essays, lectures.
2.   Public contracts—United States—Addresses, essays,
lectures. 3. Finance, Public—United States—Addresses,
essays, lectures. I. Title.
JC507.S58   322'.3'0973   74-7430
ISBN 0-470-80377-0

To the Memory of Wallace S. Sayre

Contents

Preface

This book is the second in a series of studies, sponsored by the Carnegie Corporation of New York City, dealing with the problems of accountability in what we have called the 'new political economy.' An earlier volume, *The Dilemma of Accountability in Modern Government*, edited by D. C. Hague and myself, appeared in 1971 and a comparison volume will appear shortly reporting the results of reseach conducted in the U.K. at the Manchester Business School, Essex University and Glasgow University. The term 'new political economy' is intended to convey the meaning of the large, and growing, share of the public's business that is conducted outside of the regular departments and ministries of government. The economy, and large parts of the private sector engaged in non-economic activity, have become drawn into the orbit of government influence to an unparalleled degree. So great is the interpenetration between the 'public' and the 'private' sectors that this basic distinction—on which the political rhetoric and dialogue of modern times has rested—has ceased to be an operational way of understanding reality. This book, ultimately an exercise in political theory, explores the complex inter-relationships between government and other institutions partici-pating in the policy process—universities, health care providers, corporations, voluntary societies, multinational firms, and others. We seek a formulation that will help answer the question: how, in a policy process strongly influenced if not dominated by pro-fessionals, is government responsible to the people and their traditional representatives, to be made workable? We make no pretense that a definitive answer to this question is presented here or is even an imaginable goal, but we strongly believe that this question should be debated widely and constantly in a democratic society.

Thanks are due to so many people who have participated in this project that it is impossible to mention them all by name. But I have a feeling that they know how deeply their help has been appreciated. To the contributors, and the many others in and out of government who were part of the effort, I extend my gratitude. I extend special thanks to Alan Pifer of the Carnegie Corporation for his encouragement and support. My late friend and colleague, Wallace S. Sayre, played a leadership role in the project. This book is fondly dedicated to his memory.

Paul Densen's paper appeared earlier in a National Academy of Public Administration monograph, *The Administration of Medicare: A Shared Responsibility*, which I edited with Neil Hollander. It is reprinted here with permission.

Joseph Karlesky, John Fullilove, and Sharman Mather provided valuable help as research assistants. Mary Martingale and Susan McKay assisted in typing and numerous chores connected with the project.

London
September 1973   Bruce L. R. Smith

Notes on the Contributors

Paul M. Densen is Director of Harvard's Center for Community Health and Medical Care and Professor of Community Health at the Harvard School of Public Health. He has also served as Deputy Commissioner of Health for the City of New York, and Director of the Division of Research and Statistics of the Health Insurance Plan of Greater New York.

Martin Edmonds lectures in strategic studies in the Department of Politics at the University of Lancaster. He spent the 1972–73 academic year at Columbia University's Institute of War and Peace Studies completing a study of Lockhead–Rolls-Royce as a case study in public accountability. His publications include articles in *International Affairs, Europa Archiv* and *Public Administration,* and contributions to *A Nation at War* (ed. R. Higham) and *The Military Technical Revolution* (ed. J. Erickson). His current research is in Defense Analysis and in Civil/Military Relations.

Harvey C. Mansfield is Ruggles Professor Emeritus of Public Law and Government, and presently Special Lecturer, Columbia University. He received his Ph.D. there in 1932. He has also taught at Yale (1929–42) and Ohio State University (1947–65). He is the author of *The Comptroller General* (1939), *A Short History of OPA* (1949) and co-author of *Arms and the State* (1958). He has contributed chapters in other books and articles in professional journals. He served with the Office of Price Administration during and following World War II, and for shorter periods with other federal and state agencies. He was managing editor of the *American Political Science Review* for a decade, 1956–65.

Alan Pifer is president of The Carnegie Corporation of New York and of The Carnegie Foundation for the Advancement of Teaching. He is a Director of the Federal Reserve Bank of New York, an Overseer of Harvard University, a Director of The Council on

Foundations, and a member of the Senior Executive Council of The Conference Board. He is also a Trustee of the University of Bridgeport, and of the American Ditchley Foundation. He chaired President-Elect Nixon's Task Force on Education in 1968, served on the Board of The Charles Stark Draper Laboratory of MIT from 1970 to 1973, was a Director of the New York Urban Coalition from 1967 to 1971, chairman of the Mayor's Advisory Committee for the Board of Higher Education of New York City from 1966 to 1969, and a Trustee of the African-American Institute from 1957 to 1971. From 1948 to 1953 he administered the Fulbright Program in England.

Joseph Pois is Professor of Public Administration at the University of Pittsburgh. He has served as vice-president of the Signode Corporation of Chicago; member of the Chicago Board of Education; Director of Finance of the State of Illinois; chief of the Administrative Management Division of the U.S. Coast Guard and chief of the Administrative and Fiscal Reorganization Section of the U.S. Bureau of the Budget. He has been a consultant to the Department of State, the Department of Defense, to the Governor of the Virgin Islands, and to the Indian Institute of Public Administration. He is a member of the U.S. Comptroller General's consultant panel, and has prepared a comprehensive study of the General Accounting Office.

Michael D. Reagan is a political scientist and Dean of the College of Social and Behavioral Sciences at the University of California, Riverside. His other writings include *The Managed Economy* (1963), *Science and the Federal Patron* (1969), and *The New Federalism* (1972).

Harold Seidman is Professor of Political Science at The University of Connecticut and Visiting Lecturer in development administration at the University of Leeds. He was formerly Assistant Director for Management and Organization, U.S. Bureau of the Budget. He has served as a consultant on public enterprise to the United Nations, the Economic Commission for Africa, Colombia, Guatemala, Puerto Rico, Turkey and Vietnam. He is the author of *Politics, Position and Power: The Dynamics of Federal Organization* (1970).

Ira Sharkansky is Professor of Political Science at The University of Wisconsin–Madison. His bachelor's degree is from the Wesleyan University and his doctorate from Wisconsin. He writes and teaches in the fields of policy analysis, public administration, and state politics. Among his books are *Public Administration: Policy Making in Government Agencies*; *The Maligned States: Policy Accomplishments, Problems and Opportunities*; and *The Politics of Taxing and Spending*.

Bruce L. R. Smith is Professor, Department of Political Science, Columbia University. He is the author of *The Rand Corporation* 1966), and, with George R. La Noue, of *The Politics of School Decentralization* (1973); and editor, with D. C. Hague, of *The Dilemma of Accountability in Modern Government* (1971). He received the Ph.D. in Government from Harvard University.

Elmer B. Staats is the Comptroller General of the United States, appointed by President Lyndon B. Johnson in 1966 to head the General Accounting Office. He has served as a Brookings Institution Fellow, both as Assistant Director and as Deputy Director of the Bureau of the Budget, and as Executive Director of the Operations Coordinating Board of the National Security Council. He received the Ph.D. in both Political Science and Economics from the University of Minnesota.

David Warner is a lecturer and research associate in the Health Services Research program at the Institution for Social and Policy Studies and the School of Epidemiology and Public Health, Yale University. He has been Deputy Director for Program Analysis at the New York City Health and Hospitals Corporation and an Assistant Professor of Economics at Wayne State University. He received a Master's degree in Public Administration and a Ph.D. in Economics from Syracuse University and was a post-doctoral fellow at Yale University.

Dael Wolfle is a Professor of Public Affairs at the University of Washington. Before assuming that post in 1970 he served for sixteen years as Executive Officer of the American Association for the Advancement of Science and publisher of the magazine *Science*. Earlier positions included membership on the faculty of the University of Chicago and directorship of the Commission on Human Resources and Advanced Training. He has been a consultant to numerous public and private agencies on scientific and educational affairs. Among his books are: *America's Resources of Specialized Talent* (1954), *Science and Public Policy* (1959), *The Uses of Talent* (1971), and *The Home of Science: The Role of the University* (1972).

List of Abbreviations

AAUP	American Association of University Professors
AEC	Atomic Energy Commission
AID	Agency for International Development
AMTRAK	National Railroad Passenger Corporation
COMSAT	Communications Satellite Corporation
DOD	Department of Defence
ESEA	Elementary and Secondary Education Act
GAO	General Accounting Office
HEW	Department of Health, Education and Welfare
HUD	Department of Housing and Urban Development
NASA	National Aeronautics and Space Agency
OEO	Office of Economic Opportunity
OMB	Office of Management and Budget
NIH	National Institutes of Health (Department of Health, Education and Welfare)
TVA	Tennessee Valley Authority

1 The Public Use of the Private Sector

BRUCE L. R. SMITH

The sharing of authority with private and quasi-private institutions is a central feature of modern government. Novel administrative arrangements have emerged which present intricate new problems for the public and for the private sectors. Indeed, the intermingling of functions, the relationships of financial dependence on the government, and the interpretation of highly skilled manpower cadres have obliterated many of the traditional 'public-private' distinctions. A new type of public sector has emerged, drawing heavily on the energies of society outside of the formal government.[1] This development is paralleled by the transformation of parts of the private sector into something more 'public' in character. These developments have stirred wide criticism—both from those who fear 'creeping nationalization' and the aggrandizement of public power and from those who are afraid that government will be dominated by private interests. The papers in this volume analyze various aspects of this 'new' political economy and especially seek to clarify the broad public policy issues resulting from the new developments. The aim of the introductory chapter is to provide the context so that the reader can see more easily the connecting threads among the several chapters.

It has been difficult to comprehend the impact of the new developments within our traditional concepts of public affairs. The usual Weberian notions of bureaucracy (and other older organization theories) as a hierarchy of fixed offices performing standardized tasks are clearly inadequate as a description of the new public sector in the United States. The reality, in fact, is that modern government is much more loose-jointed, with a permeable outer skin, and shot through with confusing arrangements when looked at from the traditional perspective. The simple image of the government 'at the center' directing the energies of society (and of a small layer of politicians and appointed officials controlling the 'government') is at odds with the realities of how society undertakes major social programs and manages its public affairs in the contemporary world.

A growing share of the major initiatives of government is undertaken not by civil servants with a clear mandate from their superiors. On the contrary, a complex web of professional interests, representing many sectors of society, is frequently the motive force behind a new undertaking. By a process of informal interaction, an idea gains acceptance—in something akin to the process of osmosis in the biological sphere—and gets accorded priority treatment. Universities, industry, the voluntary sector then combine to share in the implementation of the project. Having shared in the process of defining society's urgent priorities in the first place, the non-governmental actors continue to shape the evolving policy goals. The application of large-scale technology to achieve social purposes is the model of this shared public–private activity. As Gilpin has shown, most of the dramatic efforts in space, defense, and atomic energy would not have been possible without the partnership effort of industry, universities, not-for-profit laboratories, and government agencies.[2] The kinds of talent needed, and the professional administrative structures required to integrate the effort, have not been available within the formal government hierarchy.

Although modern science and technology endeavours reflect the fullest extent of public–private cooperation, they are by no means unique. Increasingly, the major activities of government reflect a similar tendency to mobilize energies throughout society and to create the amorphous administrative systems that spill over institutional boundaries. Government now appears to strive routinely for a level of mobilization of social energies previously attained only in wartime. All this has created unease, confusion, and sometimes plain incomprehension among those who view public administration from the traditional perspective. Contrast the classic view of the First Hoover Commission with a statement of the modern realities:

Responsibility and accountability are impossible without authority—the power to direct. The exercise of authority is impossible without a clear line of command from the top to bottom, and a return line of responsibility and accountability from the bottom to the top.[3]

Straight lines of authority and accountability cannot be established in a non-hierarchical system. The Federal Government is compelled to rely increasingly for accomplishment of its goals on cooperation by non-Federal institutions which are not legally responsible to the President and subject to his direction.[4]

Although many observers are dissatisfied with the textbook notions of public administration, there has been no entirely satisfactory analysis that has replaced the older ideas. Various observers have groped toward a satisfactory description, using such concepts as 'the quasi non-governmental organization,' the 'modern public sector,' the 'managed economy,' 'the contract state,' and—an older idea adapted to current use—the 'pluralist state.'[5] The failure of theory to catch up with reality is of course nothing new or remarkable. Yet even the most hard-headed practitioners have felt the need along with the theorists for some larger understanding of the complex modern trends. Pragmatic improvisation has been characteristic of both British and American administrative practices, but at certain points officials as well as scholars seem to face the need to test their working assumptions in a broad critical perspective.

Some common assumptions are found in the descriptions of the new developments: recognition that government has steadily expanded its range of function (and, equally, that improved performance in traditional areas is demanded because of greatly accelerated expectations); accompanying the growing demand for services, the extraction process whereby government draws resources and skills from the populace increases the saliency of government for the public; the recognition that bigness in itself may make some nominally private entities acquire a quasi-public character; and the resulting impact of government on the internal life of the private institutions.

These ideas begin to highlight the essential features of a 'new' political economy which differs from the managed economy of the 1930s as much as the latter differed from earlier relationships. Figure 1 sketches some of the broad features of the new political economy.

Fig. 1   The Main Features of the
'New' Political Economy in Post-Industrial Society

Early Industrialization	Managed Economy	'New' Political Economy
Early and Middle 19th century in U.S. and U.K.	Late 19th and early 20th centuries	Post-World War II
Government intervention in the provisions of social overhead capital	*Laissez-faire* gradually replaced by regulation	Massive governmental intervention in all phases of social and economic life; public-private lines blurred
Episodic *ad hoc* interest groups, beginning of mass-based political parties	National trade unions and manufacturing associations, strong parties	Looser interest groups; 'military-industrial complex,' environmental lobby; weakening of parties
Gentlemen amateur and/or 'common man' tradition in civil service	Emergence of highly-disciplined, hierarchical, and professionalized civil service	Permeable civil service drawing as professional energies outside of government
Stakes of government law and order, land grants, special charters, and other favors (distributive politics)	Conditions of labor, curbing of industrial abuses, promotion of economic growth and employment, preoccupation with standard of living (regulatory politics)	Preoccupation with quality of life, 'universal entitlement,' Spaceship Earth, price stability and 'delicate tinkering' with economy (consumer politics)

THE TRANSITION FROM THE MANAGED ECONOMY TO THE NEW
POLITICAL ECONOMY

In both Britain and the United States, the process of industrialization proceeded with government in a major, if somewhat ambivalent role. The doctrine of *laissez-faire*, in breaking away from the mercantilism of an earlier era, posited a world of individuals pursuing their own economic advantage unregulated and self-directed, and in the process creating prosperity as the maximum social benefit. There was little role for government in the theory other than the provision of a stable legal framework in which contracts were enforced so that private business relationships could be conducted. In practice, however, the role of government was substantial. The social overhead capital—canals, roads, railroads, communications, and the like—that allowed private enterprise to flourish depended on public initiative. Subsidies and grants from the sovereign were common features in the amassing of private fortunes. The lines between publicly-aided enterprise and the 'pure' private sector were blurred. Government continued to behave partly in mercantilist fashion. Lively sums up the early U.S. experience: ' "Mixed" enterprise was the customary organization for important innovations, and government everywhere undertook the role put on it by the people, that of planner, promoter, investor, and regulator.'[6]

The private associational life of society was underdeveloped while industrialism was still in its infancy. Interest group activity tended to be episodic and *ad hoc* in character. The political party system with linkages to a mass public was only beginning to emerge. The government establishment was small and was manned largely by the notables and aristocratic amateurs. The stakes of politics largely involved the securing of land grants, charters, and other favors from the Crown in the United Kingdom and from the states and federal government in the United States.

The smooth continuum of history provides few tidy lines of demarcation for the scholar's convenience. By the late nineteenth century, however, it seems reasonable to suppose that a 'managed economy' had begun to emerge in which the government's relationship to society differed in important respects from the earlier period.[7] The managed economy spanned a lengthy period and contained many internal contradictions. The early phases represented perhaps the closest approximation to the free market conditions envisaged in classical economics. The private sector was no longer an infant requiring constant nurture by a paternalistic government. The private sector grew in power and influence; business activity flourished; and the giant industrial firms emerged which limited competition in ways not foreseen in the early theories of the free market. The abuses of monopoly power and unregulated economic expansion eventually gave rise to broad government intervention into the economy. This intervention was directed mainly toward regulating the terms and conditions of the productive process, and attempting to insure economic growth when breakdowns occurred in the workings of the private market place.

The institutional landscape shifted as the managed economy evolved. The small entrepreneur was no longer the dominant form of economic activity. Powerful interest groups of labor and business arose as important participants in the political process. A great increase took place in the size of the public sector, especially stimulated by the First World War and the Depression, and a professionalized bureaucracy emerged. The New Deal Era in the U.S. was both the culmination of the managed economy and the beginnings of a shift toward the still greater role for government characteristic of the new political economy.

Although conflict was intense a common assumption even among bitter enemies in the politics of the managed economy was that there was a private sector distinct from the government. The point of contention was whether a relatively greater or a relatively smaller part of the private sector was 'affected with a public interest' and thereby subject to regulation.[8] But few in the mainstream of politics doubted that there was a sphere of activity —inevitably a substantial sphere—that was removed from the domain of public action. Indeed, the rationale for public intervention was to improve the workings of a social and economic system dominated by private energies and by the clash of private interests. The implicit assumption of both business and labor was that rapid economic expansion should be sought as the source of jobs, profits, and improvements in the standard of living for both worker and employer. The political parties, with ties to a mass constituency and to organized interest groups, helped to structure the political universe so as to provide for the orderly articulation of issues.

The transition from the managed economy to the 'new' political economy can be dated roughly from World War II. Stimulated by the Depression, the War, and the technological revolution, massive government involvement in the economy— and indeed in all phases of social life, including the cultural, educational, and charitable sectors—became the norm in the postwar U.S.[9] New functions are expected of government and, in the case of established services, new standards of performance are demanded. The government is routinely expected to curb environmental abuses, promote health, education, and scientific progress, to assimilate underprivileged groups into the mainstream of social life, to stimulate innovation, and to be concerned with the vitality of most major social institutions.

The degree of intervention in the economy now goes beyond merely regulating the conditions of economic activity. Growth is no longer the consuming goal, for growth may leave behind pockets of poverty and disrupt the life patterns of many citizens.[10]

Now balanced growth, price stability, socially responsible business activity, and other goals reflecting a more delicate tinkering with the economy have emerged as the value premises underlying the economic order. In the process the government has emerged in a role of unprecedented complexity, undertaking activities of great magnitude and novelty. The government role has acted in some respects more like its role in the early process of industrialization than its later role as manager of the private economy. As provider of venture capital, intimate partner with private interests, and pervasive influence in all aspects of social life, modern government displays the paternalism of the mercantilist era.

The political battles of the new political economy involve issues of 'consumerism' more than did the regulatory concerns of the managed economy. The lines of fracture now unite labor and management on many issues under the banner of economic growth against those who seek to limit growth in order to serve non-economic values. As church and state forces, once bitter enemies, later coalesced into an alliance of Burkian conservatives, or as the landed gentry and commercial interests eventually became allies against the labor movement, so now labor and business—still rooted to an older ethic—have seen their past antagonisms diminish in the face of threatening new political forces. Consumer interests, environmentalists, Spaceship Earth advocates, neglected minorities, and others—drawing support from some parts of the labor and business communities—surface as the opposing forces.

With affluence have come new interests no longer preoccupied with the struggle to earn a living. The political battles are not merely concerned with those activities 'affected with the public interest,' for now almost everything seems so affected. There is a rebuttable presumption in favor of wider public intervention. It is assumed as an inarticulate major premise that the government can and should direct the process of social change, force-feed the economy, and provide an unparalleled range of services.

The Apollo program in the U.S. was an important symbolic event in the new political economy, illustrating both the greater capacity of government action and the heightened expectations of what government can and should do. The moon program was perhaps more important for its effect on other areas of public policy than for the technological feat itself. People naturally ask why, if we can send a man to the moon, it is not possible also to design an urban transit system, build low-cost housing, eradicate poverty, eliminate air pollution, cure cancer, and solve myriad other problems. The spirit is one of 'universal entitlement,' a term borrowed from British labor history. It is not enough that a person has a job, he or she must have a good job. A person is entitled to the best in health care, sex life, leisure, job satisfaction, and the rest necessary to develop the human personality to the fullest. The concern with the quality of life replaces the older notion of an improved standard of living.

In the new political economy, the traditional distinction between the public and private sectors has become nearly obliterated through the flow of public funds to universities, industry, non-profit institutions, voluntary hospitals, social welfare agencies, and other quasi-public entities. As with the example of the moon landing program, massive government funding (mostly spent by private institutions pursuing public purposes) causes notable shifts in ideologies and in institutional arrangements. Whole new sectors of the economy have grown up with government as the market; such firms do not find it easy to revert to competition in the private market place.[11] The interpenetration of government and interest groups has grown. New and loose alliances, reflecting wide sectors of society, contend for proprietary influence over broad arenas of public policy. There are possibilities of conflicts of interest of a new and unusual sort through the professionalized services provided by the private sector. This is something distinct from traditional lobbying since the private interests have been delegated public responsibilities and the government has assumed an enlarged role for preserving the health and vitality of society's important 'estates.'

The public bureaucracy, thus permeated by consultants and outside experts, has lost some of the hierarchical and highly disciplined character typifying the earlier professionalized civil service. The traditional political parties have suffered a partial atrophy of their organizational strength, their ties to the citizenry, and their capacity to articulate major policy issues. Although still important as the means for organizing an orderly competition for office, the parties have been less effective in framing a coherent agenda for social action and in simplifying the vastly complex issues of post-industrial society so that the citizen can see order and intelligibility in the political universe.[12] The result of the weakening of the party system is an unstable agenda of public concerns with a tendency for issues to capture the public's attention for limited periods and then to be displaced in volatile fashion by some dramatic new concern. Once again, the analogy to a pre-industrial style of politics has some application: matters of faith, of ideology, style and symbolic commitment—issues not easy to resolve within the ordinary political processes of group interests, bargaining, and compromise—become important.

THE NEW POLITICAL ECONOMY: BRITISH AND U.S. COMPARISONS

The developments I have described above, of course, have not proceeded uniformly and evenly in all parts of the economy, geographic regions, or public policy areas. No standardized or homogeneous system exists in all institutional sectors. There is a considerable overlap of older and newer practices. When one views the new political economy from a perspective broader than that of the U.S., the ambiguities in the concept and the historical overlap of the different practices become all the more evident.

The papers in this volume, although directed toward the U.S. experience, were written with one eye on the British response to similar problems. The contributors were faced with the temptation, since the American papers grew out of a larger Anglo-American research undertaking, to expand their focus but generally resisted this temptation in the interest of achieving a disciplined and coherent research volume. Yet the basic conditions in each country that helped give rise to the project and that make British–U.S. comparisons both so tantalizing and so elusive deserve brief notice. The jolt of recognition when one expects difference, and the shock of unfamiliarity on other occasions, continue to strike the observer of the U.S. and British political cultures, their differing attitudes toward authority, institutional arrangements, and ideologies.[13]

In some respects the U.S. seems farther into the stage of the new political economy than the U.K., having earlier regularized labor-management relations, taxed capital gains and corporate income, and provided credit guarantees for ailing industries. It seems possible, perhaps surprisingly, that a greater portion of the

GNP is comprised by public sector expenditures in the U.S. than in the U.K. In other respects the U.K. is more 'socialized' than the U.S. The U.K. has large segments of its industry nationalized, an established welfare system dating back at least to the Beveridge Report, the practice of directing new industrial growth into less developed regions of the country, longer experience with a Prices and Income Policy, and numerous other examples of government intervention into the economy.

In both countries there are still remnants of earlier practices and more than vestigial traces of ideologies adapted to past circumstances. But in the central features there is a remarkable similarity in the problems facing the two countries: both are concerned with the accountability of the emerging modern public sector; both are seeking ways to manage effectively highly professionalized activities; and both are attempting to use a combination of rewards and sanctions to infuse public purposes into the activities of private institutions. In the U.S. the contract arrangement (or variant thereof) has been the principal device through which the government has sought to broaden its capacities and to invent new ways of accomplishing the public's business. In Britain, more informal arrangements are typical: the contract has its functional equivalent in informal understandings between professionals within and outside the ministry. The net effect is much the same: an exchange takes place, more or less explicitly, between officials and outside professionals which results in things getting done that would otherwise not have happened so quickly nor so effectively nor at all with equal regard for the public interest. Just as many modern government tasks can hardly be imagined without the participation of private skills, the health of private institutions increasingly depends on public assistance.

Critics on both sides of the Atlantic have vigorously attacked the developing trends. The criticism falls into familiar patterns and the British or American observer of the other country needs only change the name of the players to recognize the game. There is, on the one hand, the private sector solution—that is, those who urge the government to withdraw from extensive operations and allow the private sector to carry out tasks without public interference. The energies of a free society, under this view, will better serve social needs when the government does not intervene too directly into the private economy (though, somewhat inconsistently, government may be asked to provide subsidies, preferably disguised as tax incentives, to stimulate private enterprise.)

Coupled with the above is the idea that various functions can be 'hived off' and done efficiently in the private sector. There is some ambiguity with this concept since, for some, the hiving off may mean that the private sector is acting as the government's instrumentality, while others visualize total independence from any government direction or funding and the complete return of a function to the private market place. The advocates of the 'pure' private sector solution are especially suspicious of any partnership arrangement with the government since they fear a gradual drift toward a stultifying socialism. The government should not rescue inefficient private institutions, like Penn Central, Rolls-Royce, Lockheed, and foundering universities. Let the efficient producers survive, and let the government retain its own functions by not entering into arrangements that compromise its freedom of action. A major difficulty with this line of argument is the apparent inability of the private sector to perform many desired social functions without public stimulus. If the profit motive or private philanthropy were really able to provide the desired services, why have they not done so already? There appear to be few services that society would be willing to do without if private activity did not meet the need (postal service? health care? effective mass transit?). The need for some degree of government intervention becomes apparent.

Critics of a different sort take a dim view of the private sector and call for the government to reassert its authority—to reclaim 'sovereignty'—over activities now delegated to or partially shared with the private sector. Under this view government should do more things itself and, indeed, some form of new nationalization should take place to protect the public interest. Private business has grown so huge, and in many cases has escaped national jurisdiction through the device of the multinational firm, that the nation state is badly in need of a new assertion of its power.[14] 'Old-fashioned nationalization' is believed by many on both sides of the Atlantic to have left the essential management problems largely untouched while affecting a surface change of institutional form. At least the older socialist doctrine of controlling the 'commanding heights' of the economy seems out of touch with the modern realities. Hence there is a search for some techniques of government intervention.

Although often criticized, the public corporation demonstrates great durability as an institutional form. In the U.S., a new railroad corporation, AMTRAK, and the Public Broadcasting Corporation, have been recently created. In the U.K., nationalization has been neither abandoned nor substantially modified despite some brave talk from the conservative government. A review of the British Steel Corporation, completed in June 1971, which originally sought a greater theater of operations for the private steel makers, left the corporation about 90 percent intact, raised its borrowing capacity from public funds and authorized it to proceed with a substantial capital investment program. The policy review enlarged only in limited respects scope for private enterprise operations in the steel industry. The changes affecting the role of the private steel makers did enable the government to cut some jobs. In the U.S. the reorganisation of the railroads into AMTRAK similarly permitted the closing down of some uneconomic lines.

While talking in the abstract of new techniques of public intervention, those who have sought greater control of the economy have found it hard to specify workable arrangements. The problem has been to figure out how to achieve more effective control without merely raising costs, creating privileged claimants on the public treasury, or adding another bureaucratic layer to an already large public sector. The problem seems to be less one of inventing new ideological solutions than of making the present arrangements work in some practical sense. Liberal critics are no longer confident that an enlarged government role will produce the results they seek. The simple faith in government action was eroded over the period of great expansion in the size of the public sector with only limited improvements in critical areas of social policy. Even the severest critics of the private sector usually want certain limits on the degree of government intervention. Almost everyone in the Anglo-American context is anxious to avoid a state controlled economy or a state dominated cultural life of the Soviet or Eastern European variety. This is so both because complete state domination is believed to be inefficient, as bottlenecks in the consumer economies of the socialist countries seem to demonstrate, and because the pluralist ideology of the democracies finds massive bureaucracy unacceptable.

British and American observers tend to share certain important assumptions relating to pluralism, but it is here also that the essential differences in doctrine and in practice between the two countries are highlighted. At a general level there is agreement that democratic pluralism usually requires: (1) independent centers of initiative in the society, the existence of a 'pure' private sector, both in the profit making and not-for-profit sense, that is not controlled by government; (2) a formal government that is responsive, within some limits, to outside pressures but yet which does more than merely orchestrate the energies of the rest of society; (3) a certain amount of interaction between government and the non-government sector but neither being wholly absorbed or dominated by the other; and (4) a certain looseness in the system so that new interests, economic, political, and cultural, can organize and gain access to the system.

However, difficult questions arise when one debates in concrete terms the proper limits of pluralism as weighed against the values of coherence and orderliness in policy formation. But the normal instinct in weighing the trade-offs involved here typically differs in the two countries: a greater value is usually attached to orderliness in the British context and to openness in the American. In the U.S. there is a tendency to make the assumption that 'as between an all encompassing government which can perform a vast and increasing range of services within its own offices . . . and a smaller government that performs those services with the aid of and through a larger number of enterprises in the private sector, the preference of democratic peoples is necessarily the latter.'[15] In the U.K. the impulse in the face of the loosening of the formal government structure and the drawing in of wider social energies is to structure the process under the guiding hand of legitimate authority.

The reaction grows naturally out of tradition and constitutional doctrine. The British constitution is unitary, the U.S. plural; authority and legitimacy in the U.K. derive from the crown in Parliament as agents of the people and not from the people directly. This has the practical effect of strengthening the institutional position of central government as the embodiment of legitimacy. Americans have long been fascinated with this tidy structure of authority, as they view the amiable confusion of their loose-jointed governing system. The American system is complicated by the anti-power attitudes in the political structure as compared to the deference still accorded government officials in the U.K.[16] Americans are naturally given to wonder whether the British system provides for more effective government or whether the trappings of formal sovereignty merely provide a façade and encumbrance in dealing with the complexities of the new political economy.

There is a longing for simplistic solutions on both sides of the Atlantic. Yet informed observers have recognized the need to take stock of the pragmatic improvisations and partial solutions both countries have relied on in recent years in addressing the new range of problems. In aiding a stricken industrial giant, or in providing insurance against the failure of stock market firms, or in asking universities to promote 'affirmative action' in employment as a condition of receiving federal grants, one is making implicit judgments about social needs. How many aerospace companies, shipping yards, research universities, or commuter rail links are needed in the national interest—and what strategies and rationales guide officials in attempting to answer such questions in the context of rapid change and uncertainty? Officials have seldom had a comprehensive framework of thought for viewing such issues or any systematic way to evaluate the effects of particular techniques of public intervention. What seems called for—and what the contributors to this volume in a preliminary way seek to provide—is a new public philosophy that will encourage explicit, rather than implicit, consideration of the salient issues. An open, thorough debate of the issues in broad outline and in detail can begin to spell out the main features of a modern administrative apparatus that can mobilize wide energies in society for public purposes, but still be 'steered' by accountable officials.[17] To assume that the government can reclaim all sovereignty may seem a quaintly archaic notion given the complexity of the modern state and the variety of groups that participate in the administrative process. But a central aim of U.S. and U.K. administrative practice should be to see that public purposes dominate the orchestration of private energies.

MAJOR ISSUES

The objective of this volume is to achieve a better understanding of how the new political economy works, its advantages and disadvantages, its characteristic patterns of interaction, and the points of leverage for acting on it. The papers fall roughly into three categories: broad views of the main features of the new political economy; case studies of the workings of the new political economy in a particular area; and those mainly interested in the devices and instrumentalities for managing the new system of shared public-private activity.

Although the papers differ in approach, they share certain assumptions and each in its own way addresses a common set of problems.

The contributors recognize that the range of shared functions between government and the private sector in the new political economy is vast, and that some delimitation of our focus is necessary. The primary focus therefore is on the novel problems presented by extensive devolution of powers and the sharing of functions with non-governmental institutions where such sharing has been well established and on a significant scale. The papers are not particularly concerned with activities within the traditional private sector (e.g., the exchange of goods and services in an established market, or traditional eleemosynary-type activities conducted by established foundations and charitable institutions) or with such activities that are just moving into the mixed public-private sector. Nor are the papers concerned with the well-established functions routinely performed within the government by its own employees.

The established functions, whether governmental or private, are to be sure not free from accountability problems. A highly interesting question is how an activity, once thought to be adequately performed either by government or by the private sector alone, comes to be seen as requiring a new form of administration. Occasionally, when a spectacular breakdown in services occurs, this becomes a matter of great public concern and leads to the delegation of responsibilities to quasi-public bodies. (Such an episode occurred in the U.S. in 1966, for example, when a dramatic breakdown in Chicago's handling of the holiday mail rush focused attention on the Post Office's shortcomings and played a part in the creation of an independent U.S. Post Office Corporation in 1970.) The reverse movement is also possible, i.e., the return of a function to a more traditional administrative format or the outright abolition of the mixed public-private function (such an episode occurred in the U.K. when the Industrial Reorganization Corporation intervened in a normal stock market take-over struggle involving the J. Arthur Rank organization and, by thus frustrating the normal forces of the market place, made enemies in the London financial community whose opposition played an important part in the subsequent abolition of IRC.) The focus of the present volume is, for the most part, not directed toward these interesting dynamic questions or toward identifying the 'proper' boundaries of public and private action. The contributors assume that in a democratic society there will be some tasks that remain with the formal government, and similarly that there will always remain some sphere of purely private activity both of a profit-making and a charitable character. For present purposes, it suffices to assume that there is a significant, and possibly growing, sector of shared public-private activity, and that an important scholarly task is to gain a better understanding of its workings.

The contributors also start from the premise that the flows of public funds and the management problems associated with giving and receiving money, provide a central focus of attention. Like a barium trace in a fluoroscope, the movement of public funds to private institutions can yield important information about the workings of the system. Often a condition of financial dependence grows up between the private centers of activity and the government. The effect of that financial dependency is a subtle matter to assess, since some organizations almost wholly dependent on public funds (e.g., day-care centers) behave in a completely independent fashion and some only marginally dependent (e.g., some universities) have been forced into far-reaching internal changes through the leverage of small amounts of public funds. The growing number of claimants on government monies, and their inevitable desires to improve and expand their programs, have created novel problems. Pressures for continued growth will present issues of extraordinary complexity. Price stability is a major challenge for government in the new political economy. For the first time in modern U.S. history, the federal government has faced the dilemma experienced earlier in the states and localities of having built-in increases in expenditure exceed the growth of revenues.[18] Thus at the level of macro-economic management, and in all specific programs and government grants and contracts, there is a new concern with expenditure control and with finding new ways to increase productivity in the public sector. The contributors explore the nuances of this concern against the background of complicating political factors. The public continues to insist on high levels of service while growing increasingly resentful of taxes. Many politicians and administrators fall back on the traditional devices of financing public services in hidden and disguised ways, often creating cumbersome, costly, and confusing arrangements which erode public confidence in government over the long run despite their undoubted short-run appeal.

A further common denominator in the chapters that follow is the focus on highly professionalized services and skills that are difficult to nurture within the traditional bureaucratic setting. There is a substantial claim to self-policing by virtue of the professionalized nature of the activity or the clientele groups that must participate in policy formation. The concept of 'peer-group' or outside community of professionals appears frequently in the discussions. Indeed, the professionalization of public services might be considered a useful synonym for the new political economy. The government has been called upon to perform an esoteric range of services over the past several decades that inevitably seems to require the interaction of traditional élites like lawyers and public administrators with the newer professionals and specialists. The professionalized nature of the activity enhances the experts' claim to regulate themselves according to internal professional standards —that blessed state sought by all bureaucrats—and complicates the task of the generalist who seeks to inject wider purposes into the arena of activity.

The papers cannot be summarized in any easy fashion or their complexity reduced to a tidy formula. Several major issues, however, figure prominently in much of the discussion. The critical issues, separable in theory but interrelated in practice, include the following: (1) the ways government can sustain the institutional capacities in the private sector that are needed for public purposes; (2) the need to maintain effective expenditure control in the aggregate sense and in detailed program terms;

(3) problems of dealing with the peer-group or outside community of professionals; (4) the measurement of performance in esoteric activities; and (5) the role of the politician in a world dominated by experts and professionals.

Sustaining institutional capacity

A first major issue in the workings of the new political economy might be called the 'ailing industry problem.' The problem exists, in somewhat different form, in the case of universities, business firms, utilities, and not-for-profit entities, but there are common elements in the need to find ways to provide necessary support for industries providing goods and services considered essential to the public interest without creating unhealthy dependencies that are difficult to alter in the face of changing needs. The problem is perhaps most clearly illustrated in certain areas of industrial production and transport. In the U.S. certain industrial sectors have achieved a kind of nationalized status through the device of the administrative contract and dependence on the government as monopoly buyer of their products and services. In certain sectors of transport there has been a chronic dependence on public subsidies in one form or another, and now demands are more insistent than ever in the face of rising costs and declining patronage in an automative and industrialized society. Frequently the stricken industry provides an ancillary good or service which has less claim to be carried on by the private sector or whose size and assets are not sufficiently large to provide easy adaptability to new market conditions.[19]

The theory behind the government rescue of an ailing industry is that the nation cannot afford to have a vital service interrupted. From the standpoint of the decision-maker the choice of allowing a stricken firm or uneconomic service simply to go under is almost always unpalatable since some interest is adversely affected. Unemployment, hardship, public outrage, and interest group antagonism are the expected consequences, while there is no ready constituency or articulate support in favor of saving money (though possibly the 'taxpayer's revolt' may symbolize a latent constituency that can be mobilized).

The easy answer of returning a function 'to the private sector' is seldom a realistic alternative. It is easy to see how such tasks as the Apollo moon program and the development of complex weapon systems would be impossible without public stimulus, but it is equally true that many other services desired by the public cannot be easily provided by the 'pure' (i.e., unaided) private sector. The problem of public subsidy arises as an issue only when a firm or industry is in difficulty, and thus analogies to the flourishing sectors of the private economy are not apt. What becomes important is to judge whether an activity is so critical that it must be maintained and, if so, how this can practicably be done. In practical terms, since service demanders are typically more potent politically than budget cutters and revenue providers, the question often becomes one of how to solve the immediate problems without setting a dangerous precedent and drastically multiplying the number of claimants on public funds.

One possible answer is a government corporation, such as the Industrial Reorganization Corporation that was created in the U.K. in 1967 to assist in the reorganization of lagging parts of the economy. The great Italian enterprise of this kind, Istituto per la Ricostruzione Industriale, in 1971 was the fourth largest enterprise in Europe. The New Deal Reconstruction Finance Corporation served this function in the U.S. until its abolition in 1945. In 1971 the Senate Committee on Banking reported out a modern version of the RFC designed to save the troubled Lockheed Aircraft Company through the device of bank loan guarantees, but the idea was later abandoned in favor of a more limited proposal applying only to Lockheed. The loan guarantee, as discussed in Harold Seidman's paper, has become a widely used technique in the past decade, reaching a total of $60 billion in the 1972–3 fiscal year.[20] The difficulty with this device is that it has been employed in a piecemeal fashion without clear policy guidelines. The costs, the scope and magnitude of the activity, and the purposes to be served tend to be hidden from effective public scrutiny in the resulting complexity of the administrative arrangements.

Another indication of a somewhat haphazard approach to this range of issues is the technique of informally distributing contract awards for procurement, R and D, and the like to various firms, regions, and sectors of the economy. The contract for, say, the space shuttle went to Company X and therefore it is Company Y's 'turn' to receive the next major contract from the

Space Agency. The government may thus seek indirectly to assure the survivability of a company or even a whole institutional sector deemed important to the public interest as a by-product from the purchase of a specific good or service.

Occasionally, when a region's economy is lagging, there may be an effort to steer a number of contracts from a variety of agencies to companies in that region. Something of this sort seems to have happened in the case of Long Island in 1972 when a series of contracts were awarded to Long Island companies (the Navy Department also purchased shares in one firm to see it through a difficult financial crisis). A theory underlies policy choices of this kind— principally, a vague recognition that the government's position as buyer is so powerful that it must take responsibility for planning the overall health of the economy—but the issues are seldom dealt with explicitly. The debate is more surreptitious than open, as though constrained by the clash between solving a real problem and the remnants of an older ideology difficult to shake off in which such a problem did not exist.

Only rarely have officials felt free to ventilate such matters in public debate. The result is that no clear and consistent rationale is followed, inequities abound, and sudden zigzags in policy create confusion and even bewilderment. Government purchases for specific goods and services may also broaden gradually into a commitment for long-term support of a firm or an institutional sector. Further, there is no shared understanding among the attentive public, the general public, or even the officials themselves, as to how the game is played; as one wag is said to have noted, the trouble with informal understandings is that they are seldom understood. The impression is left, even if unwarranted, that narrow political considerations always govern the award of contracts, major procurement actions, and decisions on public subsidies. The pork-barrel mentality, with congressmen and interest groups scrambling to advantage their regions, generates a momentum that is difficult to resist. In the process public confidence in government is eroded and the capacity to resist narrow, short-term interests in favor of broader national interests is diminished.

Nationalizing the economy is no solution, for it is a myth that making an activity nominally public will always mean that the general interest and not special interests are served. Nor will efficiency always be high in public enterprises. The real issues are more subtle. There is a need, first of all, for an explicit understanding of the tacit assumptions underlying the important decisions of recent years, and for an assessment of the techniques that have been used—the public corporation, regulated industry, the administrative contract in its various forms, loan guarantees, tax advantages, direct subsidies, and other devices. The magnitude of government purchases for specific goods and services has a tendency to lead to a commitment for long-term support and thereby to create a new form of regulated monopoly industry or state enterprise which will require a clarification of the respective spheres of management autonomy on the supplier's part and of policy oversight on the buyer's part. There are some hopeful signs that the kind of systematic thinking needed has begun. The Commission on Government Procurement of the U.S. Congress in 1973 issued a lengthy report calling, among other things, for a high-level review and coordinating office for procurement policy.[21] A British White Paper on Government Organization for Defence Procurement and Civil Aerospace puts the matter succinctly:

> Those engaged in defence procurement are often monopoly buyers and have to deal with monopoly suppliers. There is insufficient forward thinking about the responsibilities which are incumbent on a procurement organization operating in such an environment. Unless there is a conscious and continuing review of forward industrial needs and strengths and a continual watch on the efficiency and financial stability of its main suppliers, defence procurement can find itself compelled to support inefficient national industries or to purchase abroad when forward thinking would have prepared energetic companies at home to be responsive to new needs. Most important of all, defence procurement must accept, and exercise, responsibility for the health of those parts of industry whose survival is paramount to the defence interests of the nation.[22]

The subtle nexus of questions concerning financial dependence on the public treasury are extraordinarily complex. A large number of institutions has been created in the U.S. almost wholly dependent on the public treasury for continued support, and other more traditional institutions in society have become partly dependent on public support. There may be a tendency for harmful intrusions into the internal life of the private organizations under such conditions of financial dependency or, conversely, for the government to be forced into the position of supporting inefficient parts of the private sector. There is a need to go beyond the mere statement of the problem toward some kind of systematic policy for dealing with it. The question of institutional support versus special project support needs to be analyzed in this context. Perhaps we may need to invent long-term funding arrangements for certain classes of institutions just as foreign aid is now thought to require long-term stability in funding.

An interesting experiment was attempted in the Defense Department in the mid-1960s with the CWAS system for defense contractors (contractors' weighted average share of risk). Controls were to be relaxed and the contractor firms were to be given wide latitude to do a good job with stable funding assumptions. Although imaginative in concept the scheme was not applied intelligently in practice and was not considered a success. Former Deputy Secretary of Defense, David Packard, initiated a more recent effort to build up a design capability with wide freedom for innovation but an assessment of this effort is not yet available.[23] The difficulties of separating the special interests from the larger public interest, and of providing necessary support without creating unhealthy dependencies, are the critical issues with such efforts. There are some 40,000 defense contractors in the U.S. but only the top 200 have a sufficient level of business with the Defense Department to have any reasonable claim for deserving some form of institutional support. Yet it is difficult to contemplate guaranteeing a certain level of public support to some contractors while denying such support to others. The same problem exists with respect to universities, non-profit corporations, and other entities. The tension between the 'trust-busting' mentality and the desire for a coordinated economy of regulated giants—contradictory and unresolved elements in the American tradition—also invariably surfaces when proposals for entering into special arrangements with major firms are discussed.

In some cases it may be appropriate to wean the private sector institutions away from overdependence on a protective governmental environment and to make them behave more like the competitive private enterprises that they think they are. This certainly seems to be the need with parts of the aerospace industry;

for example, many observers believe that there is an overcapacity in air-frame manufacturing capability. But how does one decide how much capacity in a given area is enough for the national interest? And how can resources be reallocated with a minimum of dislocation and burden when a region's economy is severely affected by a cut in government support?

Some observers have called for efforts to 'constitutionalize' those parts of the private sector engaged in public business, i.e., the same sort of norms of due procedure, public reporting, and the like that apply to public government should also apply to private governments of the large corporations, universities, and other parts of the mixed public-private sector.[24] Some observers have also called for the central government, through its powers as a purchaser of goods and services and granter of funds, to place public members on the boards of directors of private organizations in order to achieve a variety of collateral ends. Such proposals could signify drastic changes in the status of private institutions and democratic societies: they need to be explored in this context to test their realism and feasability. Perhaps more important is the wide variety of managerial reforms of a small-scale nature attempted by various agencies to achieve more effective public accountability in functions performed outside the government. At any rate, some greater degree of 'planning' or at least a clearer articulation of policy goals seems almost unavoidable, and the problems of keeping costs down and productivity high, whether one thinks of universities, multinational firms, or public corporations, will remain stubborn realities.

Expenditure Control

The problem of expenditure control follows logically from the foregoing discussion. As government gets into the business of sustaining the capacities of institutions needed for public purposes, a momentum develops for continued and even expanded support for a host of private institutions. The claim naturally is advanced that a particular service is so critical that it requires state, federal, or regional subsidy. The tactic of shifting costs from lower to higher levels of government with greater tax-raising capacities for a time postponed facing up to the ultimate issue that now confronts us—the fact that, by and large, the easy sources of revenue have now been exploited even at the level of the federal government. For the first time in modern U.S. history, the continued upward drift of expenditures has reached a point where built-in costs increases exceed the increased revenue yields accompanying the growth of the economy.[25]

The resort to 'back-door financing,' the shifting of expenditures to borrowing, and numerous other devices to disguise the full cost of program initiatives, has been a venerable part of the American tradition and doubtless new displays of virtuosity can be expected in the future. But the paramount facts remain that public sector expenditures have escalated, levels of taxation are high and intense opposition exists to further tax increases (even if, by some measures, the level of taxation in the U.S. is lower than that of most Western nations), and yet there has been no diminution in the public's desire for services. Elliot Richardson, former secretary of Health, Education, and Welfare, announced upon leaving that office, in an effort to dramatize the expenditure crisis, that if all benefits existing under current federal legislation were fully claimed, the cost would amount to over $250 billion, or the equivalent of another federal budget. The dilemma suggests that dramatic new efforts in increasing public sector productivity will be likely in the future, and that the clash between President Nixon and Congress over 'impoundment' at the start of 1973 was no mere episode but a significant feature of national politics for some time to come.

The problem of expenditure control at the macro level can be broken down into smaller and more manageable parts by viewing the problems of holding costs down and keeping productivity up in the context of government support for various institutional sectors. The overall problem has some unique characteristics, especially as it relates to the issue of maintaining general price stability in the economy, and is something more than merely the sum of smaller problems that make up the whole. Yet by looking at one institutional sector that exists in a partnership agreement with the government, we may gain a clearer view of how financial dependence affects internal management, productivity, cost control, and other salient issues of the new political economy.

The college and university sector, while not the largest in dollar amount among those parts of the private sector receiving public money, provides a fascinating glimpse of the issues. In the U.S.

as well as in other countries, the position of higher education and its educational and research functions have become the subject of broad debate. The institutions of higher learning have been caught in the squeeze of rising costs. Their traditional claims to autonomy and self-governance have been increasingly scrutinized. Influential critics have questioned whether the 'productivity' of the academic community warrants the kind and magnitude of public funds which it has received in the past decade of accelerating expenditures. Important changes, as Dael Wolfle discusses in his paper in the present volume, may occur in the compact between higher education and society in this period of reappraisal.

Understanding the higher education situation in the U.S. is complicated by problems of scale, geography, and the great diversity in educational quality and practices. There are some 2,800 colleges and universities in the country, and there is such a bewildering variety in the various parts of the higher education community as to defy easy classification. Attempts at classification would have to consider numerous dimensions (public-private, church-non-denominational, land grant is a special class, colleges-universities, technical-non-technical, etc.). There is no accepted standard of compensation for professors or educational administrators unlike the practice in many European countries. Accreditation is handled by regional bodies that have no clear criteria for their work (they have, in the past, strenuously resisted accrediting any university that was run as a profit-making enterprise and only on rare occasions have they denied or withdrawn accreditation). Patterns of funding present a complex and puzzling picture. Usually, however, some mixture of state assistance, endowment income, user charges (student tuition), and federal government and all play some part in varying degrees.

Of the total number of institutions there are perhaps 20–25 great national universities that perform most of the research in the basic sciences and other areas, and these have become (especially the private universities that do not receive large state appropriations) highly dependent on federal monies. It is not uncommon for a major university to receive from 40 to 80 percent of its budget in the form of federal money. Most of the federal assistance, again in contrast to the British and European pattern, flows to the universities in the form of research support for particular projects. There is some component that can be called institutional grants and some money channeled in the form of student aid, but these are smaller in proportion to the sums spent for these purposes in other countries. The flow of project money, however, provided in effect a form of *de facto* institutional support until the steady climb of expenditures began to bring opposing political forces into play. One result of the dominant reliance on project grant money was that the country had never developed a clear policy of how to aid higher education on a stable long-term basis.[26] The forces critical of the higher education community came from both the political Left and Right in the U.S.—the Right fearing that costs were growing out of hand and the Left attacking the lack of 'relevance' and the alleged domination of higher education by the conservative Establishment. Common to both was a pervasive lack of confidence in the quality of university administration and financial management capabilities.

With the leveling off of federal funds for research in recent years a financial crisis of major proportions has struck the American higher education community. Many universities, having grown accustomed to continued federal funding for research and having expanded their programs on that assumption, have now found that the leveling off of federal support combined with the rapid escalation in costs has placed them in a precarious position. Universities have also found that the outside sources of support have brought burdensome controls. Professors and administrators complain that the form in which federal money has been given to the universities has distorted the internal priorities of the teaching and research missions. The rejoinder to this kind of complaint is that of course priorities have been distorted but that it is society's obligation to use the leverage of federal assistance to force universities to innovate and to serve society's interests more satisfactorily. If university priorities had not been 'distorted,' some critics have contended, the university community would still be teaching only classics and theology as universities did in the early nineteenth century. Critics complain that the university wants ever-increasing levels of support without being accountable to society in any meaningful way, while university spokesmen lament that their institutions now face a situation of dwindling support at a time when government controls over the smallest details of internal management are mounting.

The cross-currents and policy conflicts surrounding the problems of controlling expenditure and yet maintaining the health of the educational sector in the U.S. are complicated by the lack of consensus within the higher education community. Like the U.S. government, the higher education community is pluralistic, and the conflicting interests of its various members make it highly difficult for any interest group or professional association to speak with a unified voice vis-à-vis the government. There is little assurance that any self-policing efforts within the university community would be effective since basic budget, accounting, and management capacities are so diverse. In general colleges and universities suffer from a severe deficiency at least at the 'middle management' levels and in some cases even at the leadership levels.

Further, there is a deep political distrust and a questioning of the value of higher education stemming partly from the student disturbances of recent years, and partly from the traditional pragmatic American distrust of intellectuals. Many obervers have come to believe that the higher educational sector is over extended and that society does not 'need' the plethora of academic institutions that it now supports, especially those modeled after the Ivy League image of exclusive devotion to pure research. Some small colleges have gone bankrupt since 1970 and some further shrinkage in the number of institutions can probably be anticipated over the next decade.

The political difficulties of framing a generally accepted body of doctrine about the role of the university and a policy for providing reasonable levels of public support are further complicated by the fact that American universities have provided a variety of services to society beyond their immediate educational tasks of teaching and research. The 'multiversity' concept in the U.S. has meant that universities have been expected, as part of the compact with society which assures them continued support, to engage in activities in the service of society going well beyond the training function. The universities have, for example, provided through university affiliated research laboratories or through direct contractual ties such services as weapons development, the administration of AID programs overseas, cultural exchange programs with foreign countries, special educational programs for the underprivileged, and numerous other service activities.

Often these programs have been administered through the professional schools and not the liberal arts part of the university, but even the traditional liberal arts departments have sometimes been involved in such programs. Moreover, the requirement that universities adopt 'affirmative action' hiring practices has placed upon them special obligations in equalizing racial and sexual employment opportunities. Although it seems fair to say that the expectations that universities can undertake, effectively, non-educational functions have have been considerably scaled down over the past decade, there is no disposition to let the academic sector return to a period of relatively little involvement with the government and with public responsibilities. The amounts of public funds involved, and the expectations which many groups have of using higher education for their purposes, precludes any halcyon role at the periphery of society's main concerns.

These trends have come together to form a crisis of higher education in the U.S. Some of the basic issues are: Can the university community itself frame a coherent position of the terms under which it would like to receive support from the government, and satisfy public officials that those terms reflect a serious effort to control costs? Can the federal government (and then the state governments) formulate a more coherent set of policies guiding the ways in which it will relate to, and provide support for, the institutions of higher learning? What should be the balance between the support provided through institutional-type grants and through research funding of individual projects? There is clearly a need for something other than project support, but the difficulties of achieving an effective program are formidable. Institutional-type support for universities has some of the same objectives as revenue sharing for states and their localities: providing stable long-term funding, holding down requests for other forms of specific aid, building up a sense of responsibility and increasing management's skills at the local level, reducing burdensome controls on the use of federal monies, and the like. Yet, as Michael Reagan discusses in his paper, the institutional or bloc formula has serious defects. Effective accountability can be lost when control over specific uses of money is surrendered—and one dramatic instance of irregularity can create political shockwaves damaging to the success of the entire program.

A particular problem with the institutional formula in the context of higher education is the tendency for such an approach to work against the interests of the higher quality institutions. Given the number of colleges and universities in the U.S., the formula for institutional support tends to result in the giving of token amounts to a great many institutions on the basis of some geographic or other objective criteria. This may result in the leveling down, rather than the leveling up, of the quality of educational programs. But there is little support in the U.S. for a planned nation-wide system of higher education with specialization of labor marking the roles of different academic institutions. This reflects in part the fear that certain institutions and regions of the country would be advantaged at the expense of other parts of the country. Americans are unwilling to think in national terms alone; each region thinks of itself as having special needs for a major university, strong economic base, and cultural resources as well as other characteristics of a distinct identity. This feeling may, indeed, be more deeply rational than any effort to create a completely planned and integrated national higher education system for a country as large and diverse as the U.S.

Some spokesmen in the university community and in government, faced with the complications of the government-university partnership, have yearned for the return of the university to a more narrow and traditional role, less involved in service activities for a society, and funded predominantly through non-government sources. Although a more modest conception of the university's capacity as an agency for social action has clearly emerged in recent years, the traditionalist outlook does not have a broad base of support within either the government or the academic community. The task therefore seems to be to rationalize the relationship so as to protect the essential independence of the universities while gearing the educational enterprise broadly to public purposes. The extent to which any institutional sector can expect to derive public support is not a matter of natural right, but a reflection of its response to legitimate concerns over expenditure control and changing conceptions of public need.

Peer Group Accountability

Closely related to the problem of expenditure control is the task of holding the professional peer group accountable. Many of the major policy initiatives of contemporary government originate with a professional peer group and then gain political salience as they attract allies. The proposals advanced by the professional peer group will: (1) almost always cost money and sometimes vast sums (e.g., early childhood education programs for $25 billion, Trident submarines for $10–20 billion, new forms of health insurance, etc.); (2) will be attractive and often meritorious and always couched in terms of appeals to the wider public interest; (3) complex and not always easy for the layman to grasp (although the essentials of any problem will always be accessible to the intelligent and prepared lay mind); and (4) involve an inescapable element of professional self-interest, either relating to jobs, influence, or merely the satisfaction of seeing one's values reflected in official policy.

Like most bureaucracies the professional peer group seeks self-regulation according to its own internal criteria. The argument is that those who have been deeply immersed in the complexities of the matter, or who have devoted their lives to the delivery of professionalized service, deserve to be seriously listened to on broad policy outlines as well as administrative detail. The argument has great force both as a description of how modern government operates and as a prescription of how sensible policy is arrived at: the task is to balance professionalism against the values of democratic control. Effective cost control, responsiveness to consumer concerns, and the weighing of conflicting functional interests can best occur in a policy process in which professionalism is partially checked at every stage as a basis for judgment.

The provision of health services, as is discussed in the papers by Paul Densen and David Warner, presents a striking instance of the intricacies of infusing public purposes into an activity dominated by the professional peer group. The concept of the peer group has been a subject of special interest throughout the Anglo-American project on accountability and is referred to by many of the contributors to this volume. Although relevant in many different policy contexts, the case of health services provides a convenient handle for grasping the essentials of the problem.

In the nineteenth century, health care was regarded traditionally as belonging to the private sector. Patients visited private physicians and paid them whatever fees the doctor and client agreed upon; for those needing hospital care, there were the private institutions and the charity hospitals for those who could not pay. There were some municipal hospitals and some government regulation of the profession (e.g., in defining and determining improper practice, licensing, sanitary inspection, and prevention of epidemics, etc.). But government intervention in general was limited. The medical profession (to the extent that it was a professionalized activity at that time) was essentially self-governing. The aura of healing and dedication, then as now, played a part in influencing the behavior of medical practitioners and shielding their profession from lay criticism. There was little direct accountability to either the government (national or local) or to the consumer. The doctors in the hospitals were accountable, instead, largely to themselves—or, in the course of time, to the professional associations which claimed to speak authoritatively for the peer group.

Although there has been an enormous increase in government aid to and regulation of health care in this century, the claim to professional peer group accountability has persisted. The idea still commands a certain respect within the government and the general populace in the current debates on health policy. A crisis of health care, however, has considerably shaken the public's confidence that the medical profession is capable of governing itself in the public interest. Cost escalation is one element of the crisis. From March 1966 to March 1970, for example, hospital costs increased 14.8 percent annually. Government expenditures for health rose to over $30 billion a year in 1972, with some observers predicting that government health expenditures will rise to $60 or $70 billion by 1980 out of a total level of public and private expenditures for health of approximately $150 billion.

While costs have soared, the quality of services in some respects has deteriorated (e.g., excessive surgery, the growth of specialisms, and the decline of general practitioners, mal-distribution of services, etc.). Overall the mixed public-private arrangements for health care delivery have created confusion and a widespread feeling that effective direction, leadership and basic accountability, are lacking in the system. The simple image of the doctor or the health scientist as the disinterested healer who knows best how to organize the health care system no longer pertains, and the public's expectations of minimum standards of health care have significantly changed. There has been a strong demand for

public intervention in the provision of health services to achieve
a variety of goals, including reduced costs, more comprehensive
coverage, better delivery of services, more equitable regional
distribution of medical facilities, and other (not always compatible)
objectives.

How can the U.S. government exercise any influence or
'control' over the health care professionals and set the main policy
objectives of the system? The difficulties are immense. Inevitably
the government must attempt to deal with the existing professionals since they are the monopoly suppliers of the service, and
this limits the leverage available to government officials from the
start. Government can influence the system only occasionally,
and at great costs in energy and political capital, and mainly by
nudging the existing vector of forces marginally in a direction
which hopefully is also favoured by some influential elements
within the health care community. A usual tactic is to align
oneself with 'enlightened' interests within the community (i.e.,
those professionals who agree with your point of view) against
other interests by some combination of sanctions for the opponents
and rewards for one's allies.

The government of course is not a simple unified authority in
health matters capable of dealing with another unified authority
in the private sector. The healing arts are highly fragmented and
have been unable to establish widely accepted standards of performance for the profession. What constitutes acceptable health
care is difficult to define, and standards of medical care vary in
different areas of the country and in the different medical speci-
alties. Moreover, 'health' is affected by a wide variety of factors
other than the quality of medical care. Thus intervening in the
health policy field and defining national needs is even more
difficult than public intervention in aerospace, transport, and
defense industries.

Most observers would agree that the system of peer group
accountability still has some role to play, especially as relates
to narrow questions within the domain of traditional medical
expertise (is surgical technique X better than Y? A particular
research project in reproductive biology more promising and deserving of support than another?). The utility of relying on peer
group review breaks down, however, when one moves away from
well-defined questions within a narrow frame of reference toward

broader managerial and policy issues. At the broadest levels of the policy debate, in the fundamental decisions affecting the relationship between government and the health care providers located mainly in the private sector, the case for specialist knowledge as a basis for judgment is least acceptable. The process most likely to produce sound judgment is the continuous reciprocal interchange between deep specialized knowledge of the subject-matter and broader lay values.

In health, as in other areas, there is a longing for simplistic solutions. Some observers have stressed the virtues of the private sector and have seen many of the problems as the result of unduly restrictive control over contractor operations. Another view suggests that the mixed public-private system has not worked in the health field and should be replaced by directly administered government programs. Yet almost any reform of the health system, whatever the formal structure of the program, seems likely to result in a pluralistic mix of institutions and a substantial range of behavior influenced chiefly by peer group norms even if there were in theory direct government ownership and management of health care facilities and public employment of doctors. The difficult questions of promoting public accountability while allowing a broad measure of flexibility and independent initiatives by the professionals in program implementation, will continue to be present in one form or another.

Administering Esoteric Services

Health care is an example of an esoteric service that increasingly has characterized government activity in the new political economy. 'Health care' is not something that can be easily defined, whether by the providers or by the consumers of the service. Simple criteria for measuring improved performance in service delivery are therefore unavailable. The Social Security Administration (SSA) of the Department of Health, Education, and Welfare was traditionally concerned with establishing standards, such as eligibility for coverage, that have uniform applicability across the U.S. In its various social welfare programs, e.g., disability and survivors' insurance and retirement insurance, the problem was to write regulations that covered statutorily defined cash benefits paid as transfer payments for all Americans within a defined category. It was possible for SSA officials to interpret the regulations with high consistency anywhere in the U.S.; the agency's main job was simply to write checks to those who met fairly clear standards prescribed by the statute.[27] When the agency became responsible for administering Medicare in 1965, the analogy was made to the other 'old welfare' type of programs administered by SSA. But it became evident almost immediately that the question of coverage of services was much harder to define and the interpretation of more complex rules by a variety of health care providers and fiscal intermediaries led to numerous problems. At the root of the difficulties was the lack of a clear definition of what constitutes health and the rapidly changing public expectations of acceptable health care standards. Originally viewed as a means of guarding against catastrophic financial loss due to illness, the Medicare program only a few years after its adoption began to be seen as a means to improve the health of all Americans, and to change the nature of the health care delivery system through the leverage of federal funds.

This transition from clearcut to esoteric goals is a central feature of the new political economy, and extends beyond health care to other areas of public policy. Indeed, the goals sought by government today represent efforts of an unparalleled complexity that would have seemed beyond the reach of government in an earlier day. The shifting conception of what is possible and even obligatory for government has occurred even though by most standards governmental performance has improved. It is comforting to suppose that a more sober and realistic set of expectations will remove the frustrations that erode the underlying stability of the political order, yet examples do not come readily to mind of a high consumption society choosing voluntarily to return to lower levels of consumption, or of a people once accustomed to a high level of public services willing to settle for fewer services. The public seems likely to insist on a continued high level of services, even if not wishing to pay for them. The public wants government somehow to improve the quality of services while holding costs under control. Clearly, the standards of performance expected of public administrators will be raised. Increased productivity will be the challenge facing public administrators in the next decades. Moreover, the challenge of increased productivity comes at a time when the easy gains have

been achieved. The shift from standardized to highly
alized activities which involve new skills, a pluralistic
stitutions, and elusive policy goals means that easy p
gains will seldom be possible. The challenge is thus a d
to increase productivity generally in government activities and
to be especially concerned with raising productivity in those
esoteric services that no one presently knows how to administer
well.[28]

The areas of community development and social services
present some of the most difficult issues in the new political
economy. Although such concerns are of relatively recent origin,
the modern issues have grown out of an older tradition of private
charity and voluntary social services for the poor. The growing
involvement of this older private sector with the new social
problems, and the implications for the traditional voluntary sector,
are discussed by Alan Pifer in this volume. The new dimension
can be dated roughly from the 1960s with the War on Poverty
in the U.S. and the rediscovery of the very poor in the U.K.
(who were found to have been relatively untouched by the decade
of the welfare state). The growing awareness of the problems of
the cities—in popular usage the 'urban crisis'—originated with
the professionals' concern with physical planning and gradually
spread to other aspects of social policy. The heightened attention
to problems of community development of social services originated with the professionals rather than with the politicians or the
clienteles served. The initial emphasis was on the relatively underprivileged populations of the central city, but later broadened
to include the working poor and the interconnection between the
problems of rural and urban development. The older notions of
aid to needy *individuals* became partly superseded by the concept of broad-scale assistance to *groups* and *communities*. But
some observers, reflecting the lack of consensus in the field,
favored plans to assist the individual consumer through voucher
devices, or income guarantees, that would enable the consumer
to rely on the market place to satisfy his or her needs for social
services, education, and housing.

The initiatives of the 1960s left a complex mixture of innovative
social programs and institutional experiments addressed to the
broad problems of community development. Policy initiatives
from central government, local governmental authorities, and

voluntary (non-profit) institutions all were involved. The resulting programs defy tidy classifications. Direct transfer payments, tax reliefs and incentives, the creation of special and charitable trusts or not-for-profit organizations, assistance from the federal government to local authorities, programs directly administered by federal grants to private bodies apart from local government, community action programs, citizen involvement, subsidies to private industries—all have been attempted with varying degrees of success.

In this complex picture, however, it is possible to single out several significant trends: (1) the traditional private non-profit or voluntary bodies have increasingly had to operate in an environment of policy direction and financial support from the formal government, central and/or local, and the voluntary bodies have now reached something of an 'identity crisis' where their future role and sources of funding require clarification; (2) the national government has discovered that it cannot reach down effectively to the sources of the problems unless it works at least in part through traditional local government (the constitutional position of the states in the U.S. guarantees them a special, and probably growing, role in solving local problems); (3) many of the practical problems center around how the ideas and money of higher levels of government with superior revenue raising capacities can be implemented effectively by the local governments that are responsible for the actual delivery of services; and (4) the newer quasi-governmental bodies, satellite institutions and special authorities, and the profit-making sector are growing in importance, but often lack a clear working relationship to other parts.

The description of the U.K. given by Gerald Rhodes in the British companion volume of this book presents a fairly accurate summary of U.S. conditions:

> The picture then is one of an intricate relationship between central apartments, local authorities, and voluntary bodies in which the latter have an accepted role, varying from organization to organization and indeed from place to place, but nevertheless falling within the sphere of 'quasi-non-governmental' activities. One of the most striking facts about these voluntary bodies is their number and range.[29]

The proper mix of responsibilities between the national government, local government, and the private bodies engaged in social services remains the central objective. There is little likelihood of a complete reliance upon a private sector solution (either profit or non-profit) or on a public sector solution. The task is not only to orchestrate a vastly complex web of institutional relationships but to do so in the context of discovering new ways to administer certain services which no one yet fully understands or knows how to administer effectively.

In recent years a good deal of emphasis has been given to the development of new management techniques, such as planning-programming-budgeting, management-by-objectives, productivity, and evaluation. Such techniques have been designed to aid central executives and policy-making officials in their quest to manage the increasingly complex tasks of the modern public sector. The practical effect has been to centralize and consolidate power. Curiously, there is a contradictory thread evident in recent administrative theory and practice. The centralizing techniques contrast sharply with the drive to open up administration— to decentralize power into smaller units, to encourage participatory arrangements that give the consumers of services and lower-level workers a share in decision-making.

President Nixon's efforts to reorganize the government in 1972, to cite one example, reflected this dual thrust in calling for 'super departments' and tighter control over the executive branch, along with revenue sharing and grant consolidation to push responsibility downward in the federal system to state and local governments. Alice Rivlin, in her lucid summary of the uses of systematic analysis for social action, urges that program evaluation be more widely used in the federal government and at the same time greater accountability be fostered (in her usage 'accountability' means wider involvement of clientele groups or consumers of government services in the policy process).[30] These seemingly conflicting tendencies need to be resolved in administrative thought and practice. They add a further complex dimension to the task of administering the esoteric services of the new political economy: can power and functions be more widely shared, by loosening up the formal government structure, while at the same time we seek to establish effective evaluation, control, and central guidance?

The politician and the expert

The twentieth century has been considered the age of the ascendency of the expert and a decline of the traditional politician as chief architect of policy. Although the generalization considerably overstates the case, there is no blinking the fact that serious issues are raised for traditional democratic theory by the emerging professionalization of public policy. As the work of modern government becomes more complex, and official ways of doing public business more numerous and subtle, there is a natural tendency for the politicians to find it harder to keep in touch with events and to follow trends, let alone to participate effectively in the policy-making process.

The role of the elected representatives—and, broadly, the relationship of Congress to the executive branch—poses a particularly difficult problem. The shifting of the day-to-day work in certain policy fields from the purely governmental arena to the quasi-governmental sector in some ways has placed the legislature at an added disadvantage vis-à-vis the executive. With a program one step further removed from direct legislative scrutiny, the capacity of congressmen to perform the vital function of intelligent lay critics in the political system may be impaired. And if the legislative role is diluted, can the other sources of intelligent lay criticism within the political system—the mass media and the specialized public opinions which follow certain policy fields— partly substitute for an active monitoring of public affairs by elected legislatures? Comment and criticism in the legislative body is made openly for the public record and within the discipline imposed by having to face re-election. It seems clear that, however active and useful the media and private watch-dog groups may be in stimulating political discussion, a special authority and legitimacy is attached to what the elected legislator does that cannot normally be matched by outsiders. It is in this context that the case for making the Congress better informed with greater staff resources has been put so often over the past decade.[31] There is no substitute for the political scrutiny of the elected representative. A serious problem exists if the legislature has been weakened by the trend toward a more complex public administration that is trying to affect a more complex world.

The actual impact of the new-style public administration is, however, more subtle and difficult to grasp than is suggested by the simple image of the legislature losing its prerogatives and powers. The legislature has in fact remarkably strengthened its role in some respects as an overseer of executive activity.[32] The new ways of accomplishing public tasks may partly work to the advantage of the legislature and enlarge its opportunities for influencing events. As the formal government is 'loosened,' and the restraints of executive secrecy and discipline are potentially weakened, the legislative body might have greater access to the policy process. One can thus imagine an effect quite opposite from the atrophy of Congress, namely, that it may unduly aggrandize its role by forming close alliances with private bodies outside the reach of executive discipline.

In speaking of the Congress, we must recognize a complex mixture of roles and interests: the elected leadership, the committees, the individual congressmen, and the Congress's own permanent bureaucracy of some 1,000 professional staffers. Staffs which grow too large present difficult managerial problems to heavily burdened congressmen, and there is already something of a problem in holding committee staffs accountable. The legislative role remains vital, and it seems clear that modern legislators need more and better information if they are to discharge their responsibilities fully toward understanding and monitoring the modern public sector. But it is difficult to come up with reforms, especially suggestions for increased staffing, data processing facilities, or specialized advisory apparatus for the Congress, which do not raise more problems than they solve. The arguments for making the Congress even better equipped than it is today with staff resources to scrutinize the details of government administration holds the danger of entangling the legislator in such a web of professional alliances that disinterested criticism becomes difficult.

The legislator's major functions in the modern period should include: injecting wider public purposes into the arenas of activity monopolized largely by professionals; reacting loudly when something goes wrong in the working of the new political economy; and in general helping to sustain general public confidence in the legitimacy of the governing system by making sure that any new program goes through a process of open debate, deliberation, and consensus building before adoption. The quasi-public sector needs to be sufficiently integrated into the regular political system so that when something goes wrong, a 'warning bell' will ring. Conversely, useful programs need to be shielded from destructive and uninformed criticism.

New government programs of recent decades are both durable and fragile: durable because they have created a broad base of political support by engaging many diverse interests in a program's administration; and fragile because they can be destroyed by muckraking enemies. A chief difficulty in balancing the objectives of program continuity and of vigorous scrutiny is the difference between the political and the scientific time constant. The politician works necessarily within a frame of reference oriented to a particular term in office or to well-defined stages in his or her political career. He or she wants to affect the world and make a difference within a limited time span, sensitive always to the evolving wishes of a constituency. The professional sees a problem from the point of view of taking limited steps over a long period of time so as eventually to reach a coherent goal. The large objectives of modern government, e.g., eliminating poverty, new energy sources, curing cancer, cleaning up the environment, clearly require under this perspective stable long-term efforts in order to achieve success. There is no easy way of reconciling these divergent but necessary perspectives in the policy process. But it is clear that there should be people who perform the task of criticism who are outside the broad 'community' of interest groups and the most involved government officials who work closely with the interest groups in a particular arena of policy. The best way to ensure penetrating criticism as well as credible support is to place the 'warning bell' function in the legislature —beyond the control either of possibly rather partial and over-sympathetic allies of the program or its muckraking enemies.

A partly alternative approach to obtaining public accountability from the modern public sector would discount political answerability in favor of commercial or objective criteria. A poor performance would automatically register when financial or technical criteria were routinely applied: failures would be dealt with by experts and officials. It is highly doubtful whether such an approach would prove viable or acceptable in the Anglo-American democracies. It is unlikely that any major public policy functions could be insulated from political debate by these advanced management techniques and virtually certain that none could be following a serious or protracted failure or crisis. The centrality of politics and of elected officials will not be eclipsed by technocratic expertise even in the complex contemporary world.

Yet great demands will be placed upon the Congress if it is to discharge its responsibilities effectively in the modern period. It is difficult to see how the Congress can have an active interest at all in the vast and loosely connected web of government-related activities (of which the formal government is itself only the relatively hard center) unless its members and committees can cope easily with such distinctions as (project-bloc-institutional-categorical' grants, 'loan guarantees-subsidies-tax reliefs,' 'statutory-proprietary-voluntary,' prices and income policies, 'multi-national-international,' and other complex ideas in their pursuit of an understanding of what is actually going on. Wherever reasonable voices are raised, calling attention to a matter of apparent public interest, the legislator should feel able to exercise his interest and scrutiny, although it would be wise to do so lightly and with discretion where largely private interests are involved. There is no reason why a free ranging, but responsible system of legislative inquiry should not manage a broad coverage of public affairs commensurate with the expanded reach of modern government.

The legislative role, finally, can be most effectively exercised if the affinity between fellow generalists in the Congress and in the high-level policy positions within the executive branch becomes fully appreciated. The recent battles between the President and Congress on war powers, executive privilege, and impoundment, create the false impression that conflict is a matter of opposing institutional perspectives. In reality, the lines of fracture in the political system are much more subtle, and place the high-level executive officials and congressmen in the position of carrying on the same dialogue if not always with shared goals. The task of the President and of Congress ultimately is to make government sensitive to popular wishes, and in this quest their common enemies are those with specialist and parochial perspectives who seek to insulate government from lay scrutiny in the interest of bureaucratic self-regulation.

CONCLUSION

Modern government is vastly more complex than the image of a central sovereign issuing authoritative orders to the periphery. Instead of standardized tasks, the novelty, complexity, and magnitude of public functions today are striking. The reality is that government in the Anglo-American pluralist democracies is loose-jointed, with a permeable outer skin, and shot through with confusing arrangements when looked at from the perspective of traditional distinctions between the public and private sectors. All this in a general way has become apparent, but the implications of these developments for the theory and practice of modern administration require clarification. A basic question is whether the partnership arrangements between the government and the private sector will endure. The modern public sector will inevitably be an arena of political controversy because many of the innovative and significant public functions will be carried out through devolution and sharing arrangements. But general public confidence in the new ways of doing government business is essential if we are to avoid drastic swings in policy and the eruption of destructive ideological conflicts.

The anti-institutional moods in the U.S. in recent years, starting with the attentive public and eventually filtering into the general public mood, have raised the question of whether any institutions, public and/or private, can be effective and whether the incentives for leadership can be nurtured anywhere in the society. The anti-institutional values—spontaneity, involvement, individual self-expression—are not to be dismissed lightly, for these have meaning for officials who administer programs and function within the institutional context. But perhaps we should be on guard against embodying all the contradictions of the age in our governing institutions. People ultimately want the government to have the capacity to govern. Tyranny is to be feared less from a strong government than from a weak government lacking the capacity to manage the explosive conflicts of contemporary society. This view suggests a process of balancing conflicting objectives within a system of mutual restraints. The absence of revolutionary zeal may disappoint some readers grown accustomed to the apocalyptic utterance in our media-conscious age. Perhaps we might do well to recall that genuine human progress seems to have been advanced most readily in those societies least afflicted by dramatic upheavals.

Notes

1. See Bruce L. R. Smith and D. C. Hague, *The Dilemma of Accountability in Modern Government: Independence vs. Control* (Macmillan and St Martin's Press, New York and London, 1971). See also Anthony Barker, D. C. Hague, and W. J. M. Mackenzie, *Public Policy and Private Interests: the Institutions of Compromise* (Macmillan, London, 1974).
2. Robert Gilpin, *France in the Age of the Scientific State* (Princeton University Press, Princeton, N.J., 1968).
3. Hoover Commission, *Report on General Management of the Executive Branch*, 1949, p. 1. See also Luther Gulick and L. Urwick (eds.), *Papers on the Science of Administration* (New York, Institute of Public Administration, 1937) pp. 1–45, esp. p. 6.
4. Harold Seidman, *Politics, Position, and Power: the Dynamics of Federal Organization* (Oxford University Press, London, 1970) pp. 29–30.
5. See *inter alia*, Don K. Price, *The Scientific Estate* (Belknap Press of Harvard University Press, Cambridge, Mass., 1965); Michael D. Reagan, *The Managed Economy* (Oxford University Press, New York, 1963); H. L. Nieburg, *In the Name of Science* (Quadrangle Books, Chicago, 1970); Alan Pifer, 'The Quasi Non-governmental Organization,' 1967 Annual Report, Carnegie Corporation of New York City; Kenneth Boulding, *The Grants Economy* (Wadsworth Press, forthcoming); and John Kenneth Galbraith, *Economics and the Public Purpose.*
6. Robert A. Lively, 'The American System: A Review Article,' in Stanley Cobin and Forest G. Hill (eds.), *American Economic History: Essays in Interpretation* (J. B. Lippincott Co., Philadelphia, 1966) pp. 178–96.
7. See Michael Reagan, *The Managed Economy* op. cit., ch. 8, 'The Expanding Economic Role of Government,' and Galvin B. Hoover, *The Economy, Liberty, and the State* (Anchor Books, Doubleday & Co., Garden City, N.J., 1961) chs. 7–10.
8. For a discussion of the early development of the doctrine of 'affected with a public interest,' see Dexter Merriman Keezer and Stacy May, *The Public Control of Business* (Harper & Brother, New York, 1930) chs. v and vi. For later cases and commentary see William B. Lockhart, Yale Kamisar, Jesse H. Choper, *The American Constitution: Cases and Materials* (West Publishing Co., St Paul, 1970) pp. 319–46, especially note *Nebbia v. New York*, 1934, p. 320: 'It is clear that there is no closed class or category of business affected with a public interest. . . .'
9. Seidman, loc. cit., p. 31. See also Galbraith, loc. cit., for a comprehensive treatment of the emergency government role.
10. See John Rawls, *A Theory of Justice* (Belknap Press of Harvard University Press, Cambridge, Mass., 1971), as an example of the changing

conceptions of equality and differential rewards as being justified only if leading to greater benefits for society's disadvantaged: in an earlier day the individual was thought to deserve whatever his efforts would gain and by advancing him or herself the overall interest of society would be advanced.

11. See Don K. Price, *The Scientific Estate*, op. cit., ch. 2.

12. Walter Dean Burnham, one of the chief advocates of the erosion-of-the-parties thesis, sees a 'top-bottom' coalition against the 'great middle' as a likely basis for future political battles in the U.S. See his *Critical Elections* (Norton, New York, 1970). This thesis is imaginative and has considerable appeal; its chief difficulty is that it does not conform to the available evidence. Cf. James Sundquist, *Dynamics of the Party System* (The Brookings Institution, Washington, D.C., 1973).

13. On Britain's 'civic culture,' see John M. Gaus, *Great Britain: A Study of Civic Loyalty* (University of Chicago Press, Chicago, 1929).

14. On the multinational firm, see Raymond Vernon, *Sovereignty at Bay* (Basic Books, Inc., New York, 1971).

15. From a background paper by John J. Corson prepared for the Anglo-American Conference on Accountability held at Williamsburg, Va., September 1971. See also Corson, *Business in the Humane Society* (McGraw-Hill, New York, 1971).

16. On the origins of the anti-power attitudes in the U.S., see James S. Young, *The Washington Community: 1800–1828* (Columbia University Press, New York, 1966).

17. What is meant by steering or 'control' is not an easy matter. The medieval Latin word for 'control' has gone separate ways in English than in other European languages. In the latter, it seems to be primarily procedural, a process of 'checking up,' relating to audit and traditional fiscal accountability. In English it has come almost to mean 'sovereignty,' a residual entitlement to assume full responsibility for command to make one's orders effective. Both elements should somehow be included, although it is clear that something is missing in each formulation. Traditional audit gets at only part of the process and, if pushed too far, may defeat the creativity and initiative that are sought.

18. Charles Schultze, *et al.*, *Setting National Priorities, the 1973 Budget* (The Brookings Institution, Washington, D.C., 1972).

19. See Weidenbaum's essay in Smith and Hague, loc. cit., pp. 129–47, for a discussion of the government-oriented corporations.

20. See the Seidman essay below.

21. *Report of the Commission on Government Procurement* (U.S. Government Printing Office, Washington, D.C., 1973), 4 vols. and index vol.

22. White Paper on Government Organization for Defence Procurement and Civil Aerospace (HMSO, London, April 1971) Cmnd. 4641, p. 23.

23. See R. W. Nichols, 'The Coming Salting of Defense R & D,' *Innovation*, No. 26 (Nov. 1971) pp. 45–56.

24. Arthur Miller, 'Accountability and the Federal Contractor,' *Journal of Public Law*, Emory University Law School, Vol. 20, No. 2 (1971) pp. 443–478.

25. See Charles Schultze, *Setting National Priorities, the 1973 Budget*, ch. 1.

26. 'The worst thing about our system of research grants,' as Don K. Price notes, 'is that it has been used to put off any federal policy for higher education.' Testimony in *National Science Policy*, Committee on Science and Astronautics, U.S. House of Representatives, 91st Cong., 2nd sess., July 7–Sept. 17, 1970 (U.S. Government Print. Off., Washington, D.C., 1970) p. 9.

27. This is the kind of case Theodore J. Lowi has in mind in his prescription for 'juridical democracy,' i.e., a bureaucracy that can function within neatly circumscribed and defined limits. See his *The End of Liberalism* (Norton, New York, 1969). It is evident that few policy areas in modern government reflect such a simple role for the administrative official.

28. On productivity and evaluation, see Alice M. Rivlin, *Systematic Thinking for Social Action* (The Brookings Institution, Washington, D.C., 1971), and 'Symposium on Productivity in Government,' *Public Administration Review*, Nov./Dec. 1972.

29. Gerald Rhodes paper in companion volume to this book, as cited in note 1.

30. Rivlin, loc. cit., ch. 6.

31. E.g., John Saloma, *Congress and the New Politics* (Little Brown & Co., Boston, 1969).

32. See, *inter alia*, Raymond H. Dawson, 'Congressional Innovation and Intervention in Defense Policy: Legislative Authorization of Weapons Systems,' *American Political Science Review*, Vol. LVI, No. 1 (Mar 1965) pp. 42–57; William E. Rhode, *Committee Clearance of Administrative Decisions* (Michigan State Bureau of Social and Political Research, East Lansing, Michigan, 1959); and Joseph P. Harris, *Congressional Control of Administration* (Doubleday and Co., Anchor Books, Garden City, New York, 1965).

2 New Problems of Accountability for Federal Programs*

ELMER B. STAATS

If I were to ask you as public administrators and political scientists what principally comes to mind when one refers to accountability, I suspect that most of you would reply in terms which would relate accountability as it bears upon our constitutional separation of powers—principally between the executive and the legislative branches.

Article II of the Constitution provides that the President 'shall take care that the laws be faithfully executed. . . .' It further provides that 'he shall from time to time give to the Congress information on the state of the Union.' In other words, he is accountable to the Congress for carrying out legislation enacted by it.

This aspect of accountability is certainly a timely one. The temptation is great to develop it at length. We hear much these days about 'executive privilege,' questions as to the President's authority to commit armed forces to combat, criticism of the President for impounding funds appropriated by the Congress, charges of a credibility gap in information made available to Congress, and so on. Concurrently, we hear more and more frequently that Congress has lost its 'coordinate' position with the executive branch, that government has become too large and too complex for adequate legislative oversight, and that the President —thanks to television—overshadows any similar figure or group of figures in the legislative branch, and thus has an overpowering natural advantage in molding public opinion.

* This paper was presented originally before the annual conference of the American Society for Public Administration in Denver, Colorado, April 21, 1971. Because of the passage of time, some of the figures in the original paper have been updated.

An equally challenging and tempting aspect of accountability is whether the Congress has weakened its capability to exercise adequate legislative oversight because of its outmoded procedures and because of its preoccupation with details and hence insufficient attention to major program issues. This is a familar story to all of us. Perhaps some of you have made these charges yourself.

But, I shall resist these temptations. Instead, I would like to develop a different but increasingly significant aspect of accountability. It is not unrelated to accountability of the Congress to the electorate, nor to the subject of separation of powers. Indeed, it is impossible to separate them. I am referring to the problem of accountability as it relates to the increasing use of organizations outside the federal establishment in carrying out governmental programs.

The idea of carrying out governmental programs through nongovernmental organizations is not a new one in our history. It is as old as the Erie Canal, land grants to the railroads, and the Morrill Act to support land-grant colleges.

What is new is the sharply increased dimension in recent years of the use of instrumentalities not directly administered by federal employees—the private corporation, the quasi-governmental organization, non-profit groups, international organizations, and state and local governments. The forms of sponsorship are many, ranging from federal charters to subsidies, from contracts to grants. But they all have a common denominator in that they are not administered directly by federal employees; they share accountability to their own management and to the federal government.

It is a fundamental tenet of democratic society that individuals, organizations, or groups entrusted with public funds and responsibilities must be held accountable for carrying out their activities faithfully, efficiently, and effectively. This need for accountability applies not only to organizations supported wholly with public funds but to those financed only in part with public funds or those established by governmental charter.

Some have described this mixture of governmental and nongovernmental arrangements as the 'contract state.' Others have described it as a blurring of the lines between the public and private sectors. Still others see it as a dangerous and unhealthy situation in which the government is in danger of losing—or has lost—its ability to act in the public interest. The phrases 'military industrial complex,' 'educational industrial complex,' and 'medical industrial complex' are used to describe what some consider to be an unholy alliance between government and industry under which the taxpayer and the general public come out as losers. Still others fear that accountability will bring with it governmental controls and the seeds of destruction of our pluralistic society.

For others, the issue—whether the growing trend is or is not desirable—is an academic one. They consider it inevitable and that the future will see an even more extensive use of such organizations.

As these people view it, the issue, therefore, is how the government can hold these organizations accountable without losing the essentials of ingenuity, creativeness, and initiative which we have associated throughout our history with independent groups in our society. This is the view which I hold.

This latter thesis has been ably voiced in the project sponsored by the Carnegie Corporation under the heading of 'Accountability and Independence.' Through joint United States-British conferences, through a series of papers commissioned for a conference at Ditchley Park in Britain, and through additional papers commissioned for a meeting in Williamsburg in 1971, the importance of preserving both accountability and independence has been underscored and highlighted.

In this fiftieth anniversary year of the Budget and Accounting Act, it is particularly timely to focus our attention on this apparent dilemma. While the subject is not exclusively one of federal concern, the extent of delegation or contracting with external groups has gone further in the federal government than in state and local governments. It is also an area of interest to me as head of the United States General Accounting Office—a major concern of which is to assist the Congress in its legislative oversight responsibilities.

A listing and highlighting of the principal forms of delegation will help emphasize the importance and ramifications of the subject.

FEDERAL SUPPORT OF INTERNATIONAL PROGRAMS

Since World War II, the United States has been a major contributor to various international organizations, especially the United Nations and its specialized agencies, and the international financial institutions.

Let me cite a few statistics:

—United States subscriptions in the International Monetary Fund stand at $6.7 billion;
—United States subscriptions to the World Bank now total $6.3 billion;
—over the last decade, U.S. contributions to other international lending institutions, such as the Inter-American Development Bank, the International Development Association, and the Asian Development Bank, totaled more than $4 billion;
—during the same period direct contributions to the United Nations and its specialized agencies, and the international organizations totaled more than $3.2 billion.

In recent years there has been a pronounced tendency toward transferring a greater portion of United States foreign assistance funds to international organizations. Certain characteristics of these organizations, particularly the *fact* of their being international, create perplexing problems in devising adequate techniques to obtain accountability. We must start by recognizing that membership in international organizations presumes a willingness on the part of member nations to rely heavily upon the management of these organizations, an agreement which severely limits action that can be taken unilaterally.

For example, developmental assistance carried out through the specialized agencies of the United Nations involves the international sovereignty, so to speak, of these agencies. But this sovereignty must somehow be reconciled with the need to obtain sufficient financial, management, and program data to assure the contributing nations that the programs of these agencies are being carried out effectively. This information is needed, of course, for the United States to determine the type and level of support it should provide these agencies. The General Accounting Office has reviewed many of these programs and in many instances concluded that not enough information is available to the United States to make a valid assessment of their operations or results.

What is needed to overcome these inadequacies? We considered the possibility of audits by the United States and other member nations but discarded the idea as unwise and impractical. We concluded that the better course for providing accountability lies in pushing for better financial controls, program evaluation, and budgetary systems within these organizations. We recommended, and the Department of State is recommending, that the United States support the establishment of a single United Nations review body to make independent evaluations of United Nations developmental activities.

Following the recent announcement by the President that the United States would seek increasingly to channel its development assistance through multilateral organizations, the Department of State reorganized its Bureau of International Organization Affairs to strengthen the Bureau's ability to monitor and evaluate the programs and activities of the United Nations and its specialized agencies. This reorganization followed closely a plan we recommended to the Department and to the House Foreign Affairs Committee. This reorganization will provide greater assurance to the Congress that channeling more aid through multilateral bodies will still afford reasonable oversight of expenditures channeled through these organizations.

With respect to the international lending institutions, GAO has similarly been concerned that there be a top level management review body in each international institution reporting to its governing board, as contrasted with the limited lower level audit activities reporting to the operating officials of the banks. This goal has already been accomplished at the Inter-American Development Bank.

FINANCIAL ASSISTANCE TO STATE AND LOCAL GOVERNMENTS

The national debate now taking place on grants-in-aid and revenue sharing is of special interest to those interested in the subject of accountability. Grant-in-aid programs increased from $2.3 billion in 1950 to $29.8 billion in 1971, an average increase of 12 percent a year. By comparison State and local revenues have increased about 9 percent a year. Approximately one-fifth of all state and local funds are now derived from federal grants. By 1973 Federal grants plus $6.6 billion of sharing amounted to $44 billion.

Human resource programs—education, manpower, health, and income maintenance—account for more than half of all federal grant funds. The Department of Health, Education, and Welfare alone made federal aid expenditures in the form of grants totaling over $12 billion in 1970, $14.7 billion in 1971, and $18.9 billion in 1972. This compares to total grant expenditures made for the entire government as federal-aid to states and local governments during 1970 of nearly $24 billion, and $36 billion during 1972. It is expected that total federal-aid expenditures will increase to over $51 billion during 1975.

For the future, the federal budget for 1972 stated that 'this year promises to be a turning point in the history of our federal system.' It notes that the President's proposals for financial assistance to state and local governments, included a program for general sharing of federal revenues for fiscal year 1972, estimated at about $5 billion during the first year.

In the debate on grants-in-aid and revenue sharing the basic question focuses on the primary purpose of such assistance. Is the primary purpose to support programs for specific *national* needs, financed in substantial part with national revenues and accounted for to the national government? Or is their prime purpose equalization of the tax burden under a system of federally-collected, locally-administered revenues?

The President, in his 1971 message to the Congress on general revenue sharing, took note of the issue of accountability. He pointed out that many people believe that the best way to hold government accountable to the people 'is to be certain that the taxing authority and the spending authority coincide.' He disagrees. His conclusion is that accountability really depends in the end 'on how easily a given official can be held responsible for his spending decisions . . . not where the money comes from, but whether the official who spends it can be made to answer to those who are affected by the choices he makes.' In brief, the President concludes that the spending rather than the taxing is crucial in the accountability issue.

The dilemma is posed by the fact that the President recommended against allowing the application of the civil rights and equal employment laws to be determined by state and local governments. These would continue to be subject to federal audit and federal control.

'Special revenue sharing,' essentially, is a program to consolidate categorical grants. The President's proposal, however, contemplates vastly increased local discretion to allow local determinations on program priorities within broad categories to replace judgments of federal agencies and to provide for minimum accountability to the federal government as to how these funds are expended.

I doubt if there is any issue in our generation which has posed the issue of accountability more sharply.

Will the Congress, which must raise the revenues, be willing to settle for the discretion and delegation to state and local government which the President's proposals contemplate? Can we find alternative ways of achieving accountability short of the detailed and burdensome requirements which we have today in so many of our grant-in-aid programs? Will the special interests—concerned with, for example, child care, aid to the mentally retarded, or water pollution control—be satisfied to allow the need for these programs to be determined by the state and local governments? Will cities who adopt 'neighborhood-level' governmental units be able to hold such units fiscally accountable?

Whichever way the issue turns, our attention has been focused sharply on the capability of state and local governments to audit programs and to evaluate their effectiveness.

The GAO took the leadership in an effort to develop auditing standards which will more clearly define the nature and quality of auditing of these programs needed to provide managers and policymakers, including legislators, with information and independent evaluations on what is done and what is accomplished with the funds expended. We also are developing a model state audit law and a model municipal ordinance. With the adoption of revenue sharing, the application of such standards may well become the major—perhaps the only—accountability tool remaining for the federal government.

FEDERAL CONTRACT RESEARCH CENTERS

Closely allied with the issues associated with grants-in-aid and revenue sharing is federal government assistance to scientific research. During the last twenty years, the federal government's assumption of expanded responsibility for scientific research has led to increased reliance on contracting with private non-profit organizations. One of the first of these was the Rand Corporation, started in 1946 as an Army Air Corps project at Douglas Aircraft Company. Two years later, it was organized as a private non-profit corporation, a model since followed in the establishment of other similar research organizations.

By the early 1960s, the number of similar non-profit corporations created by the defense agencies had expanded greatly. The increased need for strategic analysis led to the formation in 1956 of the Institute of Defense Analyses, used by the Joint Chiefs of Staff. Other well-known non-profit corporations sponsored by the defense agencies include:

Analytic Services, Inc. (Air Force)	1958
Logistics Management Institute (DOD)	1961
Research Analysis Corporation (Army)	1961
Center for Naval Analysis (Navy)	1962

During this period, the Air Force's need for systems engineering and technical management resulted in the creation of the Mitre Corporation in 1958 to serve in developing electronic and command control systems. The Aerospace Corporation was formed in 1960 to provide technical direction in missile and space programs. The System Development Corporation was spun-off from Rand in 1956 to provide operationally oriented training and other technical support for control information and processing systems. Finally, the Johns Hopkins University Applied Physics Laboratory, established in 1942, has been used by the Navy for technical advice on missile and space programs; the Laboratory is a government-financed laboratory, operated as a division of the University. Non-defense agencies such as AEC, NASA, and the National Science Foundation also sponsor non-profit research corporations.

One of the most recent non-profit research corporations is the Urban Institute, established in 1968 to study urban problems.

In 1970 the National Area Development Institute was established by Spindletop Research, a non-profit corporation in Lexington, Kentucky, with assistance from Ford Foundation, to serve a similar purpose with regard to small towns and rural areas. Recently announced are plans to create an Environmental Protection Institute to provide a similar role for the Environmental Protection Agency.

By 1967 the Office of Science and Technology and the Federal Council for Science and Technology had identified sixty-eight federal contract research centers, with varying degrees of autonomy and having highly differing purposes, including seventeen sponsored by the Department of Defense. Funding of these centers increased from $1.1 billion in 1962 to over $1.5 billion in 1970.

Much has been written and said as to the merits of these centers, sometimes referred to as 'captive' organizations. The word 'captive,'at least in the early days, was appropriate since most were not permitted at that time to undertake or receive funds from any organization other than the sponsoring agency. The policy has since changed for most of them.

Supporters of these centers argued in behalf of their establishment that they could be organized more quickly than a new unit in the governmental establishment; they frequently could borrow personnel and resources already available at a university location; and, most importantly it was argued, they would not be subject to the painstaking accountability and administrative requirements of the bureaucracy with respect to salaries, budgets, reporting, etc.—matters of long-standing concern to governmental in-house establishments.

But this very independence has also been the source of problems. How truly independent can an organization be, it is asked, if its life depends upon a year to year budget allowance from an agency or even a subordinate unit within an agency? Why should an organization fully or chiefly supported with federal funds be permitted special privileges or advantages not given to those in the federal establishment? One student of the subject summed up the dilemma of the federal contract research centers in these ironic terms: the principal issue with them currently, he said, is how to preserve the strengths which caused these centers to be established in the first place; that is, how to preserve professionalism and independence when their future is tied up so closely with the funding of a particular organization.

With increasing scrutiny and restrictions, especially from the House Appropriations Committee, these centers have been pushing for diversification of support and at least one has been cut loose from government sponsorship and functions in the private sector.

And the end of the story may not have been told. The question is asked—if we have the ingenuity to create a special purpose Langley Research Center or a National Institute of Health, why cannot we likewise establish the necessary flexibility and autonomy within government? Can the sponsored research center, in short, have it both ways—freedom from market-place competition on the one hand and relative freedom from accountability to government on the other?

RESEARCH AND DEVELOPMENT IN COLLEGES AND UNIVERSITIES

Another significant measure of federal support of science is the growth of grant and contract funds to universities. The National Science Foundation plays a major role in such support. Statistics compiled by this agency show that obligations for research and development conducted by colleges and universities more than doubled from $800 million in 1962 to $1.7 billion in 1970. The 1972 budget contemplated nearly $2 billion. Its goal is very broad: to insure the vitality of research efforts; to develop and support research efforts to increase our understanding of the problems of society and their solution; and to advance the Nation's economic growth and welfare.

This research also provides for the training of science and engineering graduate students through employment on the research projects and helps develop needed capabilities in academic institutions to undertake research on important national, regional, and local problems.

It is not possible in the limits of this paper to outline the full significance and implications of the federal government's relationship to colleges and universities as it provides funds to carry out specific projects and programs or to encourage research and training in areas of national interest. Essentially, the basic questions, however, are the same as with other organizations: What does society get from its investment? How can assurances be provided that the objectives sought with such funds are being achieved? How can assessments be made in a way which will not interfere with academic freedom or stifle initiative? Is there a choice, in other words, between the roads which lead to ever-increasing government control of our universities and falling back to the level of support which can be provided them through endowments and private philanthropy which have been relatively free from such control?

GOVERNMENT-OWNED, CONTRACTOR OPERATED PLANTS

In obtaining the goods needed by the government to carry out its programs, the question of whether to make or whether to buy is the first question that must be answered. When it decides to make, the government often invests in plants and equipment and then contracts with the private sector to operate the plants.

The Department of Defense and the Atomic Energy Commission both make extensive use of private contractors to operate government-owned industrial plants. In fact, most of the work in achieving AEC goals is performed in government-owned facilities under contracts with industrial and educational or other non-profit organizations. By the end of fiscal year 1970, these AEC contractors had approximately 106,000 employees engaged in operations and 9,000 in construction work. In comparison AEC itself had 7,548 full-time employees. Contracts with 350 prime industrial contractors in 1970 amounted to $1.6 billion. In the same period, the Department of the Army had 28 active GOCO industrial plants whose operating expenses exceeded $1.1 billion.

It can be seen that this technique is, essentially, that of procuring the management talents of the private sector. The government exerts varying degrees of control over the activities of contractors that operate GOCO plants. These controls are intended to achieve a variety of objectives. They are not necessarily directed to increasing plant efficiency. For example, needed equipment modernization or replacement that can be justified by the economics involved may be rejected by the government agency because of other demands for funds having higher priority.

The traditional incentive to efficiency—increased profit—is also absent since most GOCO contracts are cost reimbursement contracts where the contractor's profit or fee is fixed at the outset and the contractor is not rewarded for reducing costs. The government must therefore find the yardsticks to measure the management effectiveness of these contractors.

Yardsticks used by the AEC include (1) developing standards for direct labor and direct material, where applicable; (2) developing financial and personnel plans on the basis of expected workload; (3) comparing actual performance with planned performance; and (4) conducting formal appraisals of individual plant operational segments. One of the most promising objective means of measuring management effectiveness that can be used at GOCO plants and which should receive more attention is the industrial management review or 'should-cost' analysis.

NEGOTIATED PROCUREMENT

The federal government is the private sector's biggest customer. From 1949, when the Federal Property and Administrative Services Act centralized civilian procurement, the dollar value of all U.S. purchases of supplies and equipment increased from $9 billion to over $50 billion. Nearly 90 percent of these purchases is in the form of negotiated rather than formally advertised bid procurement. About one-half is negotiated with a single supplier, known as sole-source procurement.

Where the government can buy competitively in the market place, the normal market mechanisms can generally be relied upon to assure that the goods are procured at fair and reasonable prices. But negotiated procurement—especially *negotiated sole-source* procurement—requires other controls to insure reasonable prices to the government.

Some have even raised the question as to whether the major defense contractors, whose entire business depends upon government consumption and whose sales to the government are predominantly negotiated, are losing their status as private corporations.

A great deal of interest has been stimulated in improving government procurement procedures. For example, the Department of Defense is increasing its use of 'fly before you buy' procurement. GAO has recommended greater emphasis on 'should cost' analysis to find ways in which the government and the contractors can reduce the cost of weapon systems by applying improved management and engineering techniques in carrying out the contracts.

The far-ranging studies of the Procurement Commission, established by the Congress in 1969, completed its work in 1972 and produced many significant recommendations for improving government procedures for acquiring goods and services at fair prices.

GOVERNMENT UTILIZATION OF PRIVATE
ENTERPRISE FOR SOCIAL PURPOSES

A relatively new and different technique for attaining federal objectives other than through grants and subsidies to private institutions is the chartering of separate and independent organizations which may or may not receive initial or continuing funding by the federal government. Many are intended to be self-supporting. Here are two illustrations of this technique.

Job opportunities in the business sector—Jobs Program

The Jobs Program, initiated in 1968, represents a joint effort by the government and the private sector to find meaningful employment for disadvantaged persons. The National Association of Businessmen was established as a private, independent, non-profit corporation for the purpose of stimulating private business firms to hire and train the disadvantaged. The goal of the Jobs Program was the employment of 614,000 hard-core unemployed in 125 cities by June 30, 1971. The National Association of Businessmen sought to attain this objective by creating awareness, involvement, and commitment in the business community to stimulate them to provide jobs and training for such persons and advise the Secretary of Labor on how the government can help meet this objective.

GAO reviewed the operation of the Jobs Program and concluded that, in spite of growing pains and many remaining problems, it has been effective in focusing the attention of businessmen on the employment problems of disadvantaged persons and in eliciting broad responses and commitments by many private employers to hire, train and retain the disadvantaged. By the end of June 1970, more than 15,000 companies had hired persons under the Jobs Program and almost one-half million jobs had been pledged to be placed.

Medicare program

The Medicare program was established in 1966 to provide persons over the age of 65 with hospital and physician care. Physicians' services and other medical and health care is provided through a voluntary Supplementary Medical Insurance Program. This program is administered by private carriers through contracts with the Secretary of HEW. The carriers' functions include:

—determining the rates and amounts of payments on a reasonable charge basis;
—determining the medical necessity of the payments; and
—receiving, disbursing, and accounting for Medicare funds.

By the end of 1970, 19.2 million persons were enrolled in this program and forty-nine carriers had made benefit payments of about $1.5 billion.

I think we can look forward to even further use of the private sector for a range of social-purpose programs. In his Health Message to the Congress in 1971, the President called for the establishment of health maintenance organizations—known as HMOs—to upgrade the delivery of health services to U.S. citizens. The HMOs are intended to bring together a comprehensive range of medical services in a single organization so that a patient is assured of convenient access to all of them. These medical services are provided for a fixed contract fee which is paid in advance by all subscribers. There is thus a strong built-in incentive for greater efficiency.

An advantage of using private organizations for social-purpose programs is the ability to develop highly flexible relationships with the persons being served. But to the extent that delivery of services is decentralized, accountability problems become more acute. A 'built-in' accountability discipline—such as the profit incentive of the proposed HMOs—thus becomes increasingly important.

SPECIALLY CHARTERED QUASI-PUBLIC ORGANIZATIONS

In addition to the utilization of private enterprise for social-purpose programs, a number of quasi-public organizations have been established to carry out functions which traditionally have been wholly committed to the private sector. These quasi-public organizations were created to fill the gap between what the private sector had been able to deliver and what the government felt was required in the public interest. Here are three examples:

Corporation for Public Broadcasting

In 1967 Congress established the Corporation for Public Broadcasting to provide financial assistance for non-commercial educational television and radio broadcasting. This non-profit corporation seeks to strengthen and improve educational radio and television by providing an independent source of funds. It also operates and interconnects its own stations. Although independent of the government in its operations, it thus far depends upon appropriations by the Congress to finance its operations. Having no independent source of income, it remains subject to influence by the President and the Congress through the appropriation process beyond that contemplated when established.

Communications Satellite Corporation

At the dawn of the space age in the early 1960s, the Communications Satellite Corporation (COMSAT) was incorporated as a profit-making corporation with the goal of establishing, in co-operation with other countries, a commercial communications network. Financially, this corporation is completely independent of the government since it finances its operations through issuance of capital stock to the public.

Dual responsibility to its stockholders and the government can cause a dichotomy in its operations—for example, the State Department can direct COMSAT to provide communications for areas of the world that are unprofitable and therefore not in the interest of its shareholders. COMSAT also must depend upon NASA for launching of its satellites, and its operations are regulated by the Federal Communications Commission.

National Railroad Passenger Corporation (AMTRAK)

A more recent quasi-public corporation—the National Railroad Passenger Corporation—was created by the Congress in 1970 to provide intercity railroad passenger service. This action was in response to the threat that railroad passenger service might disappear. By 1970 there were only 500 passenger trains in service in the United States compared to 20,000 in 1929. AMTRAK is chartered as a private, profit-making organization financed principally by common and preferred stock; is authorized to operate intercity trains and make contracts with railroads or other companies for use of facilities and equipment; and can rely on railroads to provide manpower.

Although the accountability problems associated with the quasi-public corporations are similar to those relating to private enterprise organizations established for social purpose programs— that is, preserving independence and the advantage of market mechanisms—an additional factor to consider is that they compete with other private sector corporations. Thus there is inevitably a danger that federal support of this type of quasi-public corporation, if not carefully controlled, may tend to undermine the effect of private sector competition which may be the very reason for being of the quasi-public corporation. One way to avoid this danger is to insure that these quasi-public corporations are not too greatly dependent upon income from the federal government, at the same time recognizing that such assistance is clearly required to achieve the purposes of the corporations.

EXPANDING ROLE OF FEDERALLY SPONSORED FINANCING AGENCIES

A special type of quasi-public corporation is the federally sponsored financing agency. From their initiation in 1917, their role has grown to the extent that their operations play important roles in the allocation of monetary and fiscal resources. The five presently in existence are:

Federal National Mortgage Association,
Federal Home Loan Banks,
Federal Intermediate Credit Banks,
Federal Land Banks, and
Bank for Cooperatives.

Each was, at one time, either wholly or partly government-owned. Now they are entirely privately owned and are not included in the budget of the federal government. They were established by the Congress to meet national objectives in the area of agriculture and housing and, although now privately owned, are still under government supervision.

The Federal National Mortgage Association is the largest in scope of the federally sponsored financing agencies, being involved mainly in the purchase and sale of FHA insured and VA guaranteed mortgages. In 1970 the outstanding debt of these agencies totaled 35.8 billion. Over fiscal years 1970 and 1971, the estimated net increase in outstanding debt of these agencies amounted to more than $18 billion.

Besides affecting the housing and agricultural programs they were designed to aid, the policies of these agencies are affecting overall economic stabilization policies of the government. Some fear that these agencies, created to supplement the activities of the private sector, are becoming the dominant institutions in these areas. These people would prefer to have the operations of these institutions subject to federal budgetary control.

DELEGATION INVOLVES MIXED PUBLIC PURPOSES

The accountability issue is clouded and made more difficult by the fact that the government, in the various forms of delegation or contracting outlined above, is seeking to accomplish, in most cases, more than one public purpose. In most if not all of these arrangements, the government has the option of direct operations. Its decision not to do so may be influenced heavily by the fact that other—and frequently conflicting—objectives are sought by the use of external organizations:

—Strengthening private enterprise.
—Supporting educational institutions.
—Fostering international cooperation.
—Encouraging private investment as a means of lessening public expenditure requirements.

I would not argue, as does Peter Drucker, that government is inherently incapable of efficient management, and thus should limit itself to a policy role, but many thoughtful students of government argue that pluralism in carrying out government programs, like pluralism in the private sector, may in and of itself be an objective which should be encouraged. It would be difficult to conceive of a situation where we attempted to carry on all federal activities through direct federal operations.

There must be a balance between accountability and delegation. We now realize the Defense Department's total package procurement concept, for example, which resulted in Lockheed's problems with the C5A aircraft and the Cheyenne helicopter, is not a viable arrangement. We now recognize that the government must have a continuing, intimate, day-to-day relationship in monitoring development and production problems when a weapons system is being purchased which pushes the 'state of the art.'

The opposite extreme is the extent to which the National Science Foundation once insisted on over-detailed accountability by requiring 'total effort' reporting for academic scientists who received grants from the National Science Foundation. Either extreme is to be avoided.

THE AUDITOR'S ROLE IN MANAGEMENT AND PROGRAM EVALUATION

Perhaps some of you think of the auditor as the accountant whose role is limited to certifying as to the adequacy and completeness of financial statements. In such terms, his role is important but limited to evaluating whether there has been an adequate disclosure of financial data to the Congress, to the executive, and to the public.

This aspect of accountability, which I refer to as fiscal accountability, is only a part of the auditor's role. For example, the National Association for the Advancement of Colored People complained to our Office that a financial audit of grant-in-aid programs by state auditors was of little value if the auditor was unconcerned as to whether the program achieved the congressionally intended purpose. The stockholders of a major corporation not long ago sued a public accounting firm who certified as to the adequacy of the firm's financial statements shortly before the company went bankrupt. Their opinion was too limited, it was argued, in that it did not analyze basic management problems of the company.

Indeed, the Budget and Accounting Act of 1921 contemplated that the auditor would be concerned broadly with the 'receipt, disbursement, and application of public funds. . . .' Similarly, the Legislative Reorganization Act of 1946 directs the Comptroller General to make expenditure analyses to 'enable Congress to determine whether funds have been economically and efficiently administered and expended.' More recently, the Legislative Reorganization Act of 1970 calls on the Comptroller General to review and analyze the results of government programs and activities as well as to make studies of costs and benefits of such programs.

The responsibility of the auditor in the GAO embraces three aspects of accountability:

—fiscal accountability, which includes fiscal integrity, disclosure, and compliance with applicable laws and regulations;
—managerial accountability, which is concerned with the efficient and economical use of personnel and other resources; and
—program accountability, which is concerned with the results or benefits being achieved and whether programs are achieving their intended objectives.

An accountability system should embrace all three elements. There must be public confidence as to fiscal integrity in the spending of public funds; there must be assurance that waste does not occur through mismanagement; and, there must be a way to assess whether programs are accomplishing their intended objectives with due regard to costs.

I do not intend to imply that the auditor has an exclusive, or even necessarily the primary, responsibility for management and program evaluation. Other analytical staffs and other systems of review are also available to the administrator. Too frequently, however, such staffs have been primarily concerned with budget formulation and program planning and not sufficiently with whether on-going programs are achieving their intended result. This is the area to which the auditor has a major and increasingly important contribution to make. He has a tradition of making his findings independent of the operating officials; he is increasingly equipped with special skills which go far beyond that required for financial audits alone; and, most importantly, he is increasingly looked to by the legislature and by the executive for studies and recommendations on all three aspects of accountability.

ACCOUNTABILITY WITHIN THE EXECUTIVE BRANCH

It should be emphasized that, in any accountability system, the legislative branch is concerned with how well the manager is informed with respect to his operations; whether he has the necessary staff to deal with operating problems; and whether he is adequately evaluating his program accomplishments. When the Congress, for example, uncovers vast irregularities in the post exchanges and commissaries of the Defense Department, its natural question is why the Defense Department had not identified and dealt with the situation. When the Congress is frustrated for lack of reliable information as to whether the economic opportunity and elementary education programs are working, a natural question is what evaluations have the agencies made and what resulted from them. When the Congress is called upon to increase funding for international organizations, the natural question is how much does the State Department or the Treasury Department know about the effectiveness of international loans and technical assistance.

It is important, therefore, that the legislative auditor carry out his responsibility in part by auditing the agency's system of accountability—finding out whether internal audit is on top of its job, whether management has the information it needs to prevent cost over-runs, whether it has the analyses to justify additional funding, and so on. This concept is fundamental in that it places the emphasis on accountability at the point of primary responsibility; namely, the agency head or the President.

BY WHAT TEST SHALL WE JUDGE PERFORMANCE

Unlike the market-place test of sales and profits, the government auditor seldom can apply an equally concrete test of costs and benefits. Sometimes he can make cost benefit studies in quantative terms. Usually he must search the legislative history, the appropriations hearings, and the translation of sometimes broad statutory charters into statements of program objectives of the operating

—How do we assess the impact of a model cities or a com-

agency. He must examine evidences of program impact, of good or bad coordination, and alternately perhaps he must exercise subjective judgments based on his own experience as a trained analyst and on the conclusions reached by management or by the recipients of the benefits of the program. In short, there is frequently no established 'par for the course' by which to judge performance.

The problem is even more sharply focused when government operates through an external organization.

> munity action program designed in large part to promote citizen action and social change, complicated still further by the fact that funds may come from several agencies—public and private—under differing statutory provisions?
>
> —How do we isolate the impact of United States foreign economic assistance from the political climate and the economic development efforts within an underdeveloped nation?
>
> —How does the auditor reach a conclusion on how well research grants are administered in a given university?

The form and extent of accountability, moreover, cannot be divorced from the legislative or the political climate at a particular point of time. All of a sudden people have discovered the meaning of the words 'ecology' and 'environment.' These have now become household and schoolroom words. Ralph Nader has become something of a national ombudsman. Weapon systems, cost overruns, and efficiency have become frequent headline items and matters of concern to the entire Congress, not just to the Appropriations and Armed Services Committees.

CONCLUDING REMARKS

The conclusions for my remarks can be summed up briefly:

> —The trend toward using external groups by government will probably increase in the years ahead.
>
> —Congressional and public concern with respect to accountability systems will grow as government increases in size and complexity.
>
> —As the concern for accountability increases, we must seek

new ways to evaluate management and program effectiveness, keeping in mind that under our separation of powers the executive branch will continue to have the primary task in the accountability system, and

—Finally, as we recognize the need for, and as we can provide for an adequate and well-understood accountability system, we will also be serving the objective of a more responsive system of government, and a more democratic society.

3 The Jeopardy of Private Institutions

ALAN PIFER

Private non-profit institutions serving the public good are one of those special features of American life so much taken for granted they have long since become obscured in a haze of familiarity. And yet, if one has occasion to observe life in a nation where all activities are functions either of the state or of a single, authorized political party, the value of independent private institutions, to our perception of a good society, becomes freshly and arrestingly apparent.

Nevertheless, a high proportion of our private educational, cultural, health, and welfare institutions are heading into deep trouble increasingly affected by social and economic forces they are powerless to withstand. The steady, unrelenting deterioration of their position has now, for the first time, raised doubts about the continued public and private endeavor. For varying reasons, the American people at large and most of their political leaders seem either unaware of the situation, or unconcerned. In an age notable for the gravity and complexity of its problems, this problem, as important as many others with which we are currently obsessed, has simply failed to make its mark on the national consciousness.

Why do private service institutions matter to our society, and why is their continued existence in jeopardy.

THE PRIVATE COMMONWEALTH ENTERPRISE

The private non-profit sector of our national life can be thought of as having three parts. The first of these is the spontaneous coming together of citizens in support of causes which enlist their interest or excite their passions. These groups are often transitory, usually operate on limited funds, and seldom have professional staff. Evidence of the vitality of this part of the non-profit sector was provided in the celebration of Earth Day in April 1971. In the New York area alone, more than 200 voluntary organizations —ranging alphabetically from 'Action for the Preservation and Conservation of the North Shore of Long Island' to 'Westchester Students for Cleaner Environment'—joined in dramatizing the ecological crisis.

A second part of the non-profit sector consists of that vast array of private local and national associations, nearly all enjoying tax exemption, that are devoted to the economic or social interests of *particular* groups of the population. Here we find labor unions, trade associations, agricultural organizations, chambers of commerce, real estate boards, country clubs, fraternal and employee beneficial societies, teachers' retirement fund associations, mutual credit unions, mutual insurance companies, and many others. This portion of the non-profit sector is also thriving.

It is the third part of this sector, the part which is composed of established service institutions and organizations devoted to the common or *general* good, that is in ill health. These institutions are, roughly speaking, of five kinds: Those offering formal education, for example, private schools, colleges and universities, and special professional and vocational institutions; those providing informal education or cultural activities, such as museums, private libraries, zoological and botanical gardens, art galleries, symphony orchestras, and civic theaters; those giving health care, principally voluntary hospitals; those devoted to research; and those providing welfare services to disadvantaged or disabled members of the population.

Although there are great differences among them, private service institutions do possess a set of common characteristics. Originating generally as the fruit of some impulse of personal or religious philanthropy, they have developed into professionally administered enterprises impressed with a broad public trust. Incorporated as non-profit institutions, they enjoy federal and state income tax exemption and, in most cases, exemption from local property taxes. They are governed, almost always, by self-perpetuating boards of trustees in whom, corporately, their assets are vested. Most importantly, they exist *solely* to provide needed services to the public or some designated part thereof—services which might otherwise have to be provided by government out of tax revenues.

Traditionally, these institutions were supported almost exclusively by the income from endowments, annual gifts by individuals, corporations and foundations, and user fees; but as costs have risen and the demand for services has mounted, these sources of revenue have become increasingly inadequate. In recent years, therefore, many private institutions have begun to seek and receive a measure of governmental support, in the form of grants or contracts for specific purposes, or, indirectly, through subsidization of the purchaser of services, or, occasionally, at the local or state levels, as annual subventions.

Nonetheless, they remain *private* institutions for whose continued state of health no one is legally responsible except their boards of trustees and the administrative staffs employed by these boards. To distinguish them from private associations serving the special interests of self-selected groups, we can call them privately controlled public enterprises, or, perhaps, private commonwealth enterprises.

How many of these private institutions there are today no one is certain, although we do know that there are approximately 1,450 colleges and universities, 4,600 secondary schools, 3,650 voluntary hospitals, 6,000 museums, 1,100 symphony orchestras, 5,500 libraries, and 29,000 welfare agencies supported by United Funds. There can be no question that these institutions form a highly important piece of the fabric of American society, important enough to justify—indeed necessitate—our looking at their situations *collectively*. Together they give expression to the concept of private effort for the public good, and it is belief in the efficacy of this concept that has released untold energies and talent to the development of this nation.

PRIVATE VERSUS PUBLIC

Almost every category of private commonweal enterprise has its tax-supported, publicly controlled counterpart: public schools, colleges and universities, public museums and libraries, public hospitals, public research institutes, and public welfare agencies (albeit virtually no public symphony orchestras or public opera, ballet, and theater companies).

From time to time efforts have been made to demonstrate that the private institution is superior—or inferior—to its public analogue. Extravagant claims have been voiced on each side of the argument, and a good deal of blood, figuratively speaking, has been spilt in the sport. Common sense has always shown, however, that the question of private *versus* public, when posed as exclusive alternatives, lacks even a semblance of validity within this nation's experience. The issue is a handy one for populist or élitist polemics, but that is all. Each set of institutions has its particular strengths and weaknesses, and together they share many characteristics and goals. The case for private institutions, therefore, cannot, and should not, be made in terms of any inherent superiority they may be thought to have to public institutions.

A question that is more to the point is whether, in the aggregate, private institutions provide an essential element to the character of our national life. Would our society be as rich, as varied, as free, as lively, as it is, if these enterprises disappeared entirely from the scene—if all education took place in public institutions, if opera, ballet, drama, and music were performed only by official state companies, if medical care were provided only in public hospitals, if research were done only in governmental institutes, if welfare services were a monopoly of governmental agencies?

Put this way, the question is rhetorical and the answer, to many of us, obvious. Of course we believe in private institutions, and of course their place in the society must be preserved. But rhetoric and sentiment are not enough. A substantial new effort will be required to safeguard the future of these institutions, based on an understanding and appreciation of the unique role they play in our society. The case for a combined public-private system can no longer be assumed to rest on some sort of divine law. It must be explicitly examined and stated.

THE CASE FOR THE PRIVATE NON-PROFIT SERVICE INSTITUTION

Granting that many of the special virtues claimed on behalf of private institutions turn out not to be unique to them, and granting that some of them have in the past been less democratic and less open to change than they should have been, there are, nonetheless, at least four distinctive reasons why it is a matter of compelling importance to retain in our society service institutions that are not under public control.

The first reason is the special opportunity they offer for concerned citizens, through membership on boards of trustees and participation in a wide range of voluntary activities, to accept a significant measure of personal responsibility for the provision to the public of many kinds of essential services. Acceptance of this kind of responsibility enables lay men and women to become informed about pressing national problems. It gives them a basis for judging the performance of public officials and institutions in attacking these problems. It serves as an antidote to the all-too-frequently encountered attitude that as long as one pays one's taxes, the failures, the evils, the pathologies of the world, are someone else's responsibility.

Additionally, voluntary service by trustees and other supporters brings to these institutions special talents and experience they could not possibly command otherwise, in fields such as fund raising, legal affairs, investing, property management, and community relations. Growing recognition of the paramount importance of the last of these fields has stimulated many institutions to broaden membership in their governing boards to include more young people, more women, and more representatives of minority groups.

In this day, when it is increasingly evident that public authority, important as this is, cannot alone solve the nation's growing problems, the need is great for private individuals to accept a real measure of responsibility for these problems themselves. One of their best opportunities to do this—and an opportunity which should be extended ever more widely to all kinds of citizens—is through participation in the work of private service institutions devoted to the common good. In this respect these institutions perform an essential function in our national life.

The second notable reason private service institutions and organizations must not be allowed to disappear is the important role they play in the safeguarding of academic, professional, and artistic freedom. In periods of sharp controversy, when legislative or executive pressure on public institutions becomes intolerable, private institutions can provide essential reserve protection for these freedoms. As one looks ahead, it is hard to imagine that the tensions of our deeply divided society will not produce many new storms, each with its own particular threats to liberty of mind and conscience.

This is not to suggest that all private institutions are necessarily impervious themselves to external pressure, or that public institutions have a record of supineness in their defense of freedom. Far from it. It is simply to say that private institutions, because they are not directly dependent on public appropriations, are less immediately vulnerable to restrictions on their capacity to function effectively in the public interest.

It has therefore seemed wise to many Americans to distribute the safekeeping of their nation's most precious asset, its intellectual freedom, among a variety of institutions under the control of private citizens as well as of public authorities. In a totalitarian state, where intellectual orthodoxy is of the highest imperative, this kind of arrangement would be unthinkable because it is one designed to produce a babel of intellectual and artistic claims in the name of truth, perpetual challenges to authority, and a seeming lack of a disciplined sense of national purpose. Despite the attacks on it today by young radicals, and despite the clearly evident imperfections of our present society, our system of shared responsibility is one that has served the American people well, and we would be foolish to abandon it by allowing our private institutions to fail.

A third, purely pragmatic, reason for securing the future well-being of these institutions is simply the fact that they do exist and that if they ceased to function as a private responsibility there is no guarantee that the same kinds and quality of service they now provide could or would be provided at public expense. This is particularly true in regard to some types of services provided by religious institutions, where the doctrine of separation of church and state bars public support; but it also applies to situations in which private institutions supply services of such a controversial nature that public agencies would not dare to enter the field. There are other kinds of services, such as those offered by cultural institutions and by some kinds of research institutes, specialized educational institutions, and welfare and public affairs organizations, which many Americans would think ought not, within this nation's traditions, to be totally financed by government.

If commonweal enterprises could no longer be kept afloat through private funding and were to become entirely dependent on tax funds to continue operating, it is a fair assumption that many would have to close down or drastically reduce their services. In many cases, they would not qualify for public support, and where they did, hard-pressed public authorities would be reluctant to give them the necessary priority in the face of already established budgetary claims. It is also probable that if they were to qualify, their services would be made to conform to those offered by comparable public institutions, thereby standardizing them and very possibly destroying some of their special esprit and quality.

The building of great institutions, be they universities, museums, symphony orchestras, hospitals, or independent research facilities, is a painstaking process, almost invariably requiring many decades. Each successive generation of trustees, staff, and volunteers adds its increment to the facilities, the range of services provided, the professional standards, the esprit and the sources to the society of a value incalculably greater than simply the worth of the 'assets' which are listed in their annual balance sheets.

Such institutions are essential to an enlightened, humane, and stable society. They bring to it the perspectives of the past and of world culture. They serve as springboards from which advances are made in basic knowledge or in standards of individual and organizational performance. In an age of relentless change they provide a steadying hand of continuity. And, lastly, they serve to keep alive on a year-in year-out basis important fields of activity during the lean periods when these are out of fashion for public support.

A fourth, and perhaps most important, reason private institutions must not be allowed to decline is that they bring to our national life vital elements of diversity, free choice, and heterodoxy. These qualities are often lumped together and their identity obscured in celebration of the vague and rather overworked concept of 'pluralism.' But each, in fact, has a quite different connotation, and each has its own special importance.

Diversity suggests the existence of a variety of institutions within a given field, all rather different from one another in the way they are managed, in their perceptions of priorities, and in the kinds of service they offer. The term is value-free in that it contains no suggestion of superiority or inferiority. It says only that there are likely to be a number of ways to accomplish something and that in the long run the competition between several possible approaches is good for everybody. This prevents new ideas from being suppressed, it provides challenge to fat and complacent bureaucracies, it assures experimentation and flexibility, and it lends color to what might otherwise be a monochromatic scene.

Free choice applies to the consumer rather than to the purveyor of services. It implies the existence of a market, wherein those seeking services can shop around and take their trade where they choose. The market is, of course, not an entirely free one because the costs of private services are likely to be higher than those provided by public institutions. But the existence of the market is, all the same, important to the way the consumer feels about his life, for he knows that if a massive public agency whose services he was using were to become rigid, or inhuman, he would at least have the possibility of an alternative.

Heterodoxy describes the permitted presence in a society of unconventional ideas and philosophies and of institutions and organizations which nourish them. Tolerance of this kind is a sign of national maturity and self-confidence and indicates faith in the good sense of the average citizen to sort out what is genuine and what is specious. It also recognizes that today's iconoclasm may, as the result of changing conditions, be tomorrow's orthodoxy and that any attempt forceably to stifle the free play of ideas, however seemingly eccentric, may produce stagnation or cause the build-up of powerful social forces that will eventually result in violent upheaval. Thus, the capacity to tolerate nonconformism, trying as this sometimes becomes, is the *sine qua non* of a free society. Without it the imposition of a totalitarian state ultimately becomes inevitable.

Private institutions are not the only contributors to pluralism. Public institutions can and do play a part in it; but their vulnerability in times of crisis places a special burden on private institutions for the preservation of diversity, of free choice, and of the capacity to tolerate heterodoxy—in short, for the preservation of an open society.

CHARACTER OF THE THREAT

The developing threat to private institutions is certainly grave, but in pointing it out one risks the accusation of crying 'wolf.'

Any adequate description implies some sort of dramatic, instant fulfillment, whereas the demise of an institution is more likely to be a protracted and inconspicuous process lasting many years and encompassing several stages of progressive debility.

There may be a first stage in which the institution, for financial reasons, becomes unable to manage the growth necessary to meet new challenges. This loss of a cutting edge may bring on a second stage in which the institution's own self-confidence and the public's confidence in it begin to slip, a third in which the recruitment of capable staff becomes progressively more difficult, a fourth in which declining income begins to necessitate the curtailment of important activities and reduction of staff, and so on. Even when the institution is moribund, it may drag on for some time before it is finally forced to close down. It is at the very first stage, however, when an institution shows itself to be incapable of vigorous response to changed times, that it should be seen to be seriously ill, and it is then that remedial steps should be taken.

Many of our greatest private service institutions are now showing all the symptoms of being in this initial stage of sickness; and in seeking to understand the cause of their illness, they tend to diagnose it as essentially financial. They regard themselves as simply the victims of an inflationary spiral in which for some years now their costs of doing business have mounted more rapidly than their income. Over the past decade, expenses have at least trebled to provide the same amount of service. As service institutions, they have not been able to offset steadily rising labor costs through automation or other increases in productivity, or, alternatively, just to drop unprofitable services, as could a business enterprise. Either course would have constituted abandonment of their very *raison d'être*—to provide services they deem to be good or essential for all or many citizens, and as much as possible on terms which the less fortunate can meet.

During the past year an already serious situation for the private commonweal institution has been further aggravated by cutbacks in federal spending and by the decline in the stock market, with its consequent reduction in charitable giving. The annual operating deficit has now become an all-too-common phenomenon among these institutions. Financial exigency has, in many cases, caused positive steps to be taken, such as improvements in efficiency, new efforts at private fund raising, and efforts to reach out to meet new needs for which funding is available. It has also caused some unfortunate compromises, for example, reductions in the quality of services offered, increased charges for these services, encroachments on unrestricted endowment funds for use as annual income, and even short-term borrowing to meet payrolls. But these moves, whether sound or unsound, have provided only temporary relief, not a real solution. They have simply served to stave off the ultimate day of reckoning when many private institutions will either have to become publicly controlled and supported or go out of business.

At bottom, the problem faced by private institutions is very much the same as that faced by public institutions, except for the vital consideration that the latter's support is hitched to the tax dollar. Both have been hard hit by rising personnel costs. Both have found it impossible to offset these costs through increased productivity. More importantly, both have been seriously affected by an enormously heightened public demand, caused by affluence, population growth, changing attitudes, and related factors, for the kinds of educational, cultural, health, and welfare services which traditionally have been, and should be, supplied on a non-profit basis.

Government, quite properly, has concentrated on the staggering problem of meeting this demand and in so doing has put the major part of its effort into the development of public institutions. This approach, understandable as it is, has been built on assumptions about the continued viability of private institutions as a national resource that have become less and less justified and consequently has precluded the kind of *special* attention they urgently require.

During this period, many Americans have enjoyed an illusory confidence that private giving by individuals, foundations, and corporations, reinforced perhaps by better investment policies, by some increases in user fees, and by some limited access to funds provided through government programs, would be sufficient to maintain the strength of private institutions. They have simply failed to understand that income from private giving, essential as it is because of its unrestricted nature, represents only a small part of the annual budgets of these institutions. They have also failed to appreciate that many private institutions, because they are located in cities, have lost their traditional supporting constituencies through the migration of more well-to-do families to the suburbs. This problem particularly afflicts cultural institutions, so that just when the need for them to reach out further to serve larger numbers of urban residents is being widely recognized, their financial capacity to do so has become woefully inadequate.

If financial debility were the only problem faced by private institutions, there might be grounds for at least some degree of optimism. One might suppose that resolute action and more favorable times would, in due course, begin to restore them to a state of financial health, thus assuring the continued viability of our combined public-private system. But this future appears increasingly to be subject to more fundamental doubts having to do with the basic attitudes and beliefs of the American people. The issue now is whether a majority of our citizens still sees special merit in the retention of a combined public-private system or, conversely, whether substantial numbers would now, for varying reasons, be quite content to see private institutions generally handed over to public control.

The answers to these questions are by no means clear, however distressing this may be to those of us whose faith in our traditional system runs deep. We must recognize, for example, that millions of Americans, because of poverty, discrimination, or disillusion with the society's values, feel alienated from it. To them, private institutions, like government itself, are simply part of what they consider a rotten system and of a *status quo* which they are convinced is entrenched against the kinds of social change they advocate. We cannot expect these Americans to be the defenders of the private commonweal enterprise unless ways are found to relate it far more effectively to their needs and aspirations; but how far it can go in this direction without at the same time alienating other constituencies and jeopardizing its financial support is an even more difficult question.

Another very substantial group of citizens—fearful, insecure, disturbed by the changes that have taken place in American life and inclined to a conservative outlook—may also be disenchanted with private institutions, ironically, for almost diametrically opposite reasons. This group tends to feel that private institutions, especially colleges and universities, have gone much too far to the side of 'liberalism'—that amorphous and enigmatic force in our national life which has, in their eyes, pandered to blacks and other minorities, capitulated to student irresponsibility, undermined law and order, ignored the legitimate needs of people like themselves who are 'willing to work their way,' and generally raised everyone's taxes in the process. There certainly can be no guarantee that this large group will be passionate defenders of the independent position of private institutions in the society. On the contrary, we can expect such Americans, by and large, to favor measures which bring these institutions under ever greater public control.

Thirdly, there remain in the nation many people, especially in the nation's 'heartland,' who continue to have a kind of populist distrust of private institutions, associating them with great wealth, privilege, and a social caste system. They feel more comfortable about institutions which are the immediate responsibility of elected, publicly accountable officials. While it would be an overstatement to say that people of this outlook are downright hostile to private institutions, it would certainly be fair to suggest that one would not find among them the kind of spontaneous, fervent support these institutions now so desperately need.

Finally, there are many people who are simply indifferent to the issue, to the degree that they are even aware of it. They know little of the role of private institutions in our national life, and they care less. From time to time they benefit from what they take to be public services without realizing that these are, in fact, provided by private institutions. Unfortunately, this group probably constitutes a large part of the population.

Lack of a philosophical commitment to the idea of a combined public-private system, ignorance of private institutions and what is at stake in their preservation, and even disaffection toward them as such, among certain parts of the public at large is, not surprisingly, reflected by many public officials. Here and there one finds active and courageous supporters of the cause of private institutions, and their efforts have been helpful and appreciated. The predominant atitude of officialdom, however, is at best one of indifference to the entire issue and at worst one of skepticism bordering on hostility.

Dramatic evidence of the prevalence of these attitudes was offered in the Tax Reform Act of 1969 when Congress placed a 4 percent excise tax on the income of foundations. Foundations opposed this strenuously, pointing out that the tax would simply

deny some $50 million of much needed income to the organiza-
tions and institutions, *most of them private*, which they customarily support. The argument, though understood, was disregarded.
A desire to 'chastise' foundations, however illogical the form of
punishment, outweighed the concern that should have been felt
about those on whom the real burden of the tax would fall.
Most disquieting of all was the fact that an action as damaging
as this to private institutions could have been taken with so little
protest from the public. That surely was indicative of a state of
public apathy toward these institutions that bodes ill for their
future.

THE FUTURE

In view of the state of public opinion on the question, the general
lack of official concern, and the nation's preoccupation with other
issues, it seems unlikely that any systematic, coherent effort will
develop in the immediate future to alleviate the financial situation
of private service institutions. Their relative position in our
national life seems destined to decline and with it the special
values they bring to our society.

Some types of private service institutions will be less vulnerable
than others, particularly those which can go on raising their
prices because the consumers of their services are subsidized by
public funds or protected by insurance plans; but for other types
of institutions, especially those providing informal education and
cultural activities in which the demand for service inevitably
begins to fall off when charges are raised too high, the day of final
reckoning will come much sooner.

Private schools, colleges, and universities, while retaining a
leavening of low-income scholarship students, will do best financially by turning their backs on the hard-pressed middle class and
concentrating their admissions on the children of affluent families
which can best afford ever-rising tuition charges. In so doing,
they will pay the price of becoming estranged from the mainstream of the populace, which will only serve to increase their
growing insecurity. As for the major private research universities,
even substantial tuition increases will help only marginally, so
small a part does tuition play in their overall financing.

Any real solution to the plight of private institutions must begin with a clear appreciation by the nation's top political leaders of what the *collective* presence and vitality of these institutions mean to the nation. These leaders, rather than simply mirroring public ignorance and apathy, must educate the public and, where necessary, convert it to a sense of active concern over the future of our traditional system of shared public and private effort and responsibility; and, in this task, our political leaders must be supported and reinforced by other leadership elements in the nation. Nothing less than this kind of impetus from the top will provide the basis for the great variety of measures which will be needed to preserve and revitalize the position of our private institutions.

Much of the remedial action will, of course, have to be tailored to the special situations of specific types of institutions and will have to be taken by state and local governments as well as in Washington. But other approaches can be broad enough to affect all classes of institutions simultaneously. An example of the latter would be a totally new look at the tax laws which would approach charitable giving not simply negatively as an area for taxpayer abuse, as did the tax reform legislation of 1969, but with the positive attitude that philanthropy is a national virtue that should be given maximum encouragement. Such a reexamination has been recommended by the 'Peterson' Commission on Foundations and Private Philanthropy.

Another possibility might be a comprehensive study of the variety of ways in which private institutions could be aided as the result of public subsidization of the consumers of their services, with a view toward extending and broadening this approach. Public funds are already used extensively to provide scholarships tenable at private colleges and universities. Voluntary hospitals are assisted through medicare and medicaid to elderly and less advantaged individuals. Perhaps other kinds of private institutions, such as museums and symphony orchestras, could be assisted indirectly through public subsidy of the users of their services. This form of public support has an advantage in that it reduces the likelihood of government control of the operations of private institutions and preserves the free market.

A third possibility might be a national commission which would think through and articulate the requirements for a massive campaign to arouse public interest in the private service institution and concern over its future. Such a commission would have to determine who should be responsible for launching the campaign, how it should be organized, and how financed. And it would have to ensure that something would really happen as a result of its work.

The time for action, whether of a broad or specific nature, is extremely late. Our historic partnership of public and private commonweal endeavor is in grave danger because of the state of apathy that is permitting the decline of private institutions. Unless this decline is arrested and reversed, we, and our children after us, will almost certainly be living in a society where the idea of *private* initiative for the *common* good has become little but a quaint anachronism largely associated with the mores of an earlier age. Perhaps at that time there will be Americans who are reasonably satisfied with the kinds of lives offered them by a society which functions solely through public institutions. But there may well be others with a great yearning for more variety, more choice, more animation, and more freedom in their lives than such a system would be likely to provide. If so, they will certainly wonder at the heedlessness—the sheer negligence—of the generation before them that could have allowed a system which has these attributes to atrophy.

4 Government-sponsored Enterprise in the United States

HAROLD SEIDMAN

REDEFINITION OF ISSUE

To define the dilemma of accountability in modern government as a choice between independence and control is to pose the wrong question. Implicit in this statement is an assumption that established systems of accountability and control are fixed and immutable. Independence is equated, as it was by Dr James Killian in specifying the prerequisites for an 'independent' Corporation for Public Broadcasting, with exemption 'from civil service, public bidding, and GAO auditing requirements' and non-budgetary financing. He did not regard Presidential appointment of directors as in any way compromising the Corporation's independence.[1]

Independence in these terms is a non-solution. For the President of the United States to argue that an efficient postal service cannot be obtained without insulating the Postal Service from 'direct control by the President, the Bureau of Budget and the Congress' amounts almost to a confession of loss of faith in the democratic process.[2] The fundamental issue is whether governments have the capacity to adapt democratic institutions to the complex and varied tasks required of the modern state without sacrificing public accountability. Do governments have the will and the ingenuity to devise organization structures, administrative and personnel systems, financing arrangements and controls tailored to the needs of diverse types of government activities which provide *effective* and *meaningful* accountability and responsiveness to those officials with political responsibility and through them to the people?

Proposals for 'hiving off' in Great Britain and 'reprivatization' in the United States provide convenient rationalizations for evading the central issue. The committee chaired by Lord Fulton concluded that because 'clear delegation of authority is difficult in the Civil Service' large-scale executive operations cannot be effectively run by government departments, and they should be 'hived off' wherever possible to independent boards.[3] Peter Drucker defines 'reprivatization' as the systematic policy of using 'the nongovernmental institutions of the society of organizations, for the actual doing, i.e. for performance, operations, execution.'[4] Drucker and the Fulton Committee appear to be in agreement that the functions of governing and making political choices are incompatible with 'doing.'

Are governments inherently incapable of 'doing,' or are they merely unwilling to modify or replace outmoded means of conducting the public business? Governments tend to become prisoners of their personnel, administrative and financial control systems. To a greater or lesser degree, the systems of accountability and control in most countries are rooted in the past and were developed at a time when government functions were relatively simple and remote from the lives of the average citizen. The existing machinery of public accounting in Great Britain, under the sovereignty of Parliament and the management of the Treasury, is almost a hundred years old.[5]

The accounting, budgetary, civil service, central purchasing, and auditing systems were designed initially to prevent abuse, not to support, facilitate, and evaluate performance. If the controls constituted obstacles to effective performance, this was considered to be but a small sacrifice to place on the altar of public honesty and accountability.

Central control agencies have a vested interest in the maintenance of the *status quo*. Their considerable power and unique expertise are derived from knowledge of the system and the complex body of laws, regulations, rules, and precedents governing the public service. Proposals for fundamental reform are opposed because they may make these highly specialized skills obsolete or reduce the power of the central agencies.

PROLIFERATION OF AUTONOMOUS AGENCIES

Few governments have been willing to challenge directly the powerful central control agencies. Governments generally have found it more expedient to exempt high priority or novel types of programs from some or all of the central management controls than to attempt to reform the control system. In this they are often encouraged and abetted by the control agencies who would prefer to be by-passed than to alter existing uniform rules and traditional ways of doing business. The results are to be seen in the phenomenal growth in the number of public corporations, autonomous agencies, and recently in the United States, government-sponsored private enterprises.

At the outset, in the United States, Great Britain and elsewhere the public corporation and comparable autonomous institutions were reserved in the main for revenue-producing commercial ventures and trading enterprises. According to the criteria laid down by President Harry S. Truman in his 1948 Budget Message, use of the corporate form of organization was dedicated for government programs 'which are predominantly of a commercial character—those which are revenue-producing, are at least potentially self-sustaining, and involve a large number of business-type transactions with the public.'[6]

Increasing activities which are indistinguishable from the traditional types of government programs are being organized as autonomous or para-statal entities. Once a device is discovered for beating the system and minimizing political and fiscal accountability, it is certain to be exploited for all types of legitimate and illegitimate purposes.

Today twenty-one of the fifty-five state-sponsored bodies in Ireland are not business enterprises. Of the thirteen Puerto Rican public corporations created since 1960, only two are intended to be self-supporting from the sale of goods and services to the public. In contrast all of the Puerto Rican public corporations established prior to 1960, except the Institute of Puerto Rican Culture, were revenue producing and substantially self-sustaining enterprises. President Truman's criteria have been ignored in the United States in establishing the Community Development Corporation and the Inter-American Foundation and such government-sponsored enterprises as the National Home Ownership Foundation, National

Park Foundation, and Corporation for Public Broadcasting. Similar trends are observable in other countries, particularly in developing countries which inherited archaic control systems from their former colonial rulers.

In some countries the point has been reached where the established government departments are threatened with eclipse by the more powerful and prosperous autonomous agencies. In Puerto Rico public corporations account for 24.5 percent of Commonwealth employees. Public corporation expenditures in 1970 exceeded those for the remainder of the government by over $100 million. At the end of 1969, public corporations were responsible for 62 percent of the external debt of Puerto Rico, with outstanding bond obligations of $867 million. State-sponsored bodies in Ireland now employ 60,000 people as contrasted with 46,000 in the civil service.

The U.S. Treasury Department estimates that if federally assisted credit programs grow by approximately $30 billion, as is scheduled, then the combined total of federally assisted and direct borrowing will be about $60 billion, approximately 50 percent of all net credit demands placed on the U.S. capital markets in the fiscal year 1972–73. As Under Secretary of the Treasury Paul Volcker testified before the Senate Banking and Currency Committee in May 1972: 'Such rapid expansion of Federal credit demands should be of paramount public concern, especially because most of them are beyond the pale of budgetary review and control, while others involve awkward, expensive, and discriminatory financing arrangements.' President Nixon in his Budget Message for fiscal year 1972 ascribed this development to 'Federal credit programs which the Congress has placed outside the budget-guaranteed and insured loans, or loans by federally sponsored enterprises which escape regular review by either the executive or legislative branch.'

CAUSES OF GROWTH

The reasons advanced originally for establishing autonomous agencies to administer government-owned enterprises do not stand up when applied to functions normally performed by government bureaus. In current usage, the corporation or parastatal agency is sometimes employed as a mere convenience—a way to escape the 'civil service mentality,' salary limitations and personnel ceilings, statutory and constitutional limits on public borrowing, and central audit and management controls; to reduce the size of the budget and to finance government programs outside the budget by earmarking taxes and mortgaging future revenues; and to minimize interference by the responsible political authorities. The major motivation differs from one country to another.

The desire to exclude billions in expenditure from the federal budget and to circumvent the public debt ceiling and budgetary controls has been a major factor in the United States. Secretary of Housing and Urban Development Robert Weaver justified the conversion of the Federal National Mortgage Association from a mixed-ownership government corporation to a government-sponsored private enterprise as necessary to avoid the 'vagaries of the budget situation.' He argued that 'by putting the secondary market operations outside of the government, and thereby, outside of the budget, it would be possible for Fannie Mae to be more responsive to the needs, we believe, of the building and mortgage financing industry than it can be now.'[7] Avoidance of the 'annual battle between the Post Office Department and the Bureau of the Budget, which notoriously results in limitations upon funds available to be appropriated' was cited by the Senate Post Office and Civil Service Committee as 'the basic purpose in authorizing the sale of bonds by the Postal Service and exempting it from budget control.'[8] Legislation was enacted in 1971 (P.L. 92–126) to exclude the disbursements of the Export-Import Bank from the totals of the budget of the United States and to exempt the Bank from any annual expenditure or net lending limitations imposed in the budget. Comptroller General Elmer B. Staats suggested to the Congress that one alternative to violating the sanctity of the unified budget would be to ignore it altogether by converting the Export-Import Bank to a government-sponsored private enterprise on the FNMA Model.[9]

The exclusion of the Export-Import Bank from the budget marked the first overt departure from the unified budget concepts adopted in 1969. But the conversion of mixed-ownership corporations to government-sponsored enterprises and the creation of new government-sponsored enterprises has had the practical effect of impairing the integrity of the unified budget and limiting its effectiveness as a vehicle for bringing together competing needs and establishing overall priorities.

It is difficult to discern any consistent and logical pattern in the current proliferation of government corporations and quasi corporations and government-sponsored enterprises in the United States. (See Appendix, p. 106.) The traditional tests of a government enterprise—public purpose, government appointments of directors, and Treasury financing—are no longer rigorously applied. Under these tests such enterprises as the Corporation for Public Broadcasting, National Park Foundation, National Home Ownership Foundation, Securities Investor Protection Corporation, Student Loan Marketing Association, and the proposed National Legal Services Corporation, classified by law as not being agencies or instrumentalities of the United States, would demonstrably belong within the government sector. Confusion is compounded when the National Railroad Passenger Corporation is defined by law as both a for profit corporation, not an agency or establishment of the United States, and a mixed-ownership government corporation. There is also no consistent pattern in the measures adopted by the Congress with respect to the organization and control of such enterprises.

A few senators have expressed uneasiness about the implications of designing public institutions as non-government entities. Senator Vance Hartke said of the Corporation for Public Broadcasting: 'In other words what we are really creating here is a separate bureaucracy without the usual safeguards of a congressional watchdog looking over its shoulder, including the General Accounting Office. . . . As far as I am concerned you are creating a fiction when you indicate that you are going to take tax money and call it a quasi-government operation. It is a fiction. I don't believe that it can be maintained.'[10] Senator Claiborne Pell took a 'dim view' of the Student Loan Marketing Association because 'there is no real control by either the executive branch of government or by the Congress, and I am wondering if, as a matter of national policy, there is an argument to be made to the effect that it is a mistake to put such a public trust in an independent board.'[11]

Here, as in the area of government by contract, the distinctions between what is private and what is public are becoming increasingly blurred. These distinctions cannot be abandoned altogether without fundamental alterations in the United States constitutional system. Maintenance of this distinction is essential both to protect private rights from intrusion by government and and to prevent private usurpation of public power. Labeling as 'private' what is in fact 'public' to gain tactical political advantages or to keep expenditures out of the budget and insulate programs against control by the President and the Congress misleads the citizens and exacerbates the crisis of confidence in government. Intermingling of public and private duties places public officials in an ambiguous position and subjects them to potential conflicts of interest.

HISTORY: GOVERNMENT CORPORATION CONTROL ACT

The current situation is much the same as that which confronted the U.S. Congress when it enacted the Government Control Act in 1945. The report of the Senate Committee on Banking and Currency on the Control Act pointed out that

> with this tremendous growth in the number and importance of these corporate instrumentalities of the Government there has been increasing recognition by both the legislative and executive branches that some means adapted to the special needs of the situation must be found to coordinate the financial programs of the corporations with that of the Government as a whole. . . . Due to the piecemeal approach to the problem, the degree and character of control exercised over Government corporations by the Congress, the President, and the established fiscal agencies of the Government have varied greatly and without any real basis.

If we were to substitute the words 'Government-sponsored enterprise' for 'Government corporation,' we would be describing today's situation.

Enactment of the Government Corporation Control Act (P.L. 248–79th Congress) represented recognition by the Congress both of the need for a special type of government institution tailored to the requirements of business programs and for special types of controls over such institutions which would assure accountability without impairing essential flexibility. When it enacted the law, the Congress expressly noted that 'the corporate form loses much of its peculiar value without reasonable autonomy in its day-to-day decisions and operations.'

Title I of the Control Act is applicable to the wholly-owned government corporations listed in Section 101. It provides for an annual 'business-type' budget and an annual 'commercial-type' audit by the Comptroller General. The budget programs of the corporations as modified, amended, or revised by the President shall be transmitted to the Congress as part of the Annual Budget required by the Budget and Accounting Act, 1921. Congress is authorized to limit the use of corporate funds for any purpose, but it has rarely chosen to do so except for administrative expenses. The net outlays of government corporations are, however, subject to overall ceilings on budgetary expenditures. But, in essence, the business-type budget provides for a qualitative rather than a quantitative review of proposed corporate expenditures.

Title II of the Control Act is applicable to mixed-ownership government corporations listed in Section 201. It provides for an annual commercial-type audit for any period during which government capital is invested in a corporation. The President shall include in the Annual Budget any recommendations he may wish to make as to the return of government capital to the Treasury by any mixed-ownership corporation.

Title III of the Act contains general provisions applicable to both wholly-owned and mixed-ownership corporations. Section 303 requires:

> all bonds, notes, debentures, and other similar obligations which are hereafter issued by any wholly-owned or mixed-ownership Government corporation and offered to the public shall be in such forms and denominations, shall have such maturities, shall bear such rates of interest, shall be subject to such terms and conditions, shall be issued in such manner and at such times and sold at such prices as have been or as may be approved by the Secretary of the Treasury.

This section is not applicable to certain farm credit banks which are 'required to consult with the Secretary of the Treasury prior to taking any action' and 'to report any disagreements to the President and the Congress.'

Section 304 required liquidation by June 30, 1948, of any wholly-owned government corporation created by or under the laws of any state, territory, or possession of the United States or any political subdivision thereof, or under the laws of the District of Columbia. In the view of the Congress, it did 'not seem desirable to continue any longer this anomalous situation in which an instrumentality of the Federal Government is technically a creature of a State or local government.'

No persuasive evidence has even been presented to demonstrate that the controls established by the Government Corporation Control Act have impaired the capability of government corporations to carry out effectively the functions vested in them by law. Complaints have been made about the current practice of including net corporate outlays under an overall budgetary ceiling, but this is not a requirement imposed by the Control Act. President Eisenhower in 1957 proposed to tighten the Government Corporation Control Act by abolishing the distinction between wholly-owned and mixed-ownership corporations. In his 1958 and 1959 Budget Messages, President Eisenhower recommended that the Act be amended to provide for budget review and audit control over all government corporations which are authorized to obtain and use federal funds. He argued that the test for maintaining budget review, the annual audit by the General Accounting Office, and the controls exercised by the Secretary of the Treasury should be based not on private ownership of a portion of the capital stock, but on the use of federal funds and the assumption of financial responsibilities by the United States government. Legislation was introduced (H.R. 8332, 85th Congress) to establish and maintain budget control over any government corporation which possessed authority (1) to issue or have outstanding obligations guaranteed in whole or in part by the United States; or (2) to obtain government funds by appropriations, borrowings, subscriptions to capital stock or otherwise; or (3) to utilize government funds obtained by any of the above methods. The legislation was not enacted, due mainly to the opposition of the Farm Credit Banks.

Annexed budgets are printed in the Budget document 'as auxiliary information' for the following government corporations and government-sponsored enterprises: Export-Import Bank, Federal National Mortgage Association, Banks for Cooperatives, Federal Intermediate Credit Banks, Federal Land Banks, Federal Home Loan Banks, and Federal Home Loan Mortgage Corporation. Annexed budgets are not reviewed or acted upon by either the President or the Congress.

Enactment of the Government Corporation Control Act reduced greatly the attractiveness of either the wholly-owned or mixed-ownership government corporation as a device for 'beating the system' and escaping government controls. Many advocates of the government corporation have now shifted their affections to what they describe as a 'COMSAT-type' corporation, although it is by no means certain what they mean by the term. Confusion about the status of the Communications Satellite Corporation is understandable. It is not a covert government corporation, and the Congress, after prolonged and often bitter debate, rejected proposals for government ownership and operation of the Communication Satellite System. The Communications Satellite Act of 1962, however, does raise questions about the private character of the venture by providing for Presidential appointment, with Senate confirmation, of the Corporation's incorporators and three members of the board of directors. Attorney General Kennedy emphasized, however, that 'neither the incorporators nor the Presidentially appointed directors are to be classified as officers of the United States' and that the directors owe a fiduciary obligation to the corporation, but not to the government.[12]

COMSAT is a wholly privately owned and financed public utility subject to government regulation, and it is not a government-sponsored enterprise in the sense that that term is now employed. Nonetheless, the COMSAT model has been utilized for quite dissimilar types of activities such as the National Housing Partnerships, and the proposed National Legal Services Corporation. The National Housing Partnerships is a private corporation for profit, and the actual or potential federal interest in the venture is not such as to warrant Presidential appointment of three of the fifteen directors. In contrast, the National Legal Services Corporation was to be a government-financed public service organization.

COMSAT has been the forerunner of such government-sponsored 'private' enterprises as the Corporation for Public Broadcasting, Federal National Mortgage Association, National Homeownership Foundation, National Housing Partnerships,

National Park Foundation, National Railroad Passenger Corporation, Securities Investor Protection Corporation, and Student Loan Marketing Association.

Analysis of the charters, legislative history, and current status of these enterprises reveals:

—No criteria have been developed for the use of a government-sponsored enterprise in preference to other traditional organization forms. In most instances the choice appears to be dictated mainly by tactical considerations.

—There is no valid basis for distinguishing between many government-sponsored enterprises and other types of government activities, except for the fact that they are designed by law as 'not an agency and instrumentality of the United States Government.' Comparable powers and immunities could be granted to such agencies without characterizing them as non-government.

—'Independence' from partisan political control is not assured by vesting functions in private non-profit corporations and can be obtained by other means.

—Presidential appointment of directors does not provide satisfactory control and raises serious constitutional and legal questions concerning the removeability, role, and status of Presidentially-appointed directors of private corporations.

—The Corporation for Public Broadcasting, National Home-ownership Foundation, National Housing Partnerships, National Railroad Passenger Corporation, and Securities Investor Protection Corporation are subject to laws of the District of Columbia. This is a potential source of conflict.

—There is no uniform system of control over corporate budgets, audits, public borrowing, salaries, etc.

Absence of criteria

Government-sponsored enterprises constitute a very mixed bag. There are no established criteria for the use of such organizations and criteria cannot be developed empirically by analyzing the diverse and often conflicting reasons advanced for the establishment of each of these enterprises. It is difficult to identify any distinctive characteristics which are common to the Securities

Investors Protection Corporation, Federal National Mortgage Association, the National Homeownership Foundation, the National Park Foundation, and the proposed National Legal Services Corporation. The device is defended in some instances as a means for establishing public control and accountability, and in others for providing independence from control.

Comptroller General Elmer B. Staats suggested as criteria for excluding government-sponsored enterprises from the budget:

1. The planned ownership of the enterprise is private.
2. Its current ownership is more than 50 percent private.
3. It is not subject to the budgetary control provisions of the Government Corporation Control Act.
4. It is not otherwise subject to action on its budget by the Congress in the appropriations process.[13]

If one were to apply the Staats' criteria or the traditional tests —private stock ownership, election of a majority of directors by private stock holders, and predominantly non-Treasury financing —a logical argument can be made that such enterprises as the Federal Reserve Banks, Federal Land Banks, Federal Intermediate Credit Banks, Banks for Cooperatives and Federal Home Loan Banks belong in a class apart from other government institutions. But none of these is classified by law as a private organization. Indeed, the Farm Credit Banks and the Federal Home Loan Banks continue to be classified as mixed ownership government corporations, although the transition to private ownership has been completed.

If the criterion is the commercial profit-making character of the activity and prospective private ownership, then activities wholly dependent on federal financing and gifts, such as the Corporation for Public Broadcasting, National Parks Foundation, and National Homeownership Foundation, do not meet the test. Whatever other reasons may be cited, the single common objective in creating agencies outside the government structure is to evade some or all of the controls applicable to government agencies, funds, officers, and employees.

Government counterparts

Government-sponsored enterprises have more in common with

certain counterparts within the government structure than they have with each other. For example, it is difficult, either in terms of function, organization, and financing, to differentiate the Securities Investor Protection Corporation from the Federal Deposit Insurance Corporation and Federal Savings and Loan Insurance Corporation. Brokers and security dealers are required by law to be insured by the SIPC. FDIC and FSLIC insurance is not mandatory for state-chartered institutions. The Corporation for Public Broadcasting and the National Homeownership Foundation and the National Science Foundation and the National Foundation on the Arts and Humanities are essentially grant-giving organizations. The National Railroad Passenger Corporation is classified as a 'mixed-ownership Government Corporation,' but the Federal National Mortgage Association and Student Loan Marketing Association are not so defined although the government, either directly or indirectly, provided the initial capital. The National Housing Partnerships is the only government-sponsored enterprise without a government counterpart.

The characterization of the National Park Foundation as a 'private' non-profit corporation is clearly a legal fiction to permit gifts to the National Park Service to be invested in other than U.S. government securities. These gifts were administered formerly by a National Park Trust Fund Board within the Department of the Interior. The Foundation is in reality an agency of the National Park Service engaged exclusively in activities in behalf of and 'for the benefit' of the National Park Service. Services and facilities are provided by the Departments of Interior and Justice to the Foundation without reimbursement. If the Foundation were a private organization, then it ought not to be staffed by government employees and financed from public funds.

If the purpose is merely to grant certain powers and immunities to an organization which are not normally enjoyed by government agencies, this can be accomplished by specific statutory language without falsely labeling the organization a non-profit private enterprise. This type of misbranding is unnecessary to achieve the desired purposes and can lead to legal and organizational chaos.

Any organization which is dependent on federal financing and controlled by directors appointed by the President is not 'independent,' and the so-called 'independence' of the private non-profit corporation is an illusion. Indeed, the President and the Congress have a constitutional responsibility to oversee the expenditure of public funds by public officials appointed by the President, by and with the advice and consent of the Senate. It is by no means necessary to go outside the government to prevent improper political interference in corporate affairs. Indeed, the U.S. Postal Service and the Board of Governors of the Federal Reserve System enjoy a considerably greater measure of independence than the Corporation for Public Broadcasting and the proposed National Legal Services Corporation.

Difficulties occur when a non-profit corporation is controlled by directors and staff at political odds with the incumbent Administration. Such arrangements are not calculated to produce mutual trust and harmonious working relationships. Under these circumstances, a non-profit corporation is at a considerable disadvantage in the competition for scarce budgetary resources.

President Nixon vetoed the bill providing for two-year increased funding for the Corporation for Public Broadcasting because of 'fundamental disagreements concerning the direction which public broadcasting has taken and should pursue in the future.'[14] These represented disagreements with policies approved by a board dominated by appointees of the previous administration. John W. Macy, Jr., chairman of the Civil Service Commission under President Johnson, was forced to resign as the Corporation's president. He acknowledged that 'the endeavor to establish freedom of expression with balance and responsibility has at this point failed.'[15] Given the method of appointing the Corporation's directors and funding its operations, failure was inevitable.

Appointment of Directors

Article II, Section 2 of the Constitution provides that the President 'shall nominate, and by and with the advice and consent of the Senate, shall appoint . . . all other officers of the United States, whose appointments are not herein provided for, and which shall be established by law.' The key words are *'officers of the United States.'* As held by Attorney General Robert Kennedy, Presidentially appointed directors of a private corporation are not officers of the United States. This opinion is reinforced by language such as that in the National Parks Foundation Act to the effect that 'membership on the Board is not deemed to be an office within the meaning of the statutes of the United States.'

In appointing the directors of a non-government institution, the President is performing an extra-constitutional function. President Nixon could argue correctly when he vetoed the bill establishing the National Legal Services Corporation that to require the President to appoint eleven of the seventeen directors from lists compiled by various special interest groups was 'an affront to the principle of accountability to the American people as a whole.'[16] His contention that the proposed method of appointment was not the 'constitutional way' is, however, highly debatable. Since government-sponsored enterprises exist in a constitutional limbo, there is always a danger that a hostile Congress may seize on this device as means of circumventing the President's constitutional powers.

Intermingling of public and private duties places public officials in an ambiguous position and poses a number of unresolved ethical, legal, and constitutional questions. In the absence of statutory authorization, could the President remove a director? Directors of the Rural Telephone Bank and Student Loan Marketing Association serve at the pleasure of the President. Directors of FNMA are removable for 'good cause.' No grounds for removal of directors are specified for the Corporation for Public Broadcasting, COMSAT, National Homeownership Foundation, National Housing Partnerships, National Park Foundation, National Railroad Passenger Corporation, and Securities Investor Protection Corporation.

When Federal officers serve as directors of a non-governmental institution, do they serve in their official capacity or as private citizens? The Secretaries of Housing and Urban Development and Agriculture and the Director of the Office of Economic Opportunity are directors of the National Homeownership Foundation. The Secretary of Interior and the Director of the National Park Service are directors of the National Park Foundation. The Secretary of Transportation is a director of the National Railroad Passenger Corporation. Two of the seven directors of the Securities Investor Protection Corporation are appointed from among officers and employees of the Treasury Department and Federal Reserve. For public officials to participate in management of private institutions subject to their regulation raises ethical issues.

Normally interlocking arrangements of this type would be barred by conflict-of-interest statutes.[17]

While directors of a private corporation are not strictly trustees, they occupy a fiduciary position. Directors are agents of the corporation and as a matter of law are not permitted to enter into engagements or have any interest which might possibly conflict with the interests of the corporation. Are the public responsibilities of Presidentially-appointed directors compatible with their duties to the corporation?

For those corporations with mixed boards composed of Presidentially-appointed directors and directors elected by stockholders (FNMA, National Housing Partnerships, National Railroad Passenger Corporation, COMSAT, Student Loan Marketing Association), there are special problems. Early experiments with mixed boards ended in disaster.[18] The government was represented on the Board of the second Bank of the United States, established in 1816, by five directors. President Jackson complained in a message to Congress on December 1, 1834, of 'exclusion of public directors from knowledge' of the Bank's most important proceedings. The Presidentially-appointed directors were regarded by the other directors as government spies. The two government directors of the Union Pacific Railroad were also treated as spies and antagonists by their colleagues. The government directors in 1887 called for their abolition and their recommendation was accepted. Protection of the public interest can be better assured from the outside than from within a corporation.

The effectiveness of government directors as a means either for facilitating access to information or providing public accountability is subject to challenge. On the contrary, there is strong evidence that such arrangements tend to dilute and weaken public control. Herman Schwartz in an article in the December 1965 *Harvard Law Review* wrote:

> Both the practicalities of life and the lessons of history lead to the conclusion that the appointment of Government directors to a private board cannot effectively protect the public interest against private abuse. . . . There is also the possibility that the presence of Government will dampen the zeal of regulatory agencies. . . .[19]

The Securities and Exchange Commission is placed in a potentially embarrassing position when it is charged with responsibility for regulating the Securities Investor Protection Corporation headed by appointees of the President, Treasury, and Federal Reserve. If outvoted by his fellow directors, does the Secretary of Transportation put on his other hat in dealing with the financing of the National Passenger Corporation and in evaluating its performance?

As Senator Edmund Muskie stated with respect to the Securities Investor Protection Corporation:

> What I am fearful of is with industry representatives and public representatives on the board, that a request or application for a Treasury backup, use of the Treasury line of credit, could be interpreted as a public decision whereas actually the corporation is a private corporation, and it is a private request. . . . It seems to me the public membership on the private corporation, although it is a minority in fact, would be leaned upon as a crutch by the SEC and the Secretary of the Treasury for use of Treasury backup.[20]

More effective public control can be established by government regulation or under the provisions of freely negotiated contracts and grant agreements than by the appointment of government directors. The Opportunity Funding Corporation established under an Office of Economic Opportunity grant is more tightly controlled than most government-sponsored enterprises.

Chartering under District of Columbia laws

The 'anomalies' which led the Congress in 1945 to ban the practice of chartering Federal instrumentalities under the laws of states, local governments, and the District of Columbia have not disappeared in the intervening years. Those corporations chartered under the District of Columbia Business Corporation Law and District of Columbia Nonprofit Corporation Law are subject to dual regulation by the federal government and the district government.

It is doubtful that the Congress was fully familiar with the provisions of the District laws when it incorporated them by reference in the Acts creating such agencies as the National

Railroad Passenger Corporation and the National Homeownership Foundation. Sweeping powers are conferred upon corporations chartered under District law including power:

—to lend money to employees;
—to borrow money at such rates of interest as the corporation
   may determine without regard to restrictions of any usury
   law;
—to lend money for corporate purposes; and
—to distribute assets on dissolution.

Did the Congress intend to confer these powers on the government-sponsored enterprises?

There are a number of potential sources of conflict between the
provisions of the district laws and federal laws. For example, the
D.C. Nonprofit Corporation law (29–1019 (d)) provides: 'A
director may be removed from office pursuant to any procedure
provided in the articles of incorporation or the by-laws, and if
none is provided may be removed at a meeting expressly called for
that purpose.' Could this procedure be utilized to remove a
Presidentially-appointed director? Potential conflicts also exist
with respect to the dates for annual reports.

Government controls

Congress has pursued contradictory policies with respect to
government-sponsored enterprises. While it has defined these
enterprises as not being agencies and instrumentalities of the
United States government, the Congress increasingly has tended
to treat them as government agencies in appropriating money and
in establishing limitations on salaries and other controls. The
approach has been piecemeal, however, with the result that no
uniform system of controls has been developed.

The present crazy quilt pattern is illustrated by provisions
governing personnel and salaries. Salaries established by the
National Homeownership Foundation and National Railroad
Passenger Corporation may not exceed Level I of the Executive
Schedule, but the Corporation for Public Broadcasting is limited
to Level II. The National Legal Services Corporation would have
been required to follow the Classification Act and General
Schedule rates. No salary limitations are imposed on the other

government-sponsored enterprises. The Federal National Mortgage Association is required to make appointments solely on the basis of 'merit,' but not the other enterprises. The rationale for these differences is not readily apparent.

Decisions with regard to what programs should or should not be included in the budget totals or exempted from budget control appear to have been made on a case-by-case basis without regard to any consistent set of principles or doctrine. The rationale for exempting the U.S. Postal Service, Export-Import Bank, Corporation for Public Broadcasting, National Homeownership Foundation, and National Park Foundation from budget control, although these are either wholly-owned government instrumentalities or substantially dependent on federal funds, but maintaining budget control over the Rural Telephone Bank, a mixed-ownership corporation comparable to the Federal Intermediate Credit Banks and Banks for Cooperatives, is difficult to determine. Current practices cannot be reconciled either with concepts of a unified budget system or with the principles of an executive budget established by the Budget and Accounting Act of 1921.

Certain of the government-sponsored enterprises such as the Corporation for Public Broadcasting are treated as government agencies for purposes of appropriations. Instead of appropriating funds to a responsible and accountable federal officer, as was formerly the practice with CPB, appropriations are made directly to the non-government entity. The appropriation of money to a non-government entity raises a number of questions as to the enforceability of the Civil Rights laws and other statutory limitations on the use of appropriated funds. If funds are not appropriated to a federal officer, compliance can be obtained only by resort to the courts.

A similar unexplained diversity of provisions is to be found with respect to audit requirements. The Federal Home Loan Mortgage Corporation and National Homeownership Foundation are subject to an annual commercial-type audit by the General Accounting Office. The Corporation for Public Broadcasting, and the National Railroad Passenger Corporation are subject to a dual audit by independent certified public accountants and by the GAO 'in any year in which Federal funds are available to finance operations.' Since it is not contemplated that these corporations would ever operate without federal funds, the language with respect to the GAO audit implies an objective which appears nowhere else in the law. FNMA is subject to audit by the Secretary of HUD, not the Comptroller General. Audits by independent certified public accountants are required for the National Housing Partnerships and Student Loan Marketing Association. The Acts creating the National Park Foundation and Securities Investor Protection Corporation make no provision for an independent audit.

The Federal Home Loan Mortgage Corporation, Federal National Mortgage Association, Securities Investor Protection Corporation, and the Student Loan Marketing Association are authorized to borrow money from the Treasury or the public or both. FHLMC and Student Loan Marketing Association have an open-ended authority to borrow from the public. FNMA may issue its own securities and also has a $2\frac{1}{4}$ billion line of credit with the U.S. Treasury. The SIPC has a $1 billion call on the Treasury through the SEC. The Secretary of Transportation is authorized to guarantee loans to the NRPC of up to $450 million.

Regardless of legal status, the obligations of government-sponsored enterprises are construed to be at least moral government obligations. It would be unthinkable for the government to permit such an enterprise to default on its obligations. The financial operations of these enterprises have a direct impact on the market for government securities and without coordination can adversely affect the market for Treasury obligations.

Except for the National Railroad Passenger Corporation, the Treasury controls established by the Government Corporation Control Act have been waived. Authority to approve issuance of obligations by FNMA is vested in the Secretary of HUD, and in the Secretary of HEW for the Student Loan Marketing Association. Neither the Secretary of HUD or the Secretary of HEW has any familiarity with or responsibility for Federal debt management.

To recapture some control over Federal and Federally-assisted borrowing programs, the Treasury Department sponsored legislation to establish a Federal Financing Bank. The Bank would be authorized to purchase and sell any obligation which is issued, sold or guaranteed by a federal agency. Prior Treasury approval of the financing plans of borrowing agencies would be required with respect to method of financing, source of financing, timing, terms, and conditions. Treasury approval could not be withheld for longer than 120 days. The Bank would be capitalized by a $100 million advance from the Secretary of the Treasury and authorized to issue and have outstanding obligations not in excess of $15 billion. It is somewhat ironic that the receipts and expenditures of the proposed Federal Financing Bank would be excluded from budget totals and general limitations on expenditures and net lending, although the Bank's ostensible mission is to coordinate agency borrowing programs with 'overall Federal fiscal and debt management policies.' The legislation failed of enactment.

Half-way measures such as the proposed Federal Financing Bank are not calculated to accomplish significant improvements and contribute to the confusion. Admittedly, the controls to be vested in the Bank would have been weaker than those now possessed by the Secretary of the Treasury under the provisions of the Government Corporation Control Act. Furthermore, the Bank's authority would not extend to government-sponsored private enterprises.

CONCLUDING OBSERVATIONS

President Nixon emphasized in his message of March 25, 1971 on government reorganization that 'our entire system rests on the assumption that elected leaders can make the Government respond to the people's mandate. Too often, this assumption is wrong. When lines of responsibility are as tangled and ambiguous as they are in many policy areas, it is extremely difficult for either the Congress or the President to see that their intentions are carried out.'[21] At the same time the President has proposed measures to eliminate the *de facto* independent fiefdoms within the government structure, powerful independent *de jure* fiefdoms are being created within and outside the Executive Branch. The proliferation of autonomous agencies and government-sponsored enterprises is a threat to orderly and responsible government.

The privileged position accorded autonomous agencies has exacerbated, and sometimes created, the very deficiencies within the public service which are most often cited by those advocating the creation of autonomous agencies for important new programs. When autonomous agencies are permitted to drain away from the established departments the most challenging and innovative programs and the most ambitious and talented personnel, as has happened in some countries, then the departments should not be criticized because they have lost or cannot develop the capability to perform effectively anything but traditional tasks.

Creation of autonomous agencies and government-sponsored enterprises is a means to avoid, not to solve, the dilemma of modern governments. The issue is not independence versus control, but uniformity versus diversity. A degree of uniformity is essential, but not uniformity for its own sake. A comprehensive and critical evaluation of control systems in terms of current needs is long overdue.

United States central control agencies are more flexible and less resistant to change than most. But the last review of this type was undertaken by the General Accounting Office and Bureau of the Budget over twenty-five years ago when the Government Corporation Control Act was developed. Given a mandate from the President and the Congress, the GAO and Office of Management and Budget, the successor to the Bureau of the Budget, have the capability of conducting the necessary study and finding constructive solutions.

Such a study should concentrate on ends, not means. Controls should be evaluated in terms of their effectiveness in assuring that (1) policies established by responsible officials are implemented; (2) operations and policies are consistent with, and in furtherance of, basic objectives established by the government; (3) program goals are accomplished expeditiously and with maximum effectiveness; (4) the needs of the using public are adequately served and the rights of citizens safeguarded; and (5) sufficient information is provided to evaluate results and to make sound judgments on resource allocation. Whatever systems are devised must be sufficiently flexible to accommodate diversity—diversity in objectives and organizational, personnel, operating and financial requirements. Governments must break out of the straitjacket imposed by systems which are process rather than results oriented.

Notes

1. Hearings before the Senate Commerce Committee, Subcommittee on Communication, on S. 1160 (90th Congress, 1st Session), pp. 140–1.
2. Message of the President of the United States Relative to Postal Reform, April 16, 1970 (House Document No. 91–313).
3. The Civil Service, Report of the Committee 1966–68 (London, Her Majesty's Stationery Office), vol. 1, p. 50.
4. Peter F. Drucker, *The Age of Discontinuity* (Harper and Row, 1969) pp. 233–42.
5. E. L. Normanton, *The Accountability and Audit of Governments* (Manchester University Press, 1966) p. xv.
6. House Document 19, 80th Cong., pp. M-57–M-62.
7. Senate Committee on Banking and Currency, hearings on 1968 Housing Act, p. 59.
8. Senate Report 91–912.
9. Senate Committee on Banking and Currency, Hearings on S.19 and S.581 (1971).
10. Hearings before the Senate Commerce Committee, op. cit., pp. 116 and 161.
11. Hearings before Senate Labor and Public Welfare Committee, on S. 659 (92nd Cong., 1st Sess.) p. 619.
12. Lloyd D. Musolf (ed.), *Communications Satellites in Political Orbit*, (Chandler Publishing Corp., 1968) p. 136.
13. President's Commission on Budget Concepts, *Staff Papers*, pp. 189–90, (U.S. Government Printing Office, 1967).
14. Message Vetoing H.R. 13918—House Document 92–320.
15. *New York Times*, January 30, 1973.
16. Senate Document 92–48.
17. In an informal opinion the Department of Justice ruled that directors of the Federal National Mortgage Association were not subject to the conflict of interest statutes. Letter from William Rehnquist, Assistant Attorney General, to Under Secretary of Housing and Urban Development Richard Van Dusen, July 10, 1970.
18. See Lloyd D. Musolf, *Mixed Enterprise* (D. C. Heath and Co., 1972) pp. 54–6.
19. Herman Schwartz, 'A Dilemma for Government-Appointed Directors,' *Harvard Law Review*, Dec., 1965.
20. Senate Committee on Banking and Currency, Subcommittee on Securities, hearings on S.2348, S.3988 and S.3909, 91st Cong., 2nd Sess., p. 248.
21. Papers relating to the President's Departmental Reorganization Program, revised Feb., 1972 (U.S. Government Printing Office).

Appendix

Government Corporations and Government-sponsored Enterprises

Created since 1960

Corporation	Legal Status	Directors	Financing	Controls
COMSAT	Private for profit Corp.	12 elected by stockholders; 3 by President with Senate confirmation	No government financing	Regulation by FCC as private utility
Community Development Corporation	Not specified	Sec. of HUD, 3 by Sec. of HUD, 1 by President with Senate confirmation	None. Program financed by Appropriations to Sec. HUD and Treasury borrowing	None. Not under G.C.A. (Govt. Corp. Control Act)
Corporation for Public Broadcasting	Private non-profit Corp.	15 appointed by President with Senate confirmation	Appropriations, Grants from foundations	Audit by independent C.P.A.s and GAO in any year in which Federal funds are available
Federal Home Loan Mortgage Corp.	Not specified	Home Loan Bank Board	$100 million common stock subscribed by Home Loan Banks. Sale of obligations backed by government guaranteed securities	Not under G.C.A. Subject to commercial type audit by GAO. Operates 'without regard to any other law' applicable to public expenditure
Federal National Mortgage Association	Govt.-sponsored private corp.	10 elected by stockholders and 5 by President	$2¼ billion line of credit from U.S. Treasury. Sale of securities backed by U.S. guaranteed obligations	Subject to general regulatory power of Sec. HUD. Annexed budget. appointments to be based on 'merit'

Government Corporations and Government-sponsored Enterprises
Created since 1960

Corporation	Legal Status	Directors	Financing	Controls
Government National Mortgage Assoc.	Wholly-owned Govt. Corp.	All powers vested in Sec. HUD	Open-ended borrowing from Treasury. Commitments limited to $200 million	Subject to G.C.A.
Inter-American Foundation	Wholly-owned Govt. Corp.	7 appointed by President with Senate confirmation	Appropriations	Subject to G.C.A.
National Home Ownership Foundation	Private non-profit	Sec. HUD, Sec. Agri. Director OEO, and 15 appointed by President with Senate confirmation	$10 million appropriation	Commercial type audit by GAO
National Housing Partnerships	Private for profit	12 elected by stockholders, and 3 by President with Senate confirmation	No Federal financing	Audit by independent C.P.A.s
National Park Foundation	Private non-profit	Sec. Int., Director Park Service and 6 appointed by Sec. Int.	Services by Depts. of Int. and Justice without reimbursement	None
National Railroad Passenger Corp.	Private for profit. Mixed-ownership Govt. corp.	8 appointed by President with Senate confirmation and 7 elected by stockholders. Sec. Transp. a director	Common stock sold to railroads. $265 million U.S. grants. U.S. guaranteed loans. Treasury borrowing	Subject to G.C.A. as a mixed ownership corp. No budget control
Overseas Private Investment Corp.	Wholly-owned Govt. Corp.	AID administrator, chairman, 6 appointed by President with Senate confirmation and 4 U.S. officials designated by President	$20 million capital stock subscribed by AID. Appropriations to replenish insurance and guaranty fund	Subject to G.C.A.

Government Corporation and Government-sponsored Enterprises
Created since 1960

Corporation	Legal Status	Directors	Financing	Controls
Rural Telephone Bank	Mixed-ownership Govt. Corp.	REA Ad. and FCA Gov. ex officio. 5 designated by President, 3 from U.S.D.A. and 2 from public. 6 elected from cooperatives eligible to receive loans	$300 million in stock subscribed by U.S. Borrowers required to invest in stock and U.S. stock to be retired over a period of years. Sale of obligations to public and Treasury	Until converted to private ownership subject to G.C.A., as if it were a wholly-owned Govt. corp.
Securities Investor Protection Corp.	Private non-profit corp.	1 by Sec. Treas.; 1 by Federal Reserve; 5 by President with Senate confirmation	Authority to borrow up to $1 billion from Treasury. Assessments against members	Subject to SEC regulation
Student Loan Marketing Assoc.	Govt.-sponsored private corp.	Interim Board of 21 appointed by President	$5 million advance by Sec. HEW. Sale of stock to insured lenders. Issuance of obligations guaranteed by Sec. HEW	HEW approval of borrowing. Audit by Independent CPAs
U.S. Postal Service	Independent establishment	9 appointed by President with Senate confirmation. Postmaster Gen. and Deputy Postmaster Gen. —ex officio	Transferred assets of Post Office. Sale of obligations either to public or Treasury not in excess of $10 billion. Appropriations to pay for non-self-sustaining services	Not subject to G.C.A. GAO audit. Exempt from Federal laws with respect to contracts, property, works, officers, budgets and funds
Environmental Financing Authority	Instrumentality of U.S.	Sec. Treas. or designee chairman. 4 directors appointed by President from officers and employees of U.S.	Sec. Treas. authorized to advance up to $100 million to authority. Borrowing from Treas. or public. Sec. Treas. makes up any interest loss in purchase of state and local obligations to finance non-federal share of water pollution control projects	Subject to budget and audit provision of G.C.A. Expenditures not included in budget totals. Borrowing subject to debt limit

5 The University's Compact with Society

DAEL WOLFLE

When Daniel Coit Gilman was invited to become the first president of the new Johns Hopkins University, he rejoiced that the Johns Hopkins trustees 'are responsible neither to ecclesiastical nor legislative supervisors; but simply to their own convictions of duty and the enlightened judgment of their fellow men. . . . Their means are ample; their authority complete; their purpose enlightened. Is not this opportunity without parallel in the history of our country?'[1] Gilman's experience as president of the University of California had already persuaded him to accept any good opportunity to escape further encounters with the California legislature. When Johns Hopkins offered that opportunity he did not hesitate.

In planning the University of Chicago a few years later, President William Rainey Harper insisted that professors in all fields—theology as much as science—be free to search for the truth and to follow wherever it led. The assurance of such freedom was one of the attractions that brought the University of Chicago its distinguished initial faculty, a faculty that included nine men who had occupied presidential chairs of seminaries, colleges, or universities—all eager for the freedom Chicago promised.[2]

Academic freedom, autonomy, independence from control by church or state, the opportunity for a university to develop in accordance with its own logic and internal sense of direction—this was the ideal of Gilman and Harper, and this has been the ideal of university professors and presidents ever since.

The ideal has never been attained. Gilman and the professors he selected for Johns Hopkins had much freedom, but not complete freedom. They were responsible to a lay board of trustees.

No other pattern was really conceivable. Harvard, the first American college, adopted the well-established European custom of giving control to a lay board of trustees.

Only in its very earliest days was the European university exempt from external control. Bologna and the other earliest universities in Italy simply sprang up, without charter from pope or emperor, and without accountability to church or state. That condition was short lived, and given up voluntarily, for even then the university was not exempt from influence which the professors alone could not resist. The first lay board of trustees was appointed in Florence, and its purpose was to help the professors, who, 'trying to escape the tyranny of student guilds, appealed to the local town authorities for relief. Sympathizing with the professors, the town authorities set up a lay board of curators to administer financial subsidies to them and thus make them independent of the students.'³

The Florentine choice was not between autonomy and heteronomy, but among types and conditions of control. This is still the choice. The question to ask is not whether colleges and universities can achieve autonomy, but rather what functions should be protected against what invasions and how responsibility should be divided among faculty, administrators, and the public.

This question is as old as the Florentine decision, and it arose early in colonial America when disagreements at Harvard were resolved by giving the trustees control over external matters, such as the formation of policy and the allocation of financial resources, and giving the faculty control over the internal matters of student instruction and discipline.

THE UNIVERSITY'S COMPACT WITH SOCIETY

Custom, law, judicial rulings, and compromise gradually evolved into the sometimes uneasy, often violated, but generally workable pattern of arrangements under which American colleges and universities have been operating. These arrangements trace back to a compact between the professor and the state that originated in Germany: 'The German professor struck a bargain with the state. If the state kept its nose out of his expertise, he in turn agreed not to meddle in politics.'⁴ Under this compact, freedom to teach and freedom to learn were assured to faculty and students;

the establishment of new institutions of higher education and the conditions of public support were recognized as responsibilities of the laity; and the professors agreed to confine their activities to objective scholarship, teaching, and the search for truth.

When the idea of the German university was imported to the United States, the concept of academic freedom was as zealously sought here as in Germany and became one of the ideals of American higher education. Although the university's compact with society was never a formal agreement, on both sides it was generally recognized that academic freedom was part of a trade and not a free gift.[5] Whether the phrase 'the Ivory Tower' was spoken in pride or in derision, it was usually understood that the inhabitants of that tower had disengaged themselves from politics and the market place so that they might better fulfill their special function in society.

In both countries the compact was a success. It helped to establish the distinction between church schools which taught established ecclesiastical doctrine and universities whose professors could challenge and test ideas, teach the truth as they saw it, and seek to discover new truths. To allow independent university scholarship to flourish it was necessary to escape the control of ecclesiastical and other established doctrine.

The compact signalized this freedom

The compact has been honored, but often also it has been broken; governors, state legislatures, churches, trustees, donors, alumni, students, and the 'town' have all been guilty of intruding into the internal affairs of higher education. To protect themselves against such forays, professors banded together in 1915 to form the American Association of University Professors so that collectively they might establish investigative and punitive procedures to protect their individual freedom. This battle has been largely won; faculty control over academic affairs is a well-accepted principle in American colleges and universities.

The professors' victory on this point, however, has subjected universities to another type of external control. Indeed one of the objectives of the founders of the AAUP was to weaken the university *as an institution* and to increase the power of professional guilds in directing its development. At the beginning of the AAUP the Committee on Academic Freedom and Academic Tenure proclaimed that 'the responsibility of the university teacher is primarily to the public itself, and to the judgment of his own profession.'[6] Responsibility to the university was mentioned only later, and was clearly meant to be limited and minor. Consistent with this relative emphasis, the AAUP long ago adopted a statement of principle concerning academic freedom and tenure but has only recently given serious consideration to a companion statement on academic responsibility.

In recent years also some professors have become increasingly willing to abrogate their compact with society. In 1970 Robley C. Williams and 110 cosigners provided a useful example when they published the following letter in Science.

> We of the Molecular Biology and Virus Laboratory of the University of California (i) condemn the current U.S. policy and military activity in Southeast Asia as unwise, immoral, and dangerous; (ii) urge members of Congress to use every legal means to resist the implementation of this policy; (iii) urge immediate withdrawal of all U.S. troops and assistance from Southeast Asia; and (iv) express our intention to support only those candidates for elective office who subscribe to the above policies.[7]

Many academicians—and many others—agreed, but the existence of widespread objections to U.S. policy in Southeast Asia is not the reason for reprinting the letter here. Note that the signers were not acting as private citizens. They did not sign as individuals or identify themselves by their residence addresses. They identified themselves as 'We of the Molecular Biology and Virus Laboratory of the University of California.'

During 1969 and 1970, at the American Association for the Advancement of Science, I received a considerable number of other letters on political issues and national policies that started out: 'We the members of the Department of ——— at the University of ———.'

Rightly or wrongly, the signers of these letters were seeking to use the prestige of their positions and their universities to influence national policies. They were violating the old compact between the professors and the state.

The violation was clear and deliberate, yet it went only a few steps beyond what had already become a fairly common practice. For some years, the *New York Times*, the *Washington Post*, and other major newspapers have printed, as paid advertisements, statements concerning political issues and national policies that were signed by faculty members from many campuses, each with his institutional affiliation indicated. Some of these advertisements have included, often in small type, the not-really-sanitizing disclaimer, 'Institutional affiliations given for identification only.'

Public letters and paid advertisements have not been the only means of entering politics. During each of the last several Presidential campaigns, there have been active organizations of 'Scientists and Engineers for ————.' At several Presidential nominating conventions, university presidents have made nominating or seconding speeches. Faculty members are often in the forefront of campus protests and some have been leaders in campus disruptions.

Dr Williams[8] and his colleagues did not attempt to demonstrate that their specialized scientific competence gave them expert status on matters of international and military policy. Neither did the signers of the other letters and advertisements. Nor did they act as private individuals. They and the faculty members who have led recent campus protests might describe their motives differently; they would be supported and criticized by different groups of faculty colleagues; but all were seeking to use their university positions for political purposes.

'Keeping out of politics,' however, is a matter of degree, and one that requires closer definition. Protest leaders, letter signers, the different groups of academicians who organized in 1968 to support the Presidential aspirations of Richard Nixon or Hubert Humphrey, and others who have engaged in other kinds of political activity might respond to the charge that they had broken their social compact by claiming that conditions justified their actions or that their political engagement had been extra-curricular and had not affected their teaching or scholarly writing.

Moreover, if 'keeping out of politics' is given the extreme definition of forbidding any involvement in public affairs, the compact never could have been kept, nor was it meant to be.

For even as the first universities were being established in the United States, professors were being drawn into public affairs. The single most noteworthy example was the enactment of the Morrill Land Grant Act in 1862, which consciously and deliberately extended the function of higher education to include improvement of the practical affairs of agriculture. In an agricultural country, agriculture had long been a professorial interest. It was primary in Thomas Jefferson's list of functions of a university, and agricultural improvement was a major objective of the changes that led to the Sheffield Scientific School at Yale. The Morrill Act, however, formalized a relationship that involved both state and federal support for work intended to influence directly the practical conduct of agriculture and thus the national economy. Professors in Land Grant Colleges were not expected to meddle in the politics of election campaigns, but the Morrill Act and its subsequent extensions instructed and encouraged them to 'meddle' in the nation's economic growth and welfare.

From the Morrill Act to the present time the course has been one of greater and greater involvement of professors in public affairs. The University of Wisconsin—especially under President Van Hise—made the term 'The Wisconsin Idea' a symbol for university service to the state's government and citizens. During the 1930s, academicians were prominently involved in the New Deal agencies created to cope with national problems. Increasingly since 1940, faculty members have been providing their individual services to industry, the state or community, the federal government, and other agencies of society. They serve as advisors, consultants, and part-time or intermittent employees of a great array of agencies and institutions that are directly involved in the social, political, economic, administrative, and policy-making machinery of the nation.

Universities as institutions have also become more and more involved in public affairs. Universities serve as a principal research arm of the federal government. They administer programs of foreign assistance and international cooperation. They conduct Job Corps, Peace Corps, and other training programs. They have established consortia to manage national scientific institutions such as the National Center for Atmospheric Research and essentially governmental agencies such as the Institute for Defense Analysis. The government has sought university cooperation in these activities because of the university's special competence or its reputation for objectivity and intellectual quality.

Reactions to the university's extensive involvement in governmental affairs have sometimes been polarized. Some students, some faculty members and administrators, and some political leaders have worried about the increasing involvement of faculty members in industrial and governmental policy and practice. They see the trend as having weakened the university's educational functions, destroyed its ability to be discriminatingly critical of society and government, and robbed it of its moral influence. Theodore Roszak, one of the more extreme spokesmen for this position, thinks the university has gone so far in being willing to do whatever society will pay for that, morally speaking, it has come to resemble a 'highly adaptable brothel.'[9]

Roszak is far from being a lonely critic of the university's widening service function. Yet each new development has been welcomed by some professors and administrators as it has by the men of practical affairs with whom they have collaborated. These new developments have been welcomed not only because universities and individual professors have made important contributions to the public welfare but also because involvement in public affairs has often enriched the university's educational offerings and research opportunities. Efforts to solve practical problems have demonstrably stimulated research achievements in universities.[10] Moreover, the university professor who has had first-hand acquaintance with the workings of the Department of Defense, the Office of the President, or some other federal agency, is often a more cogent social critic than his ivory tower colleague who lacks such experience. The amount of vigorous and well-informed criticism of government policy either on broad issues such as American engagement in Southeast Asia or on specific ones such as development of antiballistic missiles both illustrates the critical role of the former government official who has become a professor, and constitutes a factual denial of Roszak's charge of moral bankruptcy.

Thus although the old compact has been useful in protecting the freedom of faculty members, never in this country has it been the only guide for relations between society and the university. Nor can it now be. The university has become dependent on federal support; the nation needs its universities, for service as well as for education; and this merging of interests and the resulting blurring of the distinction between university affairs and government affairs is but a part of a more general loss of sharpness in distinctions that once could be made more easily, for example the distinctions between government and industry, military and civilian, federal and state, or foreign and domestic.

All in all, the government has become so involved with universities, and universities so involved with government, that the nineteenth-century understanding that each would let the other alone is no longer workable.

A new compact

A new compact is needed. The old one is shattered and out of date. What should take its place? The replacement will have to go well beyond the kind of treaty that sufficed earlier. Only teaching and research needed to be considered then; the service function must now also be included, for knowledge, especially the precise, rigorous knowledge that comes from research and scholarly analysis, has become an important instrument of power.

There will be another difference between the old compact and the new one. The old compact was between the professor and the state. The concept of the university as a loose collection of independent scholars has been congenial to individual scholars. But that concept no longer suffices and the new compact will have to involve the university as an institution. Consequently there will have to be more penetrating analyses of institutional goals and of the university's relations both internally with its members and externally with society and the government.

It behooves the academic world to undertake the necessary analysis and to try to arrive at agreement upon the compact it wants with society, for in drawing up any contract, the advantage usually lies with the party that drafts the terms and knows what it wants. Of course bargaining will be necessary, but universities would do well to write the first draft. In doing that, it will be necessary to decide what responsibilities the university and the government owe each other and what protection each needs against incursions by the other.

THE UNIVERSITY AS AN AGENCY OF GOVERNMENT

The relations between the university and the government have become so many and so close that it is time to recognize the fact that in some of its functions the university has become a quasi-governmental institution.[11] Such a relationship conflicts with tradition and its existence will be denied by some people and rejected by others. Yet universities administer national laboratories; participate in government-sponsored international programs; conduct research for a variety of state and federal agencies; provide advisory, educational, and other services; and offer advanced education to career officers (civilian and military) of government departments. They educate and certify most of the people who will later occupy the seats of power throughout state and federal governments. In large numbers their faculty members sit on government policy-making bodies. Through all these means, the universities have become so widely involved in the making of government policy and in the execution of government programs that by any reasonable definition they have become agencies of government for some parts of their work.

All of this, of course, applies to the universities in their graduate and professional education functions and in their research and service programs. It applies so much less to the undergraduate college that several critics of the educational scene foresee a growing separation between undergraduate and graduate institutions.[12] The separation of graduate from undergraduate education would help to clarify the somewhat different objectives of the two levels. Cost accounting would be more honest and cost differentials more obvious. And it would be possible under such separation to distinguish more clearly between the problems and the responsibilities of the two levels. Yet there are also valid objections to separating the levels into different institutions. How soon, or indeed whether, physical separation will take place is problematical, but a clearer separation of objectives, costs, and programs—clearer in the minds of all concerned—is an objective to be emphasized in educational planning and policy making.

What should be preserved

'For seven centuries,' Eric Ashby has reminded us, 'universities have been in danger of interference from their patrons.'[13] What are the current dangers, now that government has become a major patron and universities have become agencies of government? 'Now is the time,' to quote Eric Ashby again, 'to assert what should be preserved.'[14]

What should be preserved, or perhaps regained, must be defined in terms of present realities and their logical projections. Independence from government support is no longer a realistic expectation. Amounts vary widely from one campus to another; the terms and specific purposes of support differ and will change; perhaps in the future more of the federal support will be for general rather than specific purposes. But it cannot realistically be expected that all or most of the federal monies granted to universities will have no strings attached.

What should be preserved will also have to be defined in full expectation that a variety of federal agencies will wish to use the universities for a variety of purposes, and that the agencies will define those purposes in terms of their missions and responsibilities, not in terms of university priorities.

Moreover, the definition of what should be preserved cannot assume isolation from problems society considers important. Selection and negotiation are possible, but the university must be responsive to the major needs of society. Specifically and immediately, the university cannot isolate itself from the complex and politically difficult social and environmental problems that are swirling around the country. The university must be involved in the analysis of these problems because no other institution can bring to that task an equivalent combination of intellectual standards, objectivity, expert knowledge in all of the relevant fields of theoretical and applied knowledge, and detachment from the necessity of making day-to-day decisions concerning management.

True, the university is not well organized for this kind of study, it does not have much experience in bringing its collective strength to bear on large and complex social problems, and for some kinds of applied research it is probably not the most natural or best equipped institution. The university is more adept at tearing big problems down into isolated bits than it is at treating big problems as wholes. Faculty members have more experience in working independently on selected parts of a large problem than they have in integrating their specialized knowledge into a unified treatment of the problem as a whole.

It will not be easy for a large university with all of its traditions of protecting the academic freedom of its faculty members to organize itself for collective, integrated work on such many-faceted problems. But some universities will have to make the necessary effort on some of the big social and environmental problems, for these are the problems that are high on society's current list of priorities.

It will not be necessary for all universities to become deeply involved in analyzing and studying any of these problems, or that all faculty members will have to participate, or that those who do participate must devote all of their time to the one endeavor. What is required is that a significant number of leaders, from different schools and disciplines, define and accept the task as their cooperative responsibility; that better linkages be developed between the work of individual scholars who conduct basic studies of selected aspects of the total set of problems and the problem- or system-oriented work that may perhaps best be carried forward under the auspices of engineering, medical, or other professional schools; and that methods be developed to reward faculty members for effective participation in such activities so that their professional rewards and status will not depend solely upon the standards of their individual disciplines. This latter problem may not turn out to be as difficult as it is often thought to be.

A positive reward of such an effort, to the institution and to many of its members, will be that the institution will be setting its own goals, collectively. That, too, will be something of a problem, but it should not be an insuperable one.

Moreover, collective goal setting is completely consistent with the proposition that what should be preserved is a reasonable degree of self-direction. The value is stated in this qualified fashion because self-direction is not an absolute. Historically, university development has been the product of many forces, some internal and some external. Like a living organism, a university has a heredity and an environment. It cannot take sustenance from the environment without being influenced by it. It can, however, strengthen those mechanisms of internal governance that will enable it to decide how inner nature and external influences will be combined, and to what ends. Moreover, it is not necessary—in fact not desirable—that the balance between internal and external forces be the same in all universities. Institutional variety is one of the goals to be sought. Thus what is wanted is both balance within institutions and a balance among them so that we may have a system of universities which in total meets the criterion of a balance between the current needs of society and the long-term needs of the system, including its ability to respond constructively to societal needs.

This, then, is the realistic definition of the independence that the university should preserve: a reasonable degree of freedom in determining its own ends and the means of working toward those ends, in full awareness of the demands of society and of its own abilities and limitations, and in full awareness of its niche in the higher educational system.

If this kind of independence is to be preserved, the university should undertake three interrelated tasks: analysis of the threats to independence to determine how serious each is; definition of the kinds of protection and support it needs from society; and agreement upon the kind of coin with which it will pay society for assurance of the desired independence.

Threats and possible threats to independence

Possible threats to the university's ability to set its own goals and to determine its own priorities and balance can be considered under five headings: federal government policy; the administration of federal programs; federal fiscal practices; disagreements between federal and university priorities; and other possible threats.

Of course a university could avoid any danger of federal interference simply by declining federal funds. It could also avoid danger of interference by state government, industry, private foundations, alumni, or other donors by declining funds from those sources. But then it would no longer be a university. If it wishes to remain among the productive leaders in research, a university really has no choice; it must plan to secure a substantial part of the necessary funds from federal sources. The possible dangers that accompany the benefits of federal support must therefore be considered.

FEDERAL POLICY

Direct, intentional infringement of independence by the federal government is not a serious threat. Harold Orlans summarized: 'The danger of federal control is like the danger of a dragon waking. Many academicians believe it never will wake (it has slept so long); many, that it is not asleep but awake and quite tame; others that there is no dragon at all.'[15] Even earlier, Charles V. Kidd had seen the federal requirement of security clearances for persons engaged in federally financed unclassified research as 'the one occurrence that has shaken my conviction that general federal aid to higher education poses no inherent danger to the freedom of universities.'[16]

More recently, in 1968, essentially none of the 1,200 college and university presidents who replied to a questionnaire study conducted for the Carnegie Commission on Higher Education listed federal control as one of their major concerns.[17]

Among thirty-five propositions concerning possible future trends in higher education that the American Council on Education presented to national samples of student leaders, faculty members, administrators, and trustees, one read, 'As a corollary of tax-dollar support, government agencies will have increasing influence over private colleges and universities.' All four groups ranked this hypothetical development down somewhere between eleventh and twenty-first in probability. To another hypothetical possibility which read, 'By 1978, higher education in general will be centrally planned and coordinated on some nationwide basis,' all four groups assigned ranks of thirty-four or thirty-five for probability.[18]

The absence of worry over deliberate federal control is in accord with government policy and recent experience. 'Academic freedom' is as popular a slogan in Congress as in faculty discussions. President Nixon was echoing many an earlier governmental leader when he announced in December of 1970 that 'Academic freedom is the cornerstone of the American educational system.'[19] The formal policies of recent congressional acts supporting higher education and the administrators of those acts have accepted and honored the proposition that educational decisions should be made by educators and scholars and not by the federal government.

Deliberate infringement as a matter of federal policy can be dismissed; it is not a major threat. Leaders of the federal government join with professors in repeating the hallowed principle that universities should be free from government interference.

FEDERAL ADMINISTRATION

It is sometimes charged that some of the government officials who defend the principle of non-interference fail to practice what they preach. The program officer—who is likely to be a former faculty member—has his own ideas about what is important in a field, about proper research methodology, about research or educational priorities. He helps to determine which grants are made. He discusses plans with grant applicants, and sometimes suggests ways in which he believes the proposed work can be improved. It is he to whom a grantee must go to secure approval for changes in budget allocations or work plans. If he and the grantee disagree, the grantee is in the weaker position.

There is no way to determine the extent of such 'interference' for accounts are not kept. If full accounts were available, some of the 'interference' must surely have resulted in improvements. Methodological sophistication, knowledge of sources, information about related work being carried on elsewhere, wisdom in foreseeing what work is more likely to pay off—these virtues are possessed by some bureaucrats as well as by some faculty members. The supporting agencies need and want qualified scientists as program officers. They must be expected to have ideas of their own.

Thus some of the charges of influence by program officers must be discounted, for the testimony of grantees, and particularly of disappointed applicants for grants, is not wholly trustworthy. They have lost an argument, or lost a grant, and their criticisms may not be objective.

The variety of federal programs, each with its own objectives, application procedures, and regulations, has required colleges and universities to adapt to a sometimes bewildering array of rules and regulations. And these rules and regulations have changed over time, for as national priorities have changed, so have the federal programs, the agencies that sponsored them, the amounts of money available, and the rules for their administration.

Daniel S. Greenberg concluded that 'The administrative system for providing federal support for academic research and higher education has become a monstrosity.'[20] This statement was his summary of a 1967 survey of the eighty-one universities that were receiving 65 percent of all federal monies directed to institutions of higher education. There was much complaint about the amount of paper work involved. Auditing procedures came in for specific complaint. One correspondent suggested that the federal scale of values had gotten out of balance: 'I get the impression,' he wrote, 'that the collection of *statistics* is becoming more important to the federal granting agencies than the pursuit of results. . . . It seems frighteningly clear that . . . we are going to achieve magnificently documented mediocrity.'

Diverse and changing regulations have been irritating. They have added to the cost of making and administering federal grants. But there were few complaints in Greenberg's survey of interference with the substantive conduct of scientific or educational programs. There have, however, been complaints of efforts to control the distribution of reports of work supported by federal funds. In some cases, agencies have sought to restrict the distribution. In other cases, project directors have complained of pressure to distribute reports—including sending copies to all members of Congress—before the data had been fully analyzed or the interpretation adequately reviewed and criticized.

There is no hard evidence as to which federal agencies are best and which worst in their tendencies to influence the planning and conduct of federally supported activities, but two general distinctions are possible. Close guidance is both more frequent and more appropriate in the case of contracts for work which was originally planned by a government agency than in the case of research projects initiated by members of a college or university faculty. Most contracts of the former kind are written with industry, but universities are responsible for some, and when a university accepts such a contract, guidance from the sponsoring agency should be expected.

The other distinction is less clear and less justifiable, but charges of bureaucratic interference seem more likely to be lodged against agencies which have had less experience in dealing with universities and against those that work in education, urban affairs, or other social science areas than against more experienced agencies and those that emphasize the physical and biological sciences. However, these attitudes are largely dependent upon time, place, personalities, and other individual factors. In response to the question of which agency gave the most difficulty, the Vice-President for Research of one university replied, 'Whichever one I am dealing with at the time.'

University-government relations have sometimes been strained by auditing procedures, conflicting rulings, multiple report requirements, and disagreements between university and government representatives. There has been substantial irritation at times. But these difficulties have typically affected a project or program without having had much influence on the university as a whole. In general, the relations between government officials and university representatives over the details of approved programs have not seriously damaged university independence.

FEDERAL FISCAL PRACTICES

Fiscal practices have constituted a more serious threat to university independence. The government's long-lasting refusal to reimburse universities for full indirect costs and episodic congressional insistence on cost sharing have resulted in much ill-will and have sometimes required universities to supplement federal grants with money withdrawn from other purposes.

Even if a federally-supported activity fits exactly into a university's own self-defined priorities and objectives, in starting it the university risks either financial loss or financial dependence. The management of large off-campus laboratories, such as MIT's Lincoln Laboratory, and the conduct of large on-campus programs always entails obligations to faculty and staff members and thus puts the university at the mercy of the government for fiscal continuity.

The necessary continuity has usually been provided, but not always. In 1957 the Air Force suddenly cut in half the budget of its Office of Scientific Research. Quick and vigorous repercussions forced the Air Force to restore the cut, but some projects were damaged and the episode has not been forgotten on campuses that were instructed to reduce expenditure immediately for projects that had already been financed. In 1963 the House of Representatives reduced the National Science Foundation budget by 45 percent. The Senate and the House-Senate conference committee did not let such a jolting reduction stand, but at one stage the House was willing to reduce the budget by almost half. Congress did reduce the 1969 NSF budget to approximately 80 percent of the 1968 appropriation, and then imposed on the whole Executive Branch a spending ceiling below the total of amounts appropriated. As one consequence, many grantees were not allowed to spend as much as they had been granted. Budget reductions have always been a threat and in a few cases have produced substantial dislocations and anguish.[21] In all such cases, the university is left to pick up the pieces. When a large research program is suddenly terminated it is virtually impossible to reduce supporting services with equal speed. The university has commitments and sometimes contracts that outlast termination allowances, and thus summary reductions are traumatic. However, they have been relatively infrequent, and in total have probably caused less trouble than has resulted from uncertainty and instability. Delays in renewing grants until after the previous grant period had expired have forced universities to cover interim costs and hope to be reimbursed later. The abruptness of termination of the period of regularly increasing appropriations produced some dislocations and added to the difficulties of financially hard-pressed universities —which means practically all universities. Training grants have been terminated before some of the trainees had had time to complete their approved programs.

Complaints about the disruptive effects of federal fiscal practices should not be allowed to outweigh the positive fact that much has been accomplished that could not have been done otherwise. Even so, instability and uncertainty have sometimes created serious problems for universities. Assurance of reasonably stable funding would greatly aid universities in their forward planning, and would probably increase the per dollar effectiveness of federal grants.

DIFFERENCES IN PRIORITIES

Government programs, even though well administered and consistently funded, may threaten university independence if their objectives are at variance with those of the university or if the federal priorities differ seriously from those of the university. These differences are responsible for the greatest amount of concern over the impact of federal funding on university independence.

The research interests of federal agencies are determined by their larger responsibilities—health, defense, atomic energy, or, in the case of the National Science Foundation, science itself. There is some coordination through the annual budget-making process, but to a large extent each agency sets its own priorities for the use of research funds. Many government programs have been planned without much consideration for their side effects. Budget decisions are made by agencies that have neither responsibility nor special competence for higher education as a whole. With few exceptions, government support to universities is intended to secure specified products or services, not to maintain or improve the provider of those products and services. Congress has provided the funds needed for these programs but has been much less willing to approve general support for universities and colleges.

Federal programs for higher education have been designed to support research; to educate more specialists in fields in which shortages were anticipated; to reduce financial barriers that keep able but impoverished students from entering college; to improve libraries or counseling programs; or to buy needed services. The size of these programs plus their specific nature is widely believed to have distorted university programs and to have robbed universities of the normal balance among their several activities. Harold Orlans reported a decade ago that the 'Imbalances . . . are manifest to any observer.'[22] Clark Kerr concluded that 'A university's control over its own destiny has . . . been substantially reduced.'[23] Frederick deW. Bolman lamented 'the dismemberment of our intellectual purposes in the liberal arts.'[24] These three quotations, from three quite different points of view, are typical of many reports that massive funds have distorted the balance of college and university programs. The quotations are also typical in that they offer no detailed, objective evidence of the amount and specific nature of the distortion.

Nevertheless, the charge must be taken seriously, and the seriousness of the problem increases with the amount of federal money available. When the amount of money flowing from the federal government to the campuses of colleges and universities was only a small fraction of the total higher education budget not much distortion was possible. But now that the federal government supplies a quarter of the national expenditures for higher educa-tion—and a much greater fraction on the campuses of the more prestigious universities—the purposes for which federal money is available have come to be dominant purposes on the campus.

It was intended that they be. Government agencies have actively sought to alter campus activities and sometimes to change campus priorities. They will continue to do so. Increased federal funds will become available for work on pollution abatement, waste disposal, transportation, housing, urban planning and renewal, and other social and environmental problems. These new funds will not expand as did those earlier available from the Depart-ment of Defense, the National Institutes of Health, or the National Aeronautics and Space Administration, but they will surely come to constitute a larger fraction of the total than they do now, and the federal agencies responsible for their administration will be looking for institutions qualified and willing to conduct the neces-sary studies and research.

How directly some of these newer programs are intended to influence educational as well as research plans of universities has been pointed out by Robert S. Morison:

In the last few years, numerous committees and commissions have reported on the need for breaking down the barriers between disciplines, and for developing interdisciplinary centers devoted to the solution of specific social problems. Some even go so far as to counsel the founding of whole colleges or gradu-ate schools with carefully defined missions. These proposals may be regarded as the adult form of the more spontaneous student pleas for greater relevance. It is not always emphasized that these plans seek, among other things, to take some of the responsibility for planning the instructional program away from the conventional department and to place the initiative higher in the administrative hierarchy. Although such attempts are sure to arouse anxiety and hostility within the classic departmental structure, the pressures are such as to make it highly likely that the attempts will be made.[25]

Hubert Heffner, then deputy director of the Office of Science and Technology, confirmed Morison's statement by saying that the whole concept of federal support for graduate students was being reconsidered to encourage multi-disciplinary training on practical, societal problems.[26] 'If the government does support graduate study,' he said, 'it is clear that, because of societal needs, a new type of problem-oriented training is necessary.' Heffner went on to indicate that the financing of graduate students of the kind government wanted to foster would be chiefly through multi-disciplinary research programs of a utilitarian nature. Emphasis on utility is not the idiosyncratic notion of government leaders. Congress and the executive branch both respond to the popular will, as they understand it and interpret it in terms of political and financial forces. Government actions with respect to higher education are no exception to this generalization.

That the federal government will continue to try to influence university programs and priorities can be taken for granted. Whether these efforts harm the university, distort its programs, and weaken its independence depends, however, on two character-istics of the university. One is its strength—its ability to seek and accept those forms of government support that fit its needs and to reject or persuade the government to modify those it finds objec-tionable. A few courageous institutions have rejected some forms of support. But mounting financial pressures and the diffusion of responsibility and authority throughout the faculty have usually meant that there were ready takers for any available government funds and that there were faculty members who found the objec-tives of those funds congruent with their own objectives. It must be agreed that government programs have succeeded in changing campus programs and priorities. However, the critical factor lies in the relation between the government and the university rather than in either alone. When these relations were examined a decade ago by J. Kenneth Little, most of the educational leaders con-sulted thought government domination less important than insti-tutional weakness in creating problems. The strongest institutions, they concluded, had fewer problems in assimilating federal pro-grams and support than did the weaker ones.[27]

The other aspect of universities to consider is the extent to which they have formulated their own goals. Change by itself does not necessarily indicate distortion and need not mean that university independence has been weakened. Whether federal funds have disturbed university balance depends upon how closely the changes sought by government agencies match the changes desired by universities. It is quite impossible to say how closely the two have matched, for not enough universities have had clear enough agreement upon their own objectives and priorities.

To determine the amount and kinds of distortion that have actually resulted would require agreement on what constitutes an undistorted university program. We need a baseline from which to measure the amount of distortion.

University programs as of 1940, before federal funds began to be influential, could be used as a baseline, but surely few people would defend the proposition that the proper balance within a university is timeless and unchanging.

Another possibility would be the balance that would have existed now had there been no major special-purpose federal programs. But this is obviously hypothetical, for no one can know what would have happened had history been different.

A third possible baseline would be the ideal balance among a university's activities. Ideals are, of course, always a matter of judgment, but this would be the best baseline to use if the members of a university could agree upon its own ideal of balance.

It is unlikely that they can agree. Interests are too divergent. The Professor of English and the Professor of Physics cannot be expected to view the effects of a new accelerator from the same standpoint. What they must agree upon, however, are the obvious facts that many of the changes result from decisions made at the level of the department or the individual faculty member, that departments and individuals differ greatly in their access to government funds, and that the president has only limited resources with which to redress what he considers imbalances.

Clearly, it would be desirable to have better evidence concerning the effects of federal support on higher education. To some observers this need became obvious years ago. In 1958 the National Science Foundation published a review of government-science relationships which concluded that federal support had substantially influenced the directions of scientific research, but that up to that time the redirection had neither been necessarily detrimental nor irksome.[28] Within the next few years, analyses were published by Charles V. Kidd,[29] Harold Orlans,[30] J. Kenneth Little,[31] and Homer D. Babbidge and Robert M. Rosenzweig.[32] They were followed by Clark Kerr's widely quoted work, *The*

Uses of the University,[33] a collection of papers edited by Harold Orlans,[34] and others.

These earlier studies have been useful, but it is time for further analysis. The present would seem to be a particularly appropriate time. The period of rapid increase in federal support that lasted from early in the 1950s to the middle of the 1960s has ended. Federal support will certainly increase, but priorities are changing. From within government there come statements that the project or programmatic emphasis of the past should give way to more policy orientation in planning federal activities at the same time that appropriations continue to emphasize the project approach. For all of these reasons, this would seem to be a good time to try to assess the effects of federal support on higher education.

Although the extent remains unmeasured, so many well-placed observers have said that distortion has occurred that the charge must be taken seriously. However, there are two final comments to make about this charge. First, it makes Washington, D.C. into a worse villain than the facts justify. The government programs were not conceived solely by permanent Washington bureaucrats. Bureaucrats were involved, but many of them were erstwhile faculty members and they were aided by consultants from many campuses and by the committees and staff members of the scientific and educational organizations that maintain offices in Washington for the purpose of representing educational needs and problems. Whatever disturbance of balance has resulted cannot be wholly blamed on the Washington bureaucracy unless one considers the whole elaborate machinery of educational representation in Washington to be ineffective.

As a matter of fact it has sometimes been ineffective. Congressmen and other government officials have complained that the educational world could not agree on what it wanted. Educational organizations have at times given conflicting testimony before congressional committees. Congressional witnesses and agency consultants have sometimes not distinguished between the role of advocate for particular educational goals and the political role of resolving conflict and establishing national policy.[35]

Second, the charge that universities have lost control over their professors assumes that they once had control. At the detailed level, university goals have never been institutionally determined; they have always been individualized and segmented. Teachers' colleges, theological seminaries, bible schools, technical institutes, and other specialized colleges have had institutional programs and goals. But universities have prided themselves on allowing each professor to set his own goals and to follow his own research interests. Of course there have been required courses and other shared duties, and money, equipment, and space have always been less than the sum of all the wishes of all the professors. It is also true that problems of allocation have become more acute as costs of equipment and facilities have gone higher and higher. But the entrepreneurial professor was not a new product of federal support. One cannot have it both ways. One cannot boast that the university professor is free to follow his own path and then complain if he succeeds in persuading a government agency that his path merits substantial support.

OTHER THREATS TO INDEPENDENCE

Other influences on university development cannot be considered in detail, for the emphasis here is on the federal government, but it is necessary to recognize the existence of several other forces working on the university. Financial difficulties are becoming more serious. Thus state governments, foundations, and other sources of funds tend to become more influential than they would be if money were abundant. Campus radicals and those who react strongly against their activities both wish to change the university. One group sees the university as an instrument of the goals and systems they have have rejected, while the other group sees it as a hotbed of youthful radicalism egged on by irresponsible professors. Thus both groups, for diametrically opposite reasons, exert pressure for change.

Political activism also appears to influence the ability of universities to respond effectively to external pressures. In a sociological analysis of campus problems, Seymour Martin Lipset[36] concluded that political strife widens divisions within the faculty, weakens presidential authority, makes participation in faculty government less attractive to the ablest members of a faculty and thus tends to put more of the less able and prestigious members into the faculty senate and major committees. These changes lessen an institution's ability to withstand external pressures and increase the likelihood that it will accept student demands that it act more like a secondary school or liberal arts college and less like a graduate and research university. If this happens, a university will become less attractive to research scholars and less likely to receive financial support from the federal government, foundations, industry, or individual donors.

As a result of these tensions, Kingman Brewster[37] and others have observed that universities are becoming more politically vulnerable and more fearful of political recrimination. The absence of firm agreement on university goals and priorities renders the institution more susceptible to outside pressures.

THE PRESENT STATUS

Political uneasiness, campus tensions, financial difficulties, changes in national goals, and a variety of pressures to use the university for divergent and sometimes conflicting purposes all increase the difficulty of maintaining internal balance and a reasonable degree of independence. Yet the principal threat is probably the weakness of agreement on objectives and means to their attainment.

At a federal level, no agency is responsible for overall educational planning and the general welfare of higher education. Instead, programs are developed and administered by many agencies, each for its own purposes.

Among universities, coordination is informal except within those states in which state coordinating boards are effective. But even in these cases there is little central control over the relations of individual institutions to federal agencies.

In individual universities, power is widely decentralized and faculty mechanisms which were developed primarily to make decisions concerning purely educational matters are not well designed to deal with forces that affect the institution as a whole.

In short, no one is in charge.

In the future, the universities' ability to influence government policy will depend to a substantial extent on how well they agree with each other and with the rest of higher education. Because problems and needs differ among institutions of higher education, agreement need not call for uniform treatment of all colleges and universities. But agreement within higher education on the government relationships and forms of support that seem best designed to preserve an appropriate balance between independence and responsiveness to societal needs would allow higher education to approach the federal government in unity. And in unity, as all government officials know, lies political strength.

The best guide to the constitutional doctrine that can lead to a better balance of power between the university and the federal government is Don K. Price's *The Scientific Estate*.[38] Building upon that base, it should be possible to develop a set of principles that would protect both the university and the state. Details can be left to be decided, through debate and as the collective product of many minds. But as a start, it seems that a major point of departure should be recognition of two principles: first, the university is a critically important institution that in some of its activities serves as an agency of government; and second, it is in the interests of society to keep the university reasonably independent of government control. In this context, the nature of the 'agency' relationship must be made explicit. The university works toward the achievement of some of the public purposes which are formulated or supported by the government. However, the university and the government work in quite different ways and make quite different contributions to the achievement of the purposes they share. Price was speaking of science rather than of scholarship generally, but his summary of the relationships among scholars, professionals, administrators, and politicians is still apt: 'Any constitutional system that undertakes to protect freedom by dividing powers has to be based first of all on a separation between the institutions that exercise political power and those that are engaged in the search for truth.' A following statement, slightly paraphrased, is explicit to the present context: 'Universities cannot either solve our policy problems for us or stand aside from them. And that is why the scholarly community and politicians need to develop the clearest possible idea of the working rules that govern their relationship.'[39] To agree upon these working rules is the purpose of the compact.

THE NEW COMPACT

Like its predecessor, the new compact will be an informal agreement on what the university requires of the government and on what the government, as the political representative of society, requires of the university.

In the most general terms, what the university requires is a reasonable degree of independence in managing its own affairs. The easiest aspect of independence to agree upon is that the university will retain the right to determine who shall teach, which members of the faculty are of sufficient merit to be retained or given tenure, and how approved courses, research projects, and other activities will be conducted. There will be little argument on these points.

More difficulty will arise over funding, but stable funding and internal control over a reasonable portion of a university's budget are requisites to insist upon.

Continuing obligation for stable funding

If it be accepted that universities, in some of their activities, serve as agencies of government, it follows that the federal government should accept responsibility for helping to maintain the universities as strong and effective agencies.

State governments long ago accepted continuing responsibility for state colleges and universities. The federal government has gone only part way down this road. Except for such special institutions as the military academies, Howard University, and Gallaudet College, most federal programs of support for higher education were started as if they would be temporary and as if they were merely adding a bit to the university's other funds. Clearly the relationship is no longer temporary, and obviously the amount of money involved is no longer a minor addition to other sources of support. Both the amount of money involved and the permanence of the relationships demand acceptance of continuing responsibility by the government and the development of stable policies that allow longer range planning by the universities.

Such a policy is desirable from the standpoint of the government itself, as experience with the agricultural research program long ago demonstrated. If universities are expected to work effectively on environmental problems, transportation, early childhood education, or the problems of the city, better results can be expected if they are able to interest scholars of high quality and can assure them that they will be able to work long enough to make real progress.

Multiple funding

Federal support will continue to be granted primarily for specified purposes, even if the fraction available for general institutional support is increased substantially. State governments have, in general, been less restrictive concerning the use of state appropriations, but some state governments are attempting to gain greater control over the ways universities use those appropriations. Nonappropriated funds from tuition, fees, and endowment have traditionally been wholly controlled by universities, but some state governments have given warning that they wish to control the expenditure of these funds by state institutions.

The direction of change, therefore, is toward less institutional discretion in the allocation of funds. The financial difficulties that now beset most universities give them little enough maneuvering room as things are. Proposals that would give them even less control need to be resisted if the university is to maintain the financial flexibility that is essential to a reasonable degree of freedom in deciding upon its own balance and priorities. If a university cannot be wholly independent of external financial support, at least it can strive to avoid overdependence on any one source. At the federal level, multiple sources of support is a well established practice. It is in the interests of universities to maintain that multiplicity and to work toward an increase in institutional grants. At the state level—for state universities—it is desirable to insist upon retaining institutional control over non-appropriated income, for universities would lose much of the advantage of having multiple federal sources if state authorities were to gain control over the university's non-appropriated income. Furthermore, some of the federal government's reasons for supporting the intellectual resources of state universities would diminish if those universities become captives of state political structures.

THE OTHER HALF OF THE COMPACT

Inevitably, universities and their faculties will have more trouble in agreeing upon what they are willing to give than upon what they want to receive. The harder decision cannot be avoided, however, and the first part of it concerns the responsibility that must accompany academic freedom.

Academic responsibility

The traditional academic freedom of the university should be preserved not only in the interests of the university but also in the interests of society. The university cannot be held accountable for its work unless it has authority to determine how that work is carried forward. It cannot continue to serve as an objective social critic unless it has freedom to select the scholars who will analyze and weigh the trends and processes that are important to society. It cannot retain control over its own lines of development or plan its own objectives and priorities unless it determines who will be responsible for the activities.

This traditional form of academic freedom is not sufficient, however, as a complete definition of academic freedom and responsibility. It suffices to define the freedom of the teacher within his assigned courses and of the scholar within his own research or scholarly studies. But it does not deal adequately with the professor's responsibilities to his university and to the public. Under the original Germanic compact the professor was granted academic freedom in exchange for his promise to stay out of politics. He still wants academic freedom but he can no longer promise to stay out of politics, in the broad sense, for he is often involved in policy making and sometimes in other political activities. What role does society wish him to play in the political realm, broadly defined, and what role should he play?

Only in a generalized abstraction is this question easy to answer: society wants him to act as a responsible scholar, aware of the areas in which he has expert knowledge and of those in which he does not, sensitive to the privileges of his position, and conscious of his obligation to protect the rights of other scholars, the university, and their relationships with society.

Such an abstraction is a starting point, but no more than that. The rights, obligations, and privileges involved must be agreed upon, despite current uncertainty and even disagreement over their meaning.

The reason is that knowledge is power. Knowledge has always carried power, but the power has increased and sometimes become critical as knowledge itself has broadened and led to a complex, technological, closely-interconnected society. The professor is presumed to have expert knowledge. Whether he uses that knowledge, and its power, objectively or for partisan purposes is therefore rightly a matter of public concern. The university cannot defend its claim to independence if the public cannot trust the professor to use his power objectively.

Glen Dumke, chancellor of the California State College System, has described the dangers of lapsing from objectivity:

> The college or university is the only agency in society designed to study objectively and in scholarly manner, without bias, prejudice, or partisanship, the problem of society. Because this objective analysis is so important to society, it, in turn, grants to the campus a degree of insulation from political and partisan pressures, otherwise known as academic freedom. When the state breaches its part of the contract and imposes political or other pressures on the campus, the campus has a right to complain—that is, if it is fulfilling its part of the contract. But if it is not—if the campus has abandoned objectivity in favor of partisanship, if the college or university is no longer behaving as a scholar—then society withdraws the insulation from external pressures which constitutes academic freedom.
>
> This is what has happened lately. The campus has ceased to be objective. It has joined in the fray. It has become institutionally partisan—about the Vietnam War and our foreign policy, about poverty, about racial issues. Some of the causes may well be novel and worthy, but no matter how virtuous the cause, the scholar cannot afford to take sides, because if he does, he ceases to be a scholar. Judge Learned Hand, in his little book, *Essays on Liberty*, words this concept as well as it has ever been expressed: 'You may not carry a sword beneath a scholar's gown or lead flaming causes from a cloister. A scholar who tries to combine these parts sells his birthright for a mess of pottage. When the final count is made it will be found that the impairment of his powers far outweighs any possible contribution to the causes he has espoused.'[40]

The frequency with which faculty members are trying to carry swords beneath their gowns is indicated by a recent study of faculty participants in campus protests. In a sample of 103 protests that were studied in detail by Alexander W. Astin and Ann S. Bisconti, faculty members were found to be leaders in ten, and although they managed to avoid violent incidents themselves, they played activist roles in a third of the violent protests.[41]

The extent of such activity, and the amount of concern over partisan activities by professors make it urgent that the limits of academic freedom be defined. Individual views on this point range from one pole which holds that active political involvement is a duty of the intellectual to the opposite pole represented by Judge Hand's statement that one is fit to serve as a scholar only if he restricts himself singlemindedly to that service.

Robert S. Morison has written: 'The academic community will have to recognize that academic freedom, like most other freedoms, has its limits. In the last analysis, agreement on what the limits are can only be reached by some sort of political process.'[42] Academic freedom has never meant license to do anything one wished. The old compact specifically barred political activity. Some universities—and the number is growing—bar any research whose results cannot be freely published for anyone to read. Respect for the rights of other scholars and the necessity for the university to protect itself and to assure public respect for the integrity of the scholarly community set limits which are real, though hard to define.

Agreement may be difficult to reach, but agreement on the limits of academic freedom and on the relations between the rights of the individual and the rights of the university as an institution constitute an essential part of the university's understanding with society. Definition is essential not only for the university but also for the state, for both politicians and the public should know the standards by which to judge a scholar's statements and actions. If, as some men hold, passionate commitment to action should take precedence over scholarly objectivity, the public has a right to know that this is the standard, for under this standard the public can rightfully deny the professor-politician the sanctuary of academic freedom and can insist that he be politically accountable. If, as others hold, the academic community should insist that objectivity is always expected, politicians and the public have a right to understand that this is the standard. Or, if the academic community grants to its members the right to occupy several roles, such as objective scholar in the classroom and political activist outside, politicians and the public have a right to know the conditions and standards that apply to each role.

An intermediate position is most likely to be adopted, both because it is a compromise and because there are different situations to which different standards can apply. An intermediate position will, however, be more difficult to explain to the public, for several fine distinctions are involved: the distinction between the university as an institution and its individual members; the distinction between two types of political activity by the university; and the distinction among different roles played by the men and women who serve on its faculty.

Two types of political activity by universities can be distinguished:

(1) Political activity on educational issues that affect the university; and
(2) political activity on other issues.

The first type is not controversial. An institution has a right to defend its own interests, politically as well as by other means. The section of the Internal Revenue Code that forbids tax exempt organizations such as schools and scholarly societies from all efforts to influence elections and from substantial efforts to influence legislation specifically excludes legislation that directly affects the welfare of the institution or organization.

Political activity by universities on other issues is a very different matter, so different in fact that a university endangers its own independence and the independence of its faculty members if it takes an institutional stand on such an issue.

As an institution, the university encourages free inquiry, debate, and even disagreement. It protects the right of the scholar to question, to challenge, to defend unpopular points of view—all so long as his positions result from his own research or scholarly analysis. At a time when there is so much in the world that needs criticism, the university has a special need to be able to protect the rights of its members. But this it can do only if the institution itself abstains from commitment to particular points of view. The moment a university adopts an institutional commitment on a political matter (other than one directly affecting its own welfare) it infringes the academic freedom of every member who disagrees, and it warns all of its members that their freedom may be infringed on the next occasion.

A point that is sometimes hard to explain to the public is that abstention from commitment does not mean lack of concern for the public welfare. On the contrary, this abstention is the university's way of making its best contribution to public welfare. This point is made harder to explain each time a professor tries to persuade his colleagues to adopt an institutional position on some issues of public policy.[43]

Three kinds of political activity by individual faculty members can be distinguished:

(1) Political activity of a faculty member acting as a scholar in the area of his own expertise;
(2) political activity of a faculty member acting as a scholar but outside the area of his own expertise; and
(3) political activity of a faculty member acting as a private citizen.

No hard and fast dividing lines separate these three kinds of activity. One's area of expert knowledge fades gradually into areas of superficial knowledge or ignorance. A given public issue is related more or less closely to several fields of scholarship. Public and private interests may overlap. Nevertheless, the three types of activities are sufficiently different to be considered separately.

The first type is generally accepted; scholars are expected and often invited to give the public the benefit of their special knowledge. There are many mutually agreed upon relationships in which the scholar makes his specialized knowledge available to an agency of government. Legitimate questions arise concerning some kinds of work, work for some clients, and work that detracts from the professor's primary university obligations, but relationships of this mutually agreed upon type have come to be accepted as legitimate uses of the scholar's expertise. Each is to be accepted or declined on its own merit, but each that is accepted is a mutually agreed upon relationship and the mutuality is an important defining characteristic.

In addition to the mutually arranged relationships, scholars sometimes wish to offer their expert knowledge and judgment concerning matters on which they have not been invited to contribute. There are well established procedures (e.g., publication and hearings) to accomplish this end.

The second type of individual political activity—acting as a scholar, or using one's position, in a partisan manner, outside the area of one's expertise—misleads the public and endangers other scholars and the university.

The third type of individual political activity—that engaged in as a private citizen—is commendable and to be encourged. As a private citizen the scholar has a citizen's rights. As an intelligent and informed citizen he contributes to society by exercising those rights.

It is here, however, that special care is called for in distinguishing among roles. Failure to observe the differences among these three types of political activity confuses the public, weakens public confidence in the university, and diminishes its ability to withstand external pressure and to protect the freedom of its members. Moreover, the more powerful university research and scholarship become—not powerful in the sense of challenging the right of administrators and elected representatives to make political decisions, but powerful in the sense that administrators and elected representatives cannot disregard the results of research and scholarly analyses—the more essential it becomes that the public be able to recognize the capacity in which a faculty member is speaking or acting.

Making these distinctions clear may well be the most difficult aspect of the compact on which to reach agreement. But the distinctions are essential, for their purpose is to protect the university, to protect society, and to protect the scholar's rights as an expert in his own area. Unless the distinctions are made, a scholar's rights as an expert and his different rights as a private citizen will continue to be jeopardized by every faculty member who misleads the public by acting as a scholar on matters on which he lacks expert knowledge.

University accountability

A university is accountable to government agencies for those programs and projects that are financed by federal funds. State institutions are accountable to a state board of control or some other arm of the state government. Most universities make some kind of public report of all or some of their activities. To a large extent, however, the accounts are segmental and the aspect of performance that is emphasized is the budget and the ways in which funds were used. David Z. Robinson has discussed alternative types of accountability to a federal agency for the ways in which a university has used federal funds.[44] He has pointed out that federal agencies tend to stress fiscal accountability because that is the easiest kind to assess, and has recommended that greater attention be given to accountability for the nature and quality of the work performed under federal financing.

Universities that receive federal grants must expect to be held fiscally accountable for their use of grant funds, and all universities must expect to keep good accounts and to make public reports of their financial management. But fiscal accountability is not sufficient. In all of their activities, universities are public institutions, and in some of their activities they serve as agencies of government. The support that comes through tuition and fees, state appropriations, and government grants is all public support, and even gifts and income on endowment are subject to some forms of public control, as Congress made clear in the Tax Reform Act of 1969. If, now, the government accepts partial responsibility for the continuing well-being of universities and to that end provides reasonably stable financial support, and if agreement is reached on the nature of the freedom and responsibility of academic scholars, then the public has even greater right to ask for full and informative accounts of the performance of universities.

Both the continuing university-government relationship and the legitimate interests of society call for more informative public reporting by the university concerning its accomplishments, its activities, the balance among them, and the effectiveness with which it is serving as an institution of higher education and as a continuing analyst and critic of the affairs of the nation. It will be hard for some university presidents and faculties periodically to make full and evaluative public accounts of what they have accomplished, but society can legitimately insist upon such accounts in return for the rights and support it gives to the university.

UNIVERSITY DECISION-MAKING

The final point to consider is not so much a matter for agreement between the university and the state as it is for agreement within the academic community. Yet it belongs here because society should feel assured of the university's ability to maintain its side of the agreement with society and because that ability is essential to the retention of its independence.

Decision-making within the university has purposefully been greatly decentralized. Each university has traditionally been independent of every other university. Within each university, individual schools, departments, and faculty members have been given as much autonomy as possible.

This principle is not now to be abandoned, yet great decentralization of authority is not well adapted to the making of decisions that entail institutional rather than individual or departmental responsibility; the adoption of new programs that commit institutional resources; planning institutional development and emphasis and the maintenance of what is deemed to be proper institutional balance; relations with other universities on the division of responsibility for educational programs that are too costly to be available on every campus; and negotiations with government agencies on matters of policy.

Strengthening the university administration for these purposes does not mean that all decisions will be made in the president's office or that there will be no consultation with the faculty. Any wise president will be in close consultation with faculty representatives, or the faculty may establish an executive committee or an advisory committee that works closely with the president. Whatever the details of the arrangement, it is necessary to deal with matters on which the faculty as a whole cannot act with the necessary promptness and assurance. The faculty is too prone to compromise or delay on difficult issues. And the faculty as a whole—the staunchest guardian of individual academic freedom—is too likely to approve the requests of any of its own members. Yet some decisions must be made quickly. Some must deny prized opportunities to some individuals. And some must commit the institution as a whole in its relations with government agencies or other institutions.

Many decisions, however, including some of the most fundamental ones, will continue to be responsibilities of the faculty senate, the department, or the individual professor. In fact the earlier discussion of academic freedom and responsibility implied that the faculty should accept responsibility for a kind of decision that many members would prefer to avoid. If agreement is reached on the definition and limits of academic freedom it seems altogether probable that some members of the faculty will overstep those limits. Who should then decide whether an infraction has occurred and what punishment is deserved?

The American Association of University Professors would be one logical possibility, but the AAUP has explicitly denied responsibility. The General Secretary of the AAUP has defended the Association's record of 'relative inaction' on matters of professional ethics and has assigned responsibility to the individual college or university.[45]

The American Chemical Society, the American Historical Association, and other professional guilds might be considered as possible agents to consider and to render judgment on infractions of the bounds of academic freedom. But many of these associations are too small to support the necessary machinery, and if the associations became responsible, colleagues from the same campus would have their cases heard in different courts and would be subject to different standards.

In an earlier day, the university administration might have been considered the proper authority to deal with infractions of the rules governing academic freedom and responsibility. But what faculty would now approve of such an arrangement?

The faculty seems to be left with responsibility for deciding whether one of its own members has been guilty of overstepping proper bounds, and, if found guilty, of deciding what punishment is appropriate. This disagreeable task must be accepted. Unless the faculty (or the administration if the faculty unwisely so prefers) assumes this task, statements about academic freedom and responsibility will not be credible and the compact will not be acceptable.

Above the level of the individual university there will be necessity for coordination among universities. Some of the coordinating agreements may deal with the division of responsibility among universities for different programs and activities. Others will be concerned with the use of federal funds and relationships with the federal government. Local and regional consortia are moves in the direction of coordination. So are the increasing number of state-wide boards that have been established to coordinate the work of state institutions of higher education. Beyond these, it would seem desirable for American universities to establish the means of giving them a unified and collective voice in dealing with major matters of policy in their relations with the federal government.

Government agencies administer their own programs of support for higher education and each has its own objectives. But all are parts of the federal government, and all must follow some standards and rules set by the Congress or the Office of Management and Budget. Despite their varied purposes, government agencies may therefore speak with a united voice in their relations with universities. On matters of general policy, universities will be in a better bargaining position if they have comparable unity and strength. That they cannot have if they remain independent of each other. To maintain the independence of the university as an institution may therefore require each individual university to invest some of its independence in the collectivity. Eric Ashby has argued so:

> Universities in each country must seek collective security. The days are over when each university can expect to be a fully autonomous corporation, autarchic as a medieval dukedom. In tomorrow's world there will be no security in the fragmented autonomy of scores of independent institutions. Universities, combined in this collective autonomy, could become the 'intellectual estate' of the nation, indeed still financially dependent on governments, but collectively strong enough to set the conditions under which they fulfill their function in society.[46]

The individual faculty member has had to give up some of his independence for the good of the university. Individual universities must now give up part of their independence so that together they can better preserve the independence of the university as an institution. The collectivity will strengthen the university in developing its new compact wtih the state, will help to assure the public that universities will be able to discharge their responsibilities under that compact, and will help them to retain the degree of independence required to fulfill their functions in society.

Notes

1. Fabian Franklin, *The Life of Daniel Coit Gilman* (Dodd Mead and Co., New York, 1910) p. 179.
2. Richard J. Storr, *Harper's University: The Beginnings* (University of Chicago Press, Chicago, 1966) p. 75.
3. John S. Brubacher, 'The Autonomy of the University,' *Journal of Higher Education*, vol. 38, no. 5 (May 1967) 237–49, p. 239.
4. Ibid., p. 248.
5. Ibid., pp. 237–49.
6. General Report of the Committee on Academic Freedom and Academic Tenure, *Bulletin of the American Association of University Professors*, vol. 1, part 1 (Dec. 1915) 17–43, p. 26.
7. Robley C. Williams (and 110 cosigners whose names were not published), letter to the editor, *Science*, vol. 168 (May 22, 1970) p. 917.
8. Ibid.
9. Theodore Roszak, 'The Complacencies of the Academy: 1967,' *New American Review*, no. 1 (Sept. 1967) 82–107.
10. Major developments in the social sciences during the twentieth century are analyzed in Karl W. Deutsch, John Platt, and Dieter Senghaas, 'Conditions Favoring Major Advances in Social Science,' *Science*, vol. 171 (Feb. 5, 1971) 450–9.
11. Dwight Waldo, 'The University in Relation to the Government-Political,' *Public Administration Review*, vol. 30, no. 2 (March/April 1970) 106–13.
12. This proposal has been made by a number of writers, including Carl Kaysen, *The Higher Learning, The Universities, and The Public* (Princeton University Press, Princeton, 1969); Lewis B. Mayhew, *Colleges Today and Tomorrow* (Jossey-Bass, San Francisco, 1969); Ralph W. Tyler, 'The Changing Structure of American Institutions of Higher Education,' pp. 305–20 in *The Economics and Financing of Higher Education in the United States*, Joint Economic Committee of the Congress, 91st Congress, 1st Session (U.S. Government Printing Office, Washington, 1969); and Robert Paul Wolff, *The Idea of the University* (Beacon Press, Boston, 1969).
13. Eric Ashby, in reply to letters, *Minerva*, vol. 6, no. 4 (Summer 1968) 606–7.
14. Eric Ashby, 'The Future of the Nineteenth Century Idea of a University,' *Minerva*, vol. 6, no. 1 (Autumn 1967) 3–17.
15. Harold Orlans, *The Effects of Federal Programs on Higher Education* (The Brookings Institution, Washington, D.C., 1962).
16. Charles V. Kidd, *American Universities and Federal Research* (Harvard University Press, Cambridge, 1959). In another publication, the same author has defended the proposition that the positive effects of federal research funds on academic freedom have 'far outweighed restrictions on freedom.' See Charles V. Kidd, 'The Implications of Research Funds for Academic Freedom,' *Law and Contemporary Problems* (Duke University School of Law, Durham, N.C.) vol. 28, no. 3 (Summer 1963).

17. Harold L. Hodgkinson, *Institutions in Transition* (McGraw-Hill, New York, 1971).

18. John Caffrey (ed.), *The Future Academic Community* (American Council on Education, Washington, D.C., 1969).

19. Richard M. Nixon, public letter to William W. Scranton in reply to the report of the Commission on Campus Unrest.

20. Daniel S. Greenberg, 'The Administration of Federal Aid: A Monstrosity Has Been Created,' *Science*, vol. 157 (July 7, 1967) 43–7.

21. Philip M. Boffey, a series of articles on the 1969 budget for research and development, all in *Science*: Budget Status, vol. 161 (Sept. 13, 1968) 57; Budget Paradox, vol. 162 (Oct. 18, 1968) 340–2; and Budget Trauma, no. 162 (Nov. 15, 1968) 776–9.

22. Harold Orlans, *The Effects of Federal Programs on Higher Education*, op. cit.

23. Clark Kerr, 'The Frantic Race to Remain Contemporary,' *Daedalus*, vol. 93, no. 4 (1964) 1051–70.

24. Frederick deW. Bolman, 'Fast or Famine for the Liberal Arts College,' in *Cooperative Long-Range Planning in Liberal Arts Colleges*, Earl J. McGrath (ed.) (Institute for Higher Education, Teachers College, Columbia University, New York, 1964).

25. Robert S. Morison, 'Some Aspects of Policy-Making in the American University,' *Daedalus*, vol. 99, no. 3 (1970) 609–44, p. 617.

26. Robert B. Bazell, 'Graduate Support: NIH Grants Threatened by Nixon Priorities,' *Science*, vol. 171 (Feb. 12, 1971) 554–6.

27. J. Kenneth Little, *Survey of Federal Programs in Higher Education* (United States Office of Education, U.S. Government Printing Office, Washington, D.C., 1962).

28. National Science Foundation, *Government-University Relationships in Federally Sponsored Scientific Research and Development* (U.S. Government Printing Office, Washington, D.C., 1958).

29. Charles V. Kidd, *American Universities and Federal Research*, op. cit.

30. Harold Orlans, *The Effects of Federal Programs on Higher Education*, op. cit.

31. J. Kenneth Little, *Survey of Federal Programs in Higher Education*, op. cit.

32. Homer D. Babbidge, Jr., and Robert M. Rosenzweig, *The Federal Interest in Higher Education* (McGraw-Hill, New York, 1962).

33. Clark Kerr, *The Uses of the University* (Harvard University Press, Cambridge, 1963).

34. Harold Orlans, *Science Policy and the University* (The Brookings Institution, Washington, D.C., 1968).

35. Homer D. Babbidge, Jr. and Robert M. Rosenzweig, *The Federal Interest in Higher Education* (McGraw-Hill, New York, 1962).

36. Seymour Martin Lipset, 'The Politics of Academia,' in David C. Nichols (ed.), *Perspectives on Campus Tensions: Papers Prepared for the Special Committee on Campus Tensions* (American Council on Education, Washington, D.C., 1970).

37. Kingman Brewster, 'Campus 1980,' in Robert C. Connery (ed.), *The*

Corporation and the Campus: Corporate Support of Higher Education in the 1970's (The Academy of Political Science, Columbia University, New York, 1970).

38. Don K. Price, *The Scientific Estate* (The Belknap Press of Harvard University, Cambridge, 1965).

39. Ibid., pp. 272 and 275.

40. Glen S. Dumke, 'Is Freedom Academic?' *Vital Speeches*, vol. 36, no. 9 (Feb. 15, 1970) 272–6.

41. Alexander W. Astin and Ann S. Bisconti, *Protest Behavior and Response on the U.S. Campus*, Report submitted to the U.S. Office of Education by the American Council on Education under Grant OEG-0-9-180364-44(010), Feb. 1971.

42. Robert S. Morison, art. cit.

43. Ibid., and also Kingman Brewster, Jr., 'If Not Reason, What?', *American Scientist*, vol. 58, no. 2 (March/April 1970) 171–5.

44. David Z. Robinson, 'Government Contracting for Academic Research: Accountability in the American Experience, in Bruce L. R. Smith and D. C. Hague (eds.), *The Dilemma of Accountability in Modern Government: Independence versus Control* (St Martin's Press, New York, 1971) pp. 103–17.

45. Bertram H. Davis, 'From the General Secretary,' *AAUP Bulletin*, vol. 56, no. 4 (Dec. 1970) 357.

46. Eric Ashby, 'The Future of the Nineteenth Century Idea of a University,' *Minerva*, vol. 6, no. 1 (Autumn 1967) 3–17, p. 16. For another discussion of this point see James A. Perkins, 'Reform of Higher Education: Mission Impossible?', in W. Todd Furniss (ed.), *Higher Education for Everybody? Issues and Implications* (American Council on Education, Washington, D.C., 1971).

6 Accountability and the Military-Industrial Complex

MARTIN EDMONDS

In substance, if not in detail, most studies on the American 'military-industrial complex' argue the existence of a coalescence of interest between industrial, political and military groups. This has been interpreted by some as an élite conspiracy;[1] to others it represents a form of 'subgovernment,' whose purpose is 'to strive to become self sustaining in control of power in its own sphere. (It) . . . seeks to aggregate power necessary to its purposes.'[2]

Attention has been attracted to the subject—and indeed what has made it a difficult one to ignore—by the breadth of the sphere over which these military-industrial groups have been perceived to attempt to exercise control, and the extent to which they appear to have succeeded. The dimensions of this sphere, nurtured through the 'national defense at any cost mentality that prevailed through the cold war and was kept alive by the naïve faith in the possibilities of nuclear superiority,'[3] have marked the military-industrial complex apart from all other 'subgovernments' and interest groups. Likewise, the amount of power and influence which these groups have accrued have far exceeded the immediate necessities of defense; the situation is reflected, *inter alia*, in the financial and economic dependency of many of the States of the Union upon a high level of military spending, and upon the defense industries and military installations located in them.[4] For these reasons, and others, concern has focused less in recent years on the existence of the military-industrial-complex, *per se*, and more upon the impact that it is having upon the whole American political and economic system.

The 'military-industrial complex' in the United States has generally come to be accepted as a reality. All the necessary indicators are there: the defense sector enjoys the largest share of the nation's resources, and has appropriated to it approximately half of the federal budget; there has clearly evolved a 'special relation-ship between the government and other elements of the military-industrial complex not found elsewhere; there is open and frequent mobility of senior personnel between government, the military and the private defense contractors; and there has developed a brand of 'war economy,' characterized by a network of firms which are differentiated from other enterprises by their operating procedures, and which are predominantly, if not exclusively, concerned with advanced technological weapons development and production.[5] They point to the conclusion that the perceived common ideology of the military-industrial complex, that of the maintenance and enlargement of the United States armed forces and their role in American politics,[6] continues to be upheld.

The concept of the military-industrial complex was first formulated in the United States. The overwhelming proportion of studies on the subject has been done by American scholars of their own country. It is arguably a distinctively American pheno-menon, and, *sui generis*, is recognized as a significant departure from the established structure and processes of the American political and economic system. Paramount in this is American adherence to and almost fundamentalist belief in the theory, if not the reality, of the clear distinction between the private and the public sectors of the economy.[7] After World War II, this distinc-tion was conceptualized in the defense sector in terms of the 'contract state;'[8] it denoted the contractual basis of the relation-ship between the Defense Department and the armed forces, and the private industrial corporations which developed and pro-duced the equipment to military specification and requirement. Especially, it noted the clear separation of the private and public sectors, following on, as it did, the debate at the time whether weapons development and production should be an 'in-house,' government responsibility, rather than an outside one, in the interests of curtailing excessive profits to the arms manufacturers.[9]

The military-industrial complex has itself grown out of this 'contract state' relationship. As weapons became more complex, expensive and of 'high scientific content,'[10] and as the techno-logical demands of the cold war increased, so, first the capacity, and then the potential power of the defense-oriented corporations increased. Concurrently, the nature of the relationship between the government and the large industrial corporations producing advanced weapon systems changed in degree and kind. Concern was registered at these developments, not only because of the increasing resources that were being allocated to the maintenance of an extant war potential during peacetime far in excess of any period in American history, but also because of what impact they were beginning to have on the American political system.

The earlier 'contract state' relationship changed distinctively during the late 1950s. The main input has been attributed to the growth of 'Air Force missile contracting procedures in effect during the 1950s,'[11] though the seeds of this development can be traced back to the perceived need that the aircraft industries, by dint of their situation, should be left squarely in the hands of private enterprise.[12] These procedures expanded through the 1960s, and were instrumental in the phenomenal growth of the giant aerospace corporations.[13] They also introduced a network of research and development oriented smaller enterprises, some private and some quasi-non-governmental, working on, or in support of, military contracts. The major trends set in train in the 1950s were identified in the famed Presidential farewell address in 1961, and encapsulated in the first reference to the term 'the military-industrial complex.' Included in that address was a clear warning lest these developments were allowed to go unchecked.[14] Subsequent American involvement in southeast Asia, the perceived technical requirements arising from the continuation of the cold war—themselves encouraged by some technical deception by the Soviet Union[15]—and a number of significant technological break-throughs in missilry, propulsion and electronics, accelerated, rather than checked, the drift already in motion. The military-industrial complex came to maturity by the mid-1960s.

Two broad interpretations separate the studies of the military-industrial complex in the United States. As has been noted, all recognize the military-industrial complex as a reality, however loose or unstructured it may appear to be at any one time. The split comes over the impact of the military-industrial complex on the American political and economic system. To some, the danger is the influence that private corporations exercise over the government on account of their size, wealth, and current stake in the United States economy.[16] By implication, these large defense contractors exercise influence to their own material and financial advantage. More subtly, the suggestion also is that the defense contractors in pursuing their corporate interests do not merely influence defense procurement decisions, but contribute materially and directly to the arms race as well.

The second group puts the emphasis the other way round. Accepting that the military-industrial complex has significantly altered the relationship between private and public sectors of the American economy, the concern has to do with the influence that the government has come to exercise over private enterprise. Identified in this is '. . . a continuing relationship between the Department of Defense and its major suppliers . . . which is blurring and reducing much of the distinction between public and private activities in an important branch of the American economy.'[17] This has been identified as a convergence of the two sectors, and provides the premise behind the 'state-management' concept. This suggests that a '. . . new industrial management is located in the Office of the Secretary of Defense,' and that 'basic policy decisions of the new state industrial management are also the decisions of the principal officers of the Federal Government.'[18] The argument continues that the situation is one of central control, not of ownership, of the means of production. The situation has led to excessive military spending, defense procurement decisions based on non-military criteria, the introduction of an hierarchical organizational framework superimposed over both sectors, and the emergence throughout of all the less desirable features of state management inefficiency.

Both sets of interpretations have much validity. Private corporations have exercised considerable influence over both the military and the government on questions of weapons acquisition; in a manner of speaking, that is their business.[19] But they have used their economic power and influence as major employers and as unique reservoirs of irreplaceable human and capital resources to exercise influence in areas other than defense. Conversely, the government has widened its control over the defense industrial sector, and many of the characteristics of large central management can be isolated.[20]

The purpose of this paper, however, is not to arbitrate between differing interpretations or emphasis of the implications of the military-industrial complex. Nor is it to analyze and isolate whether the military-industrial complex has any permanent structure. It is accepted that there is a loose conglomeration of institutions and individuals who have common interests in the defense sphere, and who make it their business to secure those common interests. It is also accepted that this development, at least as it became manifest in the late 1960s and early 1970s, is antithetical to the civil-military traditions of the United States and to the theory of the clear separation of function of the private and public sectors of the American politic-economic system. This paper is designed to explore the extent to which the military-industrial complex has blurred the distinction between public and private, and has shifted the loci of power from Congress and the American people in the defense procurement field to itself.

The approach has been to examine the essential nature and characteristics of the weapons acquisition process, and from there to investigate the exercise of public accountability in that area. The second is circumscribed by the first. Both focus immediately on the question of government-industry relationships in the market for military equipment. In the process of the investigation, it should also be possible to offer general judgment on the extent to which the Pentagon has usurped power from Congress, and the possibilities for the military-industrial complex to be brought back within the traditional American political framework.

THE MARKET FOR MILITARY EQUIPMENT

The premise behind the concept of the military industrial complex is that there is *a posteriori* a market for military equipment. The market itself is nothing more than the area where the demand for advanced weapon systems interacts with the supply. The military-industrial complex is located around this market, and it is in relation to the market that there is perceived to be a coalescence of interest. It is a truism that there would be no defense oriented corporation, or more simply a weapons manufacturer, if the market did not exist. Likewise there would be no real, or perceived, linkage between the military, purportedly the originators of the requirements for military equipment, the private corporations as the suppliers of that equipment, the executive departments as the monitoring and auditing agencies, and the legislature as the fund authorizing body.

The general characteristic of the weapons market is that it is closed, in the classical sense. Entry to it is difficult, if not impossible. On the demand side, at least where the expensive advanced military weapons are concerned, the government is the monopsonist. This is an acceptable assumption, despite the substantial international trade in military equipment; the understood exigencies of military and national security demand that the government is the sole originator of the demand for weapons and certainly the only recipient of the latest, most advanced equipment. More pragmatically, the government is assured of its monopsonist status on account of the costs of modern weapons. As monopsonist, the government acts not only as the principal purchaser of military equipment, but also regulates all other sources of demand.

Two major determinants of the market structure for military equipment have been identified; one is natural and the other artificial.[21] Both make for the closed character of the market and the close interaction of the institutions and people involved. The natural determinants are concerned with the properties of the products in question. The most outstanding facet of military equipment during the past two decades has been its technological and scientific content. In the formulation of military equipment requirements, the demands on technology have invariably been excessive, and have frequently stretched the state of the art beyond the immediate bounds of possibility. On account of the technical unknowns involved, this has been an unconscious rather than an intended feature. The complexity of the equipment, the time needed to research and develop it, the resources that have been required to produce it, and ultimately the cost per unit have all increased geometrically over the period in question.

The effect of technology on military equipment has served to isolate further the government as the only source of demand. As complexity increased by one factor, so costs increased by a higher one. In the case of the United States, it has almost reached the point where even the federal government can no longer equate the costs of certain weapons systems with the military advantage they might offer, irrespective of the technical feasibility. Technical complexity had also served to encapsulate prerequisite knowledge about certain categories of weapons among restricted government and military circles. The refinement of military technical expertise has heralded a further development within the weapons acquisition process: within the military, subspecialisms between and within the armed services have developed. Relatively little overlap or commonality has resulted, despite administrative attempts to enforce it.[22] Sequentially, the arms manufacturers themselves have become weapon system specific and service oriented.[23] Lastly, the demands of military secrecy, particularly, have made available huge destructive power in modern weapons, and have dictated that the government is the only source of demand.

Technical complexity and scientific content have also had immediate and important bearing on the sources of supply. The higher the scientific content and the greater the technical uncertainties, the more the likelihood of there being more than one manufacturer with the resources and capacity to develop and produce it correspondingly diminishes. Certainly the chances of two products being taken far beyond the feasibility study stage in this situation is remote; neither the government nor the competing manufacturers have the resources to do it. The demands made by modern weapons on the resources of the arms manufacturers have dictated that they become increasingly specialized and pool resources through mergers or cross-subcontracting to ensure the necessary capital to undertake long, expensive and technically complex programs. The effect has been to see in the military-industrial sector, the emergence of huge defense oriented corporations with high degrees of weapons specialism and the virtual elimination of any semblance of competition between them.[24] A concomitant of this development is that arms manufacturing companies have become increasingly government—and defense—oriented, susceptible to marginal alterations in overall defense policy and less able to diversify into fields which are less technologically oriented, less capital intensive and more competitive.[25]

Technical complexity is only one dimension of military equipment. Three others warrant inclusion, all of which have immediate bearing on the structure of the market, and the pattern of government-industry relationships. The first is the cost factor. As cost restricts the source of demand, so it has limited the source of supply of advanced military equipment. The problem is basically one of capital investment and cash flow. The total cost of major weapon system programs falls far beyond the means of a

single producer, even where risk sharing among principal subcontractors has been employed. The capital outlays on each
weapons program would normally deplete the resources of even
the largest private arms manufacturer. Exacerbating the problem
is that much of the capital is program specific, and serves no
alternate use. Even if it was possible to finance the capital
investment needed for a weapons program, the total cost of the
program would be far in excess of the equity of the company.
Commercial borrowing under these circumstances would be difficult, if not impossible, because the collateral would fall short of the
amount to be borrowed and because of the technical uncertainties
inherent in advanced weapons development. Overall costs have determined that the government has had to intervene in the market,
and that the largest corporations are the only ones to survive.

A second and frequently overlooked dimension is that of
physical size. A single major weapons system may not in itself be
physically large, though some clearly have been; more important
is the physical impact that a given weapons program has upon the
structure and manufacturing processes of a company. This can
be visualized as the degree of disruption caused within an industrial plant by a military weapons program and the internal adjustments necessary to effect completion. New technology is a major
contributory factor, since it frequently renders existing fixed
capital obsolete and requires the introduction of new manufacturing techniques. What adjustments are necessary have a further
bearing on the subsequent capacity of the manufacturer to re-
adjust to further programs upon completion, the ability to compete for follow-on contracts, and the ease with which to diversify
into other military areas or into civil work. Abnormally large
contracts, or difficult, lengthy projects, leave defense manufacturers vulnerable where future contracts are concerned.

Thirdly, there is the factor of time. Bigness and complexity
involve extensive development work over long periods of time,
making the time horizon on any major weapons system in the
order of six to ten years. Long lead times contribute to cash-flow
problems, especially during the development and early production
phases. They place a premium on the financial control abilities
of management and on cost estimating procedures. Cash-flow
problems are a major source of pressure on manufacturers and
mitigate against all but the largest and strongest. The natural lead

time of a weapons system program is invariably longer than the time horizon demanded by the military; many problems of cost escalation and technological short-fall have occurred because work on military programs has been compressed to meet the time requirements of the armed forces.

All these considerations affect the market structure. They are considered natural inasmuch as they stem directly from the nature of the product. The question that has to be asked is how is it that the characteristics of modern military equipment have been determined as technologically challenging and scientifically advanced as they have. It is perhaps in this area of weapons acquisition that there may well be collusion between the government and the weapons manufacturers.

Had there been perfect competition in the weapons market, the natural determinants discussed above would have determined that by the late 1960s few, if any, private manufacturers could have been strong enough to remain in business, alternatively, the rate of technical advance in military equipment would have been much slower. The market is far from perfect, however, and is affected artificially by extensive government involvement and interference. This has been to ensure that the private weapons manufacturers have not been too exposed to the natural influences outlined above, and more importantly to guarantee that the demands of the military in the light of perceived national security are fully met without interruption. These artificial determinants of the market structure are broadly those considerations which interfere with the free operation of market forces, and centre upon the involvement of the government in the productive capacity of the weapons manufacturing industries.

For technical reasons, the government has become involved in many ways. One has been to make available to manufacturers the facilities and findings of government research institutions. Included in this would be the quasi-non-governmental, non-profit making research institutions which make available to defense contractors both their research data and their expertise on a consultancy basis. Another has been where the government has financed pure scientific research and applied technological development within the arms industries themselves, thereby giving recipient companies competitive advantage in both development and production contracts over others in the field.

A prevalent feature of government involvement has been the provision of advanced and complex machine tools deemed necessary for particular types of advanced work. These tools are invariably expensive and specific. The majority of machine tools loaned to private industry by the government, however, happen to be of a general nature, usable on projects other than defense.[26] Evidence suggests that these machine tools are provided at a nominal rent, thereby giving the recipients financial advantage. It has also been pointed out that the installation of government owned, company operated equipment is a significant source of hidden profits to the arms industries,[27] and adds evidence of the discriminatory nature of the military-industrial complex. Government equipment specific to one program immediately creates a situation whereby a single company emerges with the know-how and expertise to fulfill one type of major task. The effect further constrains free competition in the armaments market. It also makes the follow-on imperative in weapons acquisition the more probable, since it is wasteful and not in the government's interest to duplicate expensive capital equipment and allow it to lie idle.

The government has also become involved on financial grounds. The most common manner, other than through discriminatory tax concessions on certain categories of work, has been to provide generous progress payments to defense contractors in order to minimize their exposure to financial problems through cash-flow difficulties. Frequently progress payments have been as high as 95 percent, and, according to the formula employed, even higher.[28] To compensate for the technological uncertainties of weapons programs, disruption and complex critical path problems, the government generally has employed a wide variety of contractual provisions with the arms manufacturers resigned both to give financial incentives and to ameliorate the financial impact where marginal miscalculations can result in large absolute financial losses.

The artificial and natural determinants of the weapons market have determined that the government, as monopsonist, has had to become involved in the activities of the arms manufacturers and to assume a responsibility to them over time. The military-industrial firm is not, as a consequence, autonomous. It is dependent upon the government for capital, product specification, quantity production and, to some extent, even for the management process.[29] This dependency, coupled with the perceived need for military equipment, is the basis of the military-industrial complex. Qualification of the thesis, however, rests in the pattern of government-industry relations, as manifest in the defense sector; is, for example, the relationship as favored as is assumed? Is the perceived need for military equipment the determination of those who benefit most? How subject is the military industrial complex to the regulatory and investigatory agencies of the two branches of Government? Is the power and influence of the military industrial complex inversely proportional to the extent to which it is accountable to the American people?

THE DEFENSE INDUSTRY

The defense industry is defined here as the oligopolist side of the military market for weapons systems. The military demand for equipment is extensive, as reflected in the $30 billion appropriated annually for research, development, and production. The highest proportion of that demand is for high technology equipment which concentrates in the procurement field among the large aerospace companies, electronics firms, and the shipbuilders.[30] The companies in these areas effectively form the nucleus of the defense industry. They manufacture almost exclusively for the Defense Department, produce only to customer specification and under contract. The market place at any one time is characterized by the promise of a product—a weapons system—sufficient to meet the demand—a military specification —presented in feasibility study and project design and management form. What competition there is, is confined to the credibility of those promises and the assurance of the ability to produce to time, price, and specification. These assurances are based on past performance, expertise, and, invariably a poor third, price.

Companies which receive contracts of high value fall within the parameters of what is understood by the term the 'defense industry.' They include those companies generally referred to in the context of the military-industrial complex. The structure of the defense industry, however, is not what analysts of the military-industrial complex have usually implied. First, the major defense contractors are not among the largest industrial corporations in the United States; they are, by and large, medium-sized corporations.

The largest corporations, defined as having assets over $1 billion, receive approximately 25 percent of major prime defense contract awards, while the medium firms having assets under $1 billion, receive almost 60 percent.[31] The turnover among these top medium-sized defense contractors over the past decade has been negligible.[32] Taking a cut-off point at $250 million, or more, total of prime defense contracts per annum, there emerges a modest number of 27 firms in 1970; of these, seventeen are medium sized. These twenty-seven firms accounted for 48.6 percent of the net annual total of United States military prime contract awards. Since these same corporations have received a comparable percentage during the previous decade,[33] it is appropriate to identify them as the nucleus of the defense industry.

Although the distinguishing characteristic of these companies is their position among the top recipients of military prime contract awards, more significant is their percentage of defense contracts against total sales. Of the top twenty-seven contractors receiving $250 million or more in defense contracts in 1970, twelve failed to average over 40 percent of total sales over the preceding years.[34] Figuring significantly among the twelve are the industrial giants of the United States, such as General Motors, General Electric, AT & T, Westinghouse, Ford, IBM, Standard Oil of New Jersey, and RCA. Many of these huge corporations have divisions which are almost wholly defense oriented, and have sufficient defense work to figure among the top recipients of defense prime contract awards; as a percentage of the total sales of the parent company, this defense work nonetheless remains small.

These figures, however, can be misleading. The important thing to note is that they are all for prime contractors, and that these are recipients of military prime contract awards. The prime contractor is that company which assumes overall responsibility for the technical development, and, generally, the production of a weapons system. It negotiates the price, the terms of the contract, and manages the entire program, subject to the Armed Services Procurement Regulations allowing for government supervision. Only in cases of exceptional equipment, specific subsystems, or highly secret work does the government contract outside the prime contractor on a single weapon system program.

The total costs, and annual appropriations of weapons programs are quoted in the name of the prime contractor. Profit on a contract is that considered a reasonable return for the prime contractor's responsibilities. Since virtually all of the contracts going to the large prime contractors, forming the nucleus of the defense industry, are for new equipment requiring many technical uncertainties to be overcome, and the most sophisticated of management techniques, the role and function of the prime contractor is significant. Shortfalls in a program are its responsibility, no matter where they may occur; *ceteris paribus*, the prime contractor bears the brunt of whatever penalties are contained in the contract. The variety and dimension of the problems which confront prime contractors go some way to explain why the United States government has in the past appeared over-indulgent where overruns and specification shortfalls have been concerned. Without some latitude on the part of the government, many of these prime contractors would have faced financial and contractual problems injurious to the health of the company and prejudicial to the successful completion of the defense procurement project.

Prime contractors are less vulnerable to switches in defense policy and spending compared with many second and third layers of defense subcontractors. A squeeze in defense spending has always been countered by the prime contractors with a reduction in the amount of subcontracted work. Not only is this course of action a defense mechanism for the company, but it also can effect economies as well; this is a mixed blessing, inasmuch as it cuts across government Small Business Administration policy to disseminate defense work as widely as possible.[35] The flexibility of prime contractors stems from their essential function as program managers and system assemblers, rather than as exclusive system producers. On a major aerospace system, for example, the prime contractor would be responsible for about one third of the program, by weight,[36] and approximately 50 percent by value.[37] As complexity increases *per se*, or as a particular program becomes complex, so the proportion of subcontracted work increases. Increases in the amount of subcontracted work have continued sometimes as a result of government policy, but more probably as a hedge by the main contractors to reduce their financial exposure and management problems in an increasingly difficult sphere. A counter development, and one which confuses the figures on total defense awards among prime contractors, is the increasing amount of cross-subcontracting among the prime contractors themselves.[38]

Despite these hedging mechanisms, prime contractors remain defense oriented. This is defined in terms of the extent to which a company is dependent upon defense contracts for its continued viability as an operating enterprise at least to within 75 percent of its existing size. The corollory of this is the ease or difficulty a company has in moving out of the defense field into civil markets.[39] The greater the orientation, the greater the vulnerability to changes in defense expenditure. As a simple rule of thumb, any company with more than 40 percent of its annual turnover devoted to defense is defense oriented to a significant degree no matter what the total annual turnover of the company may be.[40]

The extent of defense orientation among defense subcontractors differs in degree from the prime contractors. Their orientation depends upon their dependency upon the prime contractors, and upon the particular subspecialty they offer. Few of the estimated number of 100,000 defense subcontractors fall into the exceptional category of only producing to the immediate requirements of weapons systems. Most subcontractors have only a small proportion of their annual turnover devoted to defense; this would be the case for the 30,000 or so subcontratcors that would be associated with one major weapons system program. Subcontractors are attracted to defense work as it has proved to be a relatively secure market, with guaranteed payment and offers sometimes the opportunity for research and development work, with possible civil application, without heavy financial risk or capital outlay. These advantages are considered to outweigh the low profit percentage on defense contracts, either as a percentage on sales or as return on investment.[41]

Most of the subcontractors referred to above are mono-product companies. They work exclusively in one area, and only universify within that area. There are, however a number of subcontractors who, on account of their size, encompass a wide variety of activities, and with the trend toward merger and group operations this number is increasing. This trend has important implications for the military-industrial complex. As noted above, these subcontractors may well have defense-oriented divisions, even though the parent company itself may be far from dependent upon defense contracts. General Electric, Goodyear, the major oil companies, and the steel industries would be included in this group.

Elaboration of the types of subcontractors on weapons systems programs is significant, for it helps to establish their dependency upon the prime contractors, and their exposure to alterations in defense policy. The more product oriented the subcontractor is, and the higher the proportion of its annual turnover is to defense, the more defense oriented it is. As 50 percent of defense prime contract awards is dissipated among subcontractors, and through them to two or three further layers of subcontractors, the orientation of these thousands of companies is highly significant. The defense orientation of these subcontractors is not acute except among the hyper-specialist group; this contention is supported by the fact that only a small number of subcontractors have gone bankrupt on account of defense cut-backs after the withdrawal from Vietnam and despite a drop in subcontracting to small business from 40.8 percent to 34.8 percent between 1969 and 1971.[42]

There is a side effect of the extent of defense subcontracting which should be noted. Fifty percent of prime contract awards by value is distributed among forty to fifty major subcontractors on any one weapons program. The Defense Department has suggested that this figure should be multiplied by five, '. . . to give a true picture of the number whose livelihood is affected by this defense programme.'[43] Although the Defense Department did not elaborate how, and by how much, these subcontractors would be affected, the observation at least points out that linked to one weapons program are significant sources of income, profit, and employment to many people and industries spanning many states. The pressure for military spending does not necessarily come from either the prime contractors, or the military, but from those many subcontractors who enjoy the residual spin-offs of defense spending. None of them, however, would be included within the category of 'defense industry' or within the 'military-industrial complex;' through congressional representation and pressure, they nonetheless have the capacity to bring pressure to bear in the interests of maintained military procurement budgets.[44]

GOVERNMENT-INDUSTRY RELATIONS AND
THE MILITARY-INDUSTRIAL COMPLEX

The foregoing analysis demonstrates that government-industry relationships in the military procurement field are not on a simple one-to-one basis. They are a pattern of interlocking relationships on many levels, involving many thousands of industrial firms of all sizes and of varying degrees of defense orientation. Weapons acquisition is not simply a contractual matter between prime military contractors and the appropriate defense department agency.

In an operational sense, the basis of government-industry relationships concerning weapons acquisition in the United States are the Armed Services Procurement Regulations. These cover purchasing regulations and provide for the appointment of Defense Department personnel to operate within prime defense contractors in a monitoring and general supervisory capacity. These appointments afford to the Defense Department significant control over the defense related operations of the prime contractor.[45] Only for a short trial period during the 1960s under the 'Total Package Procurement' system did these Defense Department personnel not take a fully active role in the management of weapons development and production, leaving the responsibility predominantly to the contractor. The experiment has been terminated following a number of major miscalculations.[46]

At a lower operational level, that of the defense subcontractors, the Armed Services Procurement Regulations still apply. Here, however, the principal lines of communication are not usually with the Defense Department, but instead with the prime contractor. Consequently the ties between defense subcontractors and Defense Department procurement agencies is not as close. It is a major problem in all government contracting that civil servants monitoring the performance of a contractor for any length of time tend to become product and company oriented. The tendency is to take the contractor's interpretation of a situation to the detriment of objective reporting. The effect, however, confirms the apparent special relationship between the government and the prime contractor, rather than the subcontractor.

With regard to decision-making, the mobility of personnel between the government, the executive departments, the military and industry is significant. The numbers of military officers who are appointed on retirement to senior executive posts in the defense industries is noticeable. The numbers seem to speak for themselves, but how to interpret them is not so easy. It is impossible, for example, to determine whether or not these appointments are on account of military expertise, or because of their familiarity with the people and processes within the top decision-making circles of the Pentagon.[47] Either way, there is no question that the defense industries try to influence the Defense Department with new ideas and products, and are not averse to employing all methods of persuasion and salesmanship at their disposal. Since this pressure is virtually constant, the impression at least is of a high degree of collusion.

There are many links, direct and indirect, between the government, the defense contractors and the military. Because of the market structure, they are 'locked in' together;[48] the links are therefore not only clearly visible, but also virtually permanent.[49] Superimposed on this interlocking relationship is the cementing effect of advanced technology, which has a form of imperative of its own.[50] It gives those defense contractors currently involved a uniqueness and an exclusivity which is hard to contest. For as long as the United States perceives that it is necessary to maintain a war potential, and that technological expertise in weapons development and production should be retained and not allowed to atrophy, the government is obliged to sustain both the demand for advanced military equipment at a given level, and to continue its involvement in the military market.

This 'given level' has to be seen both quantitatively and qualitatively. Quantitatively, a ceiling has to be sufficient in the short run to offset the more drastic consequences of a cut in defense spending, such as unemployment and regional disruption. This argument has more political weight than economic due to the political interests of congressmen whose electoral districts are major beneficiaries of defense spending.[51] Qualitatively, the need is to keep abreast, or ahead, of perceived enemies, and to provide scientific challenge for defense scientists and technologists.

For essentially negative reasons, the possibility of any significant alteration in the defense procurement budget, and hence any alteration in government-industry relations, is small. In the long run, defense industries might convert to civil work provided the incentives were there and they had the flexibility and capacity to do so. The incentives would have to be substantial, and technology oriented. They would probably involve the creation of a demand from the civil agencies of the government. But this market is only latent, and for as long as the perception of defense needs remains as consistent as it has done for the past two decades, the likelihood of making any switch, with all the problems associated with it, is remote. A break, or change in government-industry relations would have to come within; the *positive* reasons for change seem remote which suggests that it would be for *negative* reasons if any alteration in government-industry relations were to be introduced.

Over the past twenty years in the United States there has been a conspicuous absence on the part of the government to introduce a policy to restructure and reorganize the major defense-oriented industries. The principal areas for concern have been effect improvement in the existing weapons procurement process. These have included mechanisms to detect, prevent, or ameliorate cost overruns, ways of stopping waste, duplication and shortfalls in delivery time and equipment performance, improvements to the mechanisms and processes of contract negotiation, cost-estimating procedures and weapon system management and control, and methods of standardizing reporting, accounting, and information gathering. Little has been done to put the defense industries on a national footing where the needs of the armed services are better equated with industrial potential. This perhaps would strike too close to the heart of the existing procurement system; consequently there is a running battle to keep abreast through adjustment and adaptation, with the many complex problems that arise. The effect has been twofold: the prime contractors, all under private ownership, if not control, continue to receive favored treatment almost as a matter of expediency, and the government and the defense contractors are drawn closer administratively, operationally, and spiritually.

This is the fundamental paradox of weapons procurement in the United States today. The more that the free enterprise system in weapons procurement is made to work, the more adjustments have to be made. These adjustments lock the government and the defense contractors closer together, confirming outside impressions of coalescence of interest and collusion between them. The stage has now been reached where the government in recent years has been forced out of conviction, to camouflage major procurement errors,[52] lobby Congress for additional billions of dollars to see programs through to completion,[53] 'bail-out' a number of major contractors faced with bankruptcy,[54] and continue with programs which have no longer immediately served the tactical and strategic needs of the armed services.[55]

An important question is how much room does there remain for adjustment to the present procurement system without further compromising the principles of private enterprise. The indicator of the impact of these adjustments on the defense subcontractor might provide a lead. Two statistics suggest that there is not much more room: the first is that the percentage of business devolving upon the small business defense subcontractor has been falling consistently over the past five years; the second is that among defense subcontractors, there is 65 percent under-utilization of productive capacity. At present the margin falls among these less defense-oriented firms, but the margin is moving up all the time.

The relationship between government and industry remains premised on private ownership of the defense industries, despite government control over price, product, and production. The relationship is under pressure, not because of attacks on the 'military-industrial complex,' but because of the combined effect of the natural determinants of the product and the constraints which are building up within the United States economy as a whole. To date, the response has been for the government and industry to close ranks, even to the detriment of smaller members of the defense industries. As the government has moved further and further to protect the arms manufacturers, and in consequence become more closely allied to them, the question of public accountability becomes more pertinent.

ACCOUNTABILITY AND THE MILITARY-INDUSTRIAL COMPLEX

Accountability in defense procurement falls broadly into two broad areas. The first is the accountability of the defense contractors to the government; this is the residual element of the early 'contact-state' relationship and before the military-industrial-complex situation today. The second is the accountability of the defense contractors and the government to the American taxpayer and to Congress. Whilst the foci of interest for accountability in both cases may be the same, their applicability and operation are significantly different. Both the government and the defense industries, depending on the prevailing relationship between them, are accountable for the choice of weapons system program; the choice of contractor; the conduct of the program; and finally the fiscal control over the expenditure of public money.

First, there is the whole area of the accountability of the major contractors to the government. In theory, if the market structure had been free, the contractor should have little say in the choice of weapons systems. In practice, the expertise of the contractor and the long-standing relationship with the Defense Department offers opportunity to exercise considerable influence. As long as feasibility studies by prime contractors—and proposals for modifications once a contract is under way—are accepted by the Defense Department, accountability for weapons choice in one sense is the responsibility of the government. But contractors participate in the decision-making process of weapons choice; the lengthy process of discussion, analysis and synthesis of scientific and technical alternatives between the contractor and both the military and the Defense Department brings the contractor into the heart of the weapons definition and selection process. It is this close participation which partially explains why the government has come to the support of contractors when unforeseen problems on weapons systems start surfacing. The extent of the influence of the contractors on weapons choice can be seen in recent policies by the government to reduce contractor involvement in weapons choice; these have been to try to reintroduce competition between prime contractors, and to introduce a 'fly before you buy' principle in weapons purchase.[56]

Over the choice of contractor, it might be assumed that a defense contractor can hardly be held accountable, since contractors do not choose themselves. They can, however, influence their being selected, and for the exercise of this influence, they can be held accountable. Accepting that relatively few major contracts are competed for, and that contractors are, on account of their expertise and capabilities, monopolists in an area of defense specialism, there have been occasions when there has been competition. The C-5A contract would be a recent example. Lockheed, the eventual winners, were accused of having deliberately underestimated the costs of development and production, and of effecting a 'buy-in.' The company was thought to have relied on the magnanimity of the Defense Department, the inability of the government auditors to detect cost overruns unil at least sunk costs on the program would render cancellation more easily than continuation, and the re-pricing formula which they insisted was included in the contract, in the event that their low estimates got them into trouble.[57]

It was in reference to this sort of situation, and others like it, when contractors have been less than honest in their estimates of costs, time schedules and performance guarantees, that the Deputy Secretary of Defense, David Packard, registered a hope for more 'integrity' in government-industry relations.[58] On evidence, the Truth in Negotiations Act of 1962, which was designed to obviate such problems, has not worked as well as was intended. The reason is a difference in interpretation of what is 'proprietary commercial information,' and what is permissible for government scrutiny.[59] The situation reveals that whilst there are close relations between government and industry, they are certainly ambivalent. If anything, it would appear that the defense contractors are the capricious ones. The Government has recently responded to overcome problems in this area by introducing the 'should-cost' principles in cost-estimating for major weapons systems.[60]

Contractors' accountability to the government for program management becomes confused by the immediate involvement of the Defense Department itself. On any major defense contract, a Systems Program Office is located in the prime contractor's factory. Its responsibility is to monitor the conduct of the prime contractor, and judge on the spot, appropriate action to keep the program on schedule.[61] The SPO's function is to report back to a Defense Department Designated System Management Group progress, decisions, and problems. The ability of the SPO to fulfill its function effectively depends on the quality of the information fed back to it by the contractor. The experience to date in this has not been good, and by the time cost overruns, or technical problems have been isolated, the sunk costs in the program have amounted to a high percentage of the whole program.[62] Many problems complicate this information feed-back, not least of which is the combination of civil and military work done by most defense contractors, and the hazy definition of what is proprietary information.[63]

Defense contractors are accountable to the government for their use of public money; they have to submit their books for audit. Since 1964 the relevant agency in the Defense Department has been the Defense Contracts Auditing Agency (DCAA). It is a central auditing agency responsible for all defense audits, and it reports to the Secertary of Defense. The effect has been to shift responsibility for audit from the General Accounting Office, a body which reports to Congress.[94] Since the significance of audit lies in the public dissemination of the findings, the role of the DCAA adds weight to the contention that many contractors' misappropriation of funds are buried in the Pentagon away from public scrutiny. Another factor which militates against the fiscal accountability of defense contractors to the Defense Department, is the lack of any enforcement in accounting methods and standards, which makes comparisons difficult and fiscal maneuver hard to isolate.

As the relations between the government and industry become closer, and as information about contracts, contractors, and the conduct of procurement programs becomes more and more difficult to unearth, so the important focus of accountability has to be that of the accountability of the Defense Department and the defense contractors to Congress, and to the American public. Again there is the paradox, that the more Congress demands to know what is going on in the area of defense procurement, the closer the Defense Department and the contractors become.

Program accountability is the idea that the government is accountable for selection of weapons systems, and that it is getting what it is paying for. A major problem in this area is the question of national security and secrecy. Secrecy is a basic consideration where weapons systems are concerned, even at the development and production stage. There has to be an element of trust that the weapon in question is 'cost-effective' and is essential to the overall military posture of the state. Before funds are appropriated to a major weapons system program, it is the responsibility of the Congressional Committees, especially those of the Armed Services and Appropriations Committees, to satisfy themselves about weapons choices and their relevance to overall defense policy. The record of these committees has not been impressive, and it is often assumed that their uncritical view reflects the separate interests of the members in keeping defense expenditure up, especially in their home states. The only committees which have assiduously investigated weapons procurement programs have been the Joint Economic Committee and the House Government Operations Committee. The subpoena powers of these committees—or the lack of them—limit their effectiveness which has rested very heavily on the industry of their respective staffs and the particular enthusiasm of the committee chairman and members.[95]

The choice of contractor, and the performance of that contractor on a weapons system program, are certainly areas for accountability. The exercise of accountability is an entirely different matter. Mismanagement is only heard about long after the deed has been done, and only then when additional funds are requested from Congress. Information is the essential consideration, and for this, Congress is dependent on the Defense Department. As noted above, the cooperation of the defense contractors themselves in providing information—if they have it themselves—leaves much to be desired. The General Accounting Office is the auditing arm of Congress, and should have access, though for reasons of security or 'proprietary information,' the Defense Department has frequently obstructed the work of the GAO in the weapons procurement field. The importance of the GAO has further been undermined by the DCAA and the sense that it would be unnecessary to duplicate defense audits.[66] But even when the GAO has turned attention to weapons programs, it has been mainly dependent on information supplied by the Department of Defense, and all that has been asked for has not existed, or not been forthcoming.[67] The principal area where the GAO has done valuable work has been in investigating procurement problems and suggesting remedies. While these may be critical analyses, they do not represent a threat to the fundamental relationship between government and industry, nor to the prevailing procurement system.

A second agency of note which can effect some answerability from defense contractors is the Renegotiation Board. The Board's responsibility is to check profits made on defense contracts to insure that none is excessive. It is a relic of the pre-Second World War when problems of weapons procurement were simpler and the relationship between government and industry less interwoven. Whilst many feel that the Renegotiation Board has outlived its usefulness, the inescapable fact is that the Board's post-contract auditing still reveals millions of dollars in excessive profits on defense contracts.[68] Post-contract auditing has its usefulness, inasmuch as it is a threat to prime defense contractors who may try to take advantage of the government; but it is a last resort. It does not directly help to tackle the immediate problems of contractor inefficiency, waste, cost escalation, and poor estimating, so endemic in the defense industry today.

A third watch-dog over the activities of the defense contractors but for entirely different reasons, is the Securities and Exchange Commission. The SEC's responsibilities to the general public are to insure that all business corporations give full and accurate information concerning their financial standing and operations. This is to insure that privileged information is not used to private advantage, thereby jeopardizing confidence in the various dealings in securities in the several exchanges throughout the United States. Defense contractors are not exempt, as demonstrated by the thorough investigation undertaken by the SEC into the Lockheed Corporation when it was suspected *inter alia* that some senior Lockheed officials had sold shares in the company on the basis of privileged information about the difficulties being encountered on the C-5A contract.[69] Significantly, the information gathered by the SEC in that report was superior and more detailed than any other publicly available report up to that time. As with the Renegotiation Board, however, the SEC only functions *ex post facto*, and only then when there is good reason to suspect wrong dealings. But the concept of accountability is not premised on wrong doings and the apportionment of blame; it is concerned with the right to know what is going on, both good and bad, at the earliest opportunity.

The problem is basically one of information. The American taxpayer is paying for the acquisition of sophisticated weapons systems and should be assured of the right to know, within the bonds of national security, of any misappropriation of funds, of ill management of weapons programs, when costs escalate beyond reason, and when funds are being appropriated to keep the arms manufacturers in business more than to procure arms for essential military needs. The requisite information has to come from two sources: the defense contractors themselves, and the Defense Department. Many considerations mitigate against full information being forthcoming, which do not in themselves constitute either a conspiracy or government-military-industrial collusion: the first must be the question of national security and the need for secrecy. This has prevented access to contractors' books in many cases, since they contain information which could lead to military disadvantage if discovered by perceived enemies. Much, of course, does not fall within this category, but is wrongly given blanket classification as a security measure. Secondly, there is the question of proprietary information, which is defined, invariably, by the contractor and not the Defense Department, as anything which may put the company at a competitive disadvantage with other manufacturers in the field. No official definition of proprietary information exists, which has meant that contractors have shielded, both from the public and the Defense Department, pertinent information on the management and fiscal control of major weapons systems programs. Third, the feed-back process on weapons systems programs is slow and complex. Although the Department of Defense has a computerized 'progress payments model' which has been operational since 1967 designed to keep track of the day-to-day performance of defence contractors,[70] the feed-back of information on the progress of weapons systems is slow. The problem is endemic in the size and the complexity of a weapons systems program, involving many thousands of sub-contractors, technical unknowns, and fiscal and administrative imponderables. It is perfectly possible for the lag to be at least up to one year, or more.[71] Finally, there is the simple fact that military contracts are never static; over the six or seven years of a weapons system development, amendments are made to the original specification by the military and sometimes on the recommendation of the contractor. These alterations not only contribute to rising costs, but also to the length of time before the weapon enters operational service. Cost escalation need not necessarily be the result of poor management entirely; invariably it is the result of military intransigence when requests for alterations to specifications are made in the interests of the contractor meeting time and cost requirements. The adage that the best is the enemy of the good is never more apposite than in weapons development.

To suggest a coalescence of interest and collusion among the 'military-industrial complex' on the basis of the inaccessibility of the public to gain access to information is to overlook the important point that the information is not always readily available This, however, is not to deny that there could be more public-mindedness of the Defense Department and the defense contractors when it comes to keeping Congress and the public informed of what is going on. On the other hand, those bodies empowered with duty to investigate the executive agencies which are responsible for the spending of public money are not altogether without blame either. The relevant committees in Congress could well have been more persistent and penetrating in their inquiries into defense spending and procurement. Likewise, Congress could have given the General Accounting Office more support on those occasions when the GAO has encountered opposition from the Defense Department. In defense of the GAO, however, it should be pointed out as well that its responsibility goes far beyond merely the Defense Department, and that it has not the resources to pursue every scandal which surfaces—civilian or military— where public money is concerned, and act as a recommending body to Congress on questions of financial control and management.

Perhaps to the embarrassment of the Defense Department, or indeed to the General Accounting Office and Congress, information on poor management on weapons systems in recent years has come from disclosures from within the Defense Department and the defense contractors. The dangers that those who release information on mismanagement of public funds on defense, or even civil, programs can face are enormous, and have been well documented.[71] But it is a poor reflection on the present situation in the United States where accountability for defense procurement spending is concerned, when information on cost escalation, or overruns above target cost, in one case to the amount of $2 billion, has to come from inside sources or what might pejoratively be classified as 'administrative leaks.'

In recent months a Report of the Commission on Government Procurement was published. The study had been commissioned as part of an Act, Public Law 91–129, which was passed by Congress in November 1969, to establish a Commission on Government Procurement. The Commission's Report, a mammoth four-volume study, was published in early 1973; of note is the absence throughout the study of any reference to accountability, or the feed-back of information on government procurement for congressional, executive, or public scrutiny.[73] The report falls very much within the old pattern of working continually at the margin of procurement processes and procedures to effect improvement in choice, capital utilization, etc; it evades the basic issue that the efficiency of a corporation, whether government oriented or in open competition, is enhanced by the threat of public exposure.

The last area of accountability is fiscal. Here the problem revolves around the relative powers and responsibilities of the General Accounting Office, the Defense Contract Auditing Agency and the professional responsibilities of the contractors' accountants. The DCAA has duplicated the function of the General Accounting Office which has meant that unless the GAO has the backing of Congress to go over the DCAA work, and has the same access to information, the fiscal accountability of the contractors ends there. This effectively keeps the contractors' books away from public scrutiny. By law, all corporations are required to have their books audited, summaries of which appear in the annual report to stockholders. Different accounting methods and general summaries help to disguise the financial state of a company, especially when auditors are concerned with the total affairs of the company and not with specific projects.

CONCLUSION

The military-industrial complex has been seen as a coalescence of interest among the government, the military, and the defense contractors. The structure of the defense market demonstrates that this apparent coalescence is premised upon the natural and artificial determinants of the market, and not necessarily mutual interest. Mutual interest itself is tempered by the fact that the defense industry, being the third element in the complex, comprises more than just the major defense contractors, though these emerge as the ones closest to the government. What matters more, where the pressure for continued defense spending is concerned, is the defense orientation of the company, and in this the major contractors are often better off than many second and third rank subcontractors. The subcontractors cannot be overlooked, since they collectively receive almost 50 percent of the government's annual defense procurement bill of $30 billion.

The core element in continued defense procurement spending is a military perception of a need for advanced weapons systems. This fact is inescapable. In a negative sense, military requirements are likely to be favorably met on account of the current impact, both political and economic, on the different states of the Union. To some extent a blind eye has been turned to the question whether continued military spending at a $30 billion annual level is needed.

The test of whether the military-industrial complex is really a coalescence lies in the extent to which it is accountable to the general public. As government-industry relations are getting closer and closer on account of the natural determinants of the market, the public is becoming more and more separated from having any idea of what is going on, at least until it is too late. The institutional bodies—Congress, the GAO, etc.—with the public responsibility to find out what is going on in the interests of holding the defense contractors and the government accountable, have not, for many reasons, been as assiduous in their duties as they might. This does not mean that accountability in this area is a dead issue; it means that the dissemination of information has to be more widespread, and that this has to be recognized by both the Defense Department and the contractors.[74] This ultimately may well be a condition of keeping the current government-industry relationship and procurement system the way they are, rather than being forced to introduce a nationalized defense armaments industry.

Notes

1. C. Wright Mills, *Power Elite* (Oxford University Press, New York, 1959); Richard L. Heilbroner, *The Limits of American Capitalism* (Harper Row, New York, 1965).
2. D. Cater, *Power in Washington* (Vintage Books, New York, 1965) p. 17.
3. A. Yarmolinsky, *The Military Establishment* (Perennial Library, New York, 1973) p. 67.
4. James R. Anderson, 'The Balance of Payments among States and Regions,' in S. Melman (ed.), *The War Economy of the United States* (St Martin's Press, New York, 1971) pp. 137–47.
5. S. Melman, 'Ten Propositions on the War Economy,' *American Economic Review* (May 1972), p. 312.
6. J. K. Galbraith, *How to Control the Military* (New American Library, New York, 1969) p. 27.

7. This sentiment was perhaps most emphatically expressed during the Emergency Loan Guarantee hearings during June and July, 1971. See Hearings before the Committee on Banking, Housing and Urban Affairs, United States Senate, 92nd Congress, 1st Session on *Emergency Loan Guarantee Legislation*. June–July, 1971 (Government Printing Office, Washington, 1971) pp. 1157–92.

8. H. L. Nieburg, *In the Name of Science* (Quadrangle Books, Chicago, 1966 cit. A. Yarmolinsky, op. cit., p. 66.

9. R. Kaufman, *The War Profiteers* (Doubleday Anchor, New York, 1972) pp. 17–23.

10. M. Wiedenbaum, 'The Government oriented Corporation,' in B. Smith and D. Hague (eds.), *Dilemmas in Accountability in Modern Government* (Macmillan, London, 1971) p. 129.

11. Yarmolinsky, op. cit., p. 66.

12. Kaufman, op. cit., p. 23.

13. M. Reich, 'Does the US Economy need Military Spending?', *American Economic Review* (May 1972) pp. 296–303.

14. D. Eisenhower, Farewell Address, Jan. 1971.

15. H. Horelik and M. Rush, *Strategic Power and Soviet Foreign Policy* (Chicago U.P., Chicago, 1966) p. 225.

16. W. Proxmire, *Report from Wasteland* (Praeger, New York, 1970).

17. M. Wiedenbaum, address before the American Economic Association 1967, cit., S. Melman, *Pentagon Capitalism* (McGraw-Hill, New York, 1970) p. 12.

18. Melman, *Pentagon Capitalism*, op. cit., p. 17.

19. J. Donovan, *Militarism, USA* (Scribners, 1970) p. 47.

20. Melman, 'Ten Propositions on the War Economy,' op. cit., p. 312–18.

21. Walter Adams and William J. Adams, 'The Military Industrial Complex: A Market Structure Analysis,' *American Economic Review* (May, 1972) pp. 279–87.

22. E.g., The TFX decision. See R. Art, *The TFX Decision* (Boston, 1968).

23. J. Kurth, 'The Political Economy of Weapons Procurement: the Follow-on Imperative,' *American Economic Review* (May, 1972) pp. 307–309.

24. M. Wiedenbaum, 'Concentration and Competition in the Military Market,' *Quarterly Review of Business and Economics*, vol. 8 (1968) p. 7.

25. *Vide* Lockheed experience with the L-1011. See S. Melman, 'The characteristics of the industrial conversion problem' in S. Melman (ed.), *The War Economy of the United States*, op. cit., pp. 201–7.

26. Kaufman, op. cit., p. 142.

27. Ibid., p. 153.

28. Statement of Elmer B. Staats before the Subcommittee on Priorities and Economy in Government, Joint Economic Committee, Dec. 1972, U.S. General Accounting Office, Dec. 18, 1972, pp. 8–11.

29. Melman, 'Ten Propositions on the War Economy,' op. cit., p. 313.

30. U.S. Department of Defense List of Companies and their subsidiaries according to net value of military prime contract awards, Fiscal year 1970, cited in Kaufman, op. cit., p. 49–65.

31. Ibid. The top ten companies received in 1970 28% of military prime contract awards; the top 20, 40% and the top 100, 60%. See also, F. M. Scherer, 'The Aerospace Industry in Walter Adams (ed.), *The Structure of American Industry*, 2nd edn (Macmillan, New York, 1971) pp. 341–4.

32. Yarmolinsky, op. cit., p. 245.

33. Ibid., p. 242.

34. Melman, *Pentagon Capitalism*, op. cit., pp. 77–8; see also Scherer, op. cit., p. 343.

35. Report of the Subcommittee on Government Procurement to the Select Committee on Small Business, 'The Position and Problems of Small Business in Government Procurement, House of Representatives, 92nd Congress, 2nd Session, Oct. 1972 (Government Printing Office, Washington, 1972) p. 2.

36. Warren Kraemer, 'The high technology gap, too much too soon,' in *Dealing with Technological Change* (Auerbach, New York, 1971) p. 29. Mr Kraemer is referring to advanced technology civil aircraft, but the general point still stands.

37. Melman, *Pentagon Capitalism*, op. cit., p. 52.

38. Kaufman, op. cit., p. 270.

39. E.g., the Lockheed L-1011 program which was primarily responsible for the ratio of defense work to civil work to be reduced from 90%: 10% in 1967 to virtually 50%:50% in 1971.

40. M. Wiedenbaum, 'The Government oriented Corporation,' op. cit., p. 136. However, the GAO study on Defense Industry Profits defines High Volume Defense Contractors as those having 10% of total sales in defense.

41. General Accounting Office, *Defense Industry Profits Study* B-159896, March 17, 1971, p. 55.

42. Barry Shillito, Statement before the subcommittee on Government Procurement of the House of Representatives Select Committee on Small Business, 92nd Cong., 1st Sess., Sept./Nov. 1971, p. 466.

43. The Defense Industry, Bulletin. Feb. 1966, cited in Melman, 'Pentagon Capitalism,' op. cit., p. 81.

44. M. Reich, 'Does the U.S. Economy require military spending?' in *American Economic Review*, May 1972, pp. 296–303. Reich makes the important point that many corporations wish to keep military spending up in order to keep the defense oriented corporations from turning their resources and talents in the direction of civil production. He cites the example of the development of mass transportation systems would deal a body blow to the U.S. automobile industry.

45. Melman, *Pentagon Capitalism*, op. cit., pp. 37–45.

46. *Policy Changes in Weapons Systems Procurement*, 42nd report by the Committee on Government Operations, Dec. 10, 1970, pp. 11–14.

47. Yarmolinsky, *The Military Establishment*, op. cit., pp. 73–5.

48. Wiedenbaum, 'The Government oriented Corporation,' op. cit., p. 129.

49. Ibid., p. 142.

50. Ralph E. Lapp, *The Weapons Culture* (W. W. Norton, New York, 1968).

51. See M. Barone, G. Ujifusa, and D. Matthews, *The Almanac of American Politics* (Gambit, New York, 1972).

52. E.g., the Lockheed C-5A program. The Defense Department tried to disguise the extent of the cost overrun, even after it had been revealed to the Joint Economic Committee in late 1968.

53. E.g., the 'restructured contract' of May 1971 in which the government would, after a fixed loss of $200 million to Lockheed, complete the C-5A program on a cost reimbursement basis. The estimated cost to the tax-payer was appoximately $2 billion over original estimates.

54. *New York Times*, May 1, 1973. The authority for this is Public Law 85–804.

55. The Pentagon Office of Systems Analysis did a study on the C-5A in June 1969, and recommended that only three (58 planes) squadrons would be sufficient. This suggests that the additional planes were (a) not required militarily and (b) were only procured in order to bring into operation the re-pricing formula in order to minimize Lockheed's losses. B. Rice, *The C-5A Scandal* (Houghton Mifflin, New York, 1971) p. 112.

56. *Policy Changes in Weapons Procurement*, Hearings before a Sub-committee of the Committee on Government Operations, House of Representatives, 91st Cong., 2nd Sess., Sept. 1970, pp. 16–17.

57. Rice, *The C-5A Scandal*, op. cit., p. 26.

58. Emergency Loan Guarantee Legislation, Hearings before the Com-mittee on Banking, Housing and Urban Affairs, U.S. Senate, Part 1, June, 1971, 92nd Cong., 1st Sess., p. 161.

59. General Accounting Office Report to Congress. *Effectiveness of Revised Procedures Implementing the Truth in Negotiations Act* B-39995, Washing-ton, Dec. 29, 1970, p. 2 and pp. 26–7.

60. General Accounting Office Report to Congress on *The Feasibility of Using 'Should-Cost' Concepts in Government Procurement* B-159896, May 20, 1970 (Washington).

61. *Government Procurement and Contracting*. Hearings before the Sub-committee on Government Operations, House of Representatives 91st Cong., 1st Sess., April 29, 1969, Part IV, pp. 1163–6.

62. Interview. By the time that the full extent of the cost overruns on the C-5A had been established by the Pentagon, $2 billion in sunk costs had already gone into the program.

63. *The Acquisition of Weapons Systems*. Hearings before the Sub-committee on Priorities and Economy in Government of the Joint Economic Committee, 92nd Cong., 1st Sess., May 25, 1971, Part IV, pp. 1178–80.

64. C. Mollenhoff, *The Pentagon* (Putnam, New York, 1967) p. 22.

65. Outstanding in this respect are the following: Senator William Proxmire (author of *Report from Wasteland*), Congressman Richard Moorhead; Richard Kaufman of the Joint Economic Committee Staff (author of *The War Profiteers*); Ernest Fitzgerald, also on the Joint Economic Committee Staff (author of *High Priests of Waste*); Peter Stock-ton on Congressman Moorhead's staff (author of articles on the military-industrial complex) and Merton Tyrell, of Performance Technology Corp. consultants (author of *Pentagon Partners*).

66. Kaufman, op. cit., p. 171.

67. *The Acquisition of Weapons Systems*, op. cit., Part I, p. 7. There is also here the question of executive privilege; it was an issue in 1959 when the Defense Department objected to GAO investigations into Navy expenditure. See Mollenhoff, op. cit., p. 228.

68. M. Edmonds, 'Government contracting and Renegotiation,' *Public Administration* (Spring 1972).

69. *Report of Investigation in Re Lockheed Aircraft Corporation* HO-423, Vols I and II (May 25, 1970. Securities and Exchange Commission, Washington.

70. E. A. Fitzgerald, *The High Priests of Waste* (Norton, New York, 1972) p. 293.

71. GAO Report to Congress, *Need to improve effectiveness of contractor procurement system reviews* B-169434, Aug. 18, 1970, p. 38.

72. *The Dismissal of E. A. Fitzgerald by the Department of Defense.* Hearings before the Subcommittee on Economy in Government of the Joint Economic Committee, 91st Cong., 1st Sess., Nov. 1969, pp. 5–55. Another example is that of a Lockheed employee, Henry Durham; see the *New York Times*, Mar. 7, 1973, p. 85.

73. *Report of the Commission on Government Procurement: Summary*, Dec. 1972, p. 143.

74. *The Acquisition of Weapons Systems*, op. cit., Part I, Dec. 1969, pp. 2–3. GAO recommendations in testimony were to this effect.

7 Accountability and Independence in Federal Grants-in-aid

MICHAEL D. REAGAN

My purposes here are primarily analytic and secondarily programmatic. I hope to present a framework for analysis, which will include elaboration of some of the dimensions and problems involved, and to argue in favor of emphasis upon one particular kind of accountability and the need for the training of professional program evaluators to do the job of program evaluation that is required.

Although all operations of government give rise to problems of accountability and independence, grant-in-aid programs do so more patently and more urgently, presumably, than do operations that are entirely executed by agents and agencies within the same level of government that has authorized the program. Of course, the hierarchic authority of organization charts does not always work out in practice, with the result that various divisions and bureaus within federal departments are notoriously autonomous of and unaccountable to their nominal superiors in the cabinet offices. Nevertheless, it is probably reasonable to assume that as between running the same congressionally-approved program through a federal civil service operation, or through grants to state or local governmental units whose personnel are administratively accountable to the political leadership of their own jurisdiction, the latter type of operation will typically raise more severe problems of accountability than the former.

Whether, on the other hand, accountability in grant programs is more or less difficult to achieve than in 'administration by contract' programs would be hard to say. Offhand, grant programs would appear to fall somewhere in between direct civil service operations and the execution of federal government programs by private contractors. It might be fruitful to hypothesize, however, that from the viewpoint of the federal government, state and local government agencies are perhaps just as external and autonomous as are private institutions. Or does the public-private distinction, which has clearly been eroded in many respects, still have sufficient meaning to warrant the supposition that state and local government officials would, more than the employees of private institutions, have a 'public benefit' orientation such as to constitute a kind of built-in voluntary accountability?[1]

As we shall see, there are so many different kinds of grant-in-aid programs that the variations among them may give rise to as great a spread of accountability problems as would be found between grant programs, contract programs, and direct federal programs. Here, at any rate, we look only at the grant-in-aid part of the picture.

DIMENSIONS OF ACCOUNTABILITY

Since accountability is an aspect of a relationship in which one person is subject to the authority of another in such a way that redress may be exacted in case of default, the first question to ask is, 'Accountable to whom?' Those engaged in the management and operation of a government program might be accountable to the electorate, the legislators, or to higher administrative authority. Only those who are themselves elected by the people can truly be said to be accountable to the electorate. An appointed official may be *responsible* to the electorate, but not *accountable*. That is, he may have an ethical obligation to the electorate, and he may feel within himself that he wants to carry out the electoral will as he understands it. No matter how strong his sense of obligation, however, he is not accountable because the electorate has no means by which to exact redress in case he defaults on his obligations. The electorate itself, that is to say, cannot exercise sanctions over him.

In a parliamentary model, one can also say that the administrator is not accountable (though he may again be responsible) to the legislature. In the United States, some academic analysts would say that an administrator's responsibility runs only to higher executive authority, with the elected chief executive being accountable in some respects (perhaps primarily through the budget) to the legislature as well as to the electorate, in turn. Writers in the public administration field (who have generally tended to favor the executive branch and be sceptical of the talents and often even the motivation of the legislature) have often held that view. Other analysts, including many political scientists outside the public administration field, have argued that ours is a system of dual administrative accountability in which administrative control is in some forms exercised directly by the legislature, as well as through the general regulations, statutory controls, and budgetary limits which it imposes on the chief executive, to guide him in holding administrative subordinates within assigned limits, in turn. The device of the legislative veto,[2] for example, places certain congressional committees in a position of direct administrative supervision over discrete bureaucratic decisions. The function of legislative oversight, whose purpose is to ensure that authority delegated to administrators is used only in effective pursuance of congressionally mandated objectives, may be the most important aspect of Congress's role today. Under direct federal program operation, legislative oversight sometimes provides rather strong and direct accountability over administrators. In the area of grants-in-aid, however, oversight by Congress can only hold accountable the federal officials charged with disbursing the grant funds; it cannot hold accountable the state and local government employees who actually execute the programs. Perhaps one can say that Congress can hold the program accountable, although not the program operators. That is to say, the primary legislative sanction is withdrawal of funds and the termination of aid. That does not constitute, except indirectly, a sanction over the persons involved at the state-local level.

In grant-in-aid programs, therefore, accountability runs to a higher administrative authority, rather than to a legislature or an electorate. At least, that is the case so far as the federal level is concerned. If one talks about all levels simultaneously, the state or local official operating a federally aided program may or may not be accountable in more than one way. For example, when a grant is given to a general jurisdiction city government, the mayor is electorally accountable to his local constituency as well as being administratively accountable—within the sphere of the grant program—to whatever federal agency has awarded the grant. Or, he may be a city manager accountable to the local legislature (i.e. the city council), as well as to the granting agency at the federal level. In either of these instances, however, his electoral or legislative accountability is not precisely his accountability for the grant-in-aid. With respect to that, his accountability is executive only. It may still, however, be multiple in nature. That is, a state health services director will be administratively accountable to his governor as one higher executive, and also to, say, the Social Security Administration as grantor agency for a Medicaid program.

The next question is, 'Accountable for what?' What are the purposes of accountability? In what aspects of a program's operation do we seek accountability? In a formal, financial sense, the purpose of accountability is often seen as the prevention of embezzlement or other malfeasance on the part of those spending funds. This purpose, which is pursued much more vigorously by public agencies than in the private sector, has led more than any other single factor to the phenomenon of bureaucratic 'red tape.' Forms, requisitions, affidavits, etc., are filled out in quintuplicate and filed for every purchase of a box of paper clips in order that the managers at the top will not be blamed for a theft or misappropriation of three-dollars' worth of funds at the bottom—even if such prevention costs five dollars for each transaction processed.

A related purpose of accountability is to prevent waste of public monies. Waste is a word of many meanings. It means inefficiency of procedures in ways that cost more money than need have been spent to achieve the same objective. It means 'frills' that constitute gold-plating but are not functionally necessary to the completion of a project. It means expenditures in pursuit of projects whose attainment is simply not feasible in a given state of technology—such as the nuclear airplane project cancelled at the beginning of the Kennedy Administration after an expenditure of more than a billion dollars in R & D funds. It means, in short, a variety of ways of using money that do not contribute effectively, or at all, to the attainment of the primary objective. When anything experimental is at stake, it is, of course, a difficult question whether the greater waste occurs through a bold experiment that doesn't work, or through bureaucratic timidity that maintains such close controls over the experimenters that they are never free to give their proposed innovation a real try-out. A third purpose of accountability is to ensure that administrative interpretation of the goals of a program as laid down by the legislator or by higher executive authority remains in close congruence with those goals as seen by the originators of the program. For example, when OEO funds were used to develop the political strength of minority groups, objections were raised that this was not what was meant by a war on poverty in the minds of those who declared the war. OEO guidelines regarding what maximum feasible participation is and is not supposed to mean have been intended as a device of accountability in this sense.

Related but broader is the notion of accountability for the purpose of ascertaining the degree of attainment of the original objective for which the grant program was set in motion. Program accountability in this sense, as Bruce Smith has noted, 'is addressed to the question of whether the government is actually getting the results it sought through the program apart from the conformity to standards of propriety in disbursements of funds.' Illustrations are easy to cite: Has the War on Poverty reduced the number of those measured as poor by whatever monetary standard for family income is used? Have federal grant funds for public assistance programs been successful in enabling the states to provide incomes of at least minimal adequacy to the aided clientele groups—the blind, the aged, the families of dependent children? Has the community facilities program enabled more towns to build sewage treatment plants than would have managed to do so in the absence of such aids? Are blighted downtown areas getting a new lease on life through urban renewal grants? Is domestic transportation improved through federal grants for airport construction? Although measures of success are not always easy to devise, it is easy to define the difference between programmatic accountability and merely fiscal accountability. Programmatic accountability does have a sub-category we should mention. In addition to concern with the question, 'Are the objectives of the program being achieved?' there is also the question: 'Are the funds all being expended in programmatically rational, functional ways?' For example, when one reads that ESEA funds allocated for the purpose of improving the education of children from poverty families have been used by a school district simply to buy a television set for each room, one doubts the programmatic rationality of the expenditure.

Achievement of a program's goals is surely the 'name of the game,' and therefore should be at the nub of accountability. But, strange as it may seem, the greatest difficulty in achieving programmatic accountability may lie less in the difficulties of controlling the behavior of local officials at some geographic distance from the office of the granting agency than with the problem of defining the program goals in a sufficiently operational manner to permit measurement of the degree of their achievement. One of the problems here, as we shall see, particularly when we discuss the various types of grant programs, is that some grants-in-aid are seen as being for the purpose of helping state and local governments to achieve *their* goals, while others are for the purpose of achieving *federally defined* goals by buying the cooperative activity of state and local agencies. 'The essence of the grant system is that it entails the achievement of federal purposes by proxy,' says Martha Derthick,[3] while James L. Sundquist thinks that most of the programs inaugurated prior to the 1960s entail the achievement of state and local purposes with the aid of federal funds.[4] Apart from this problem, there is also the matter of defining just what the programmatic goals of the grantor agency are in a given instance. From the viewpoint of the general public, and from the viewpoint of the ultimate beneficiary-clientele of a program, there is probably a single objective for each program to eliminate poverty, improve education, obtain jobs, finance needed health services, etc. From the viewpoint of the granting agency, however, there are likely to be multiple objectives. The substantive program objective is likely to carry along with it ancillary 'boiler-plate' objectives that are common to many federal programs. These latter include the improvement of state and local personnel systems, using the grant as leverage; more efficient administration; more equitable treatment of persons similarly situated but in different local jurisdictions; or the coordination of the program being aided in a particular instance with related programs.

Sometimes the purpose of accountability is defined broadly as being to insure 'full value' for the expenditure of taxpayers' funds. Full value, however, means both goal achievement and efficiency in the achievement of goals. Grantees are likely to stress goal achievement as being adequately accountable; grantors are likely to want to insist also an efficiency along the way. Agreement between grantor and grantee as to what constitutes adequate fulfillment of one's responsibilities, therefore, is not easy to achieve.

The means of accountability

The kind of means used to achieve accountability naturally varies with the purposes of the review. If one objective is that of preventing malfeasance, an audit in the usual fiscal sense of verifying accounts is appropriate, and a substantive program review would be useless. On the other hand, if what one wants to hold the grantee accountable for is the successful attainment of the social objective of the grant program, then a fiscal audit may be only peripherally useful as an instrument of accountability. If one wants to prevent waste and emphasize efficiency, however, one may wish to employ both programmatic and financial means.

If we use the verb 'to audit' in a broad sense, to include review of adherence to the social objective of the grant as much as fiscal integrity, we can say that the kind of audit desired will depend on who is asking for the review. Program directors, whether at the level of the federal bureau chief or the local government person in charge of actually providing the service to the ultimate clients, will usually be oriented both by professional training and by the nature of positions to emphasize the social audit. Budget directors, representatives of the General Accounting Office, and congressmen are more likely to be interested in fiscal integrity, and to think that all is going well if that has been attained and the paperwork is flowing freely.

The divergent purposes of different groups are exemplified in the public assistance programs. Martha Derthick reports, for example, on what has taken place in the public assistance programs. Starting from the premise that the federal administration needs to find out whether each state is keeping the promises it has made when it filed its state plan (public assistance is an area in which the design of the programs has, until recently, been left largely up to the states), a system of 'audit exceptions'—the disallowance of matching funds for particular expenditures—was instituted. If, for example, a state aids a child who is over the age limit set in the AFDC program, then the federal government will not share the cost of payments for that individual. Although this system remains in use, it is now on a spot-check basis. Says

Derthick: 'It caused tension within the federal administration because accountants rather than social workers were dominating supervision of the states. Social workers regarded the procedure as too negative—so much focused on fiscal regularity that social progress was slighted.'[5] Fiscal auditors, operating out of the Office of the Comptroller in HEW, continue to spot-check cases, but an administrative review in the hands of social workers from the substantive division of HEW handling public assistance has become the primary tool of accountability. The programmatic emphasis is strengthened even further than one would expect because administrative review, says Derthick, 'became a device for prodding the states to liberalize their programs as well as to abide by the canons of fiscal regularity and orderly administration.' Merely fiscal audits would, of course, not be able to serve as an additional programmatic prod upon the grantee. Substantive reviews conducted by the professionals of the field involved thus become a way of holding the grantees accountable to the professional values of the grantor representatives as well as to the former legislative requirements.

Although one might think that Congress would be most interested in knowing whether programmatic success had been achieved or not (since that is, after all, what the money is appropriated for), the fact of the matter seems to be that the legislators pay more attention to 'proper and efficient operation' (the phrase contained in the Social Security Act of 1935). Derthick points out[6] that a stress on administrative conditions develops partly because they are seemingly neutral and do not involve controversial value choices. These the congressmen have preferred to leave to politicians at the state level to wrestle with, at least in the public assistance program. It may be that as a national consensus emerges in a given programmatic area, there is a greater tendency for both legislators and administrators in Washington to impose their value choices, while areas of greater dissensus are ones in which more independence is left to the grantee level.

A congressional predilection for fiscal and administrative over programmatically substantive auditing and accountability may be explained also, perhaps, by the greater operationality of the former kinds of requirements. The congressional preference has long been for the 'line item' or 'object of expenditure' budget as opposed to the program budget or the more recent PPBS system.

With the former kind of budgeting it is easier to tell how many paper clips are being purchased and how many people are being hired, rather than to define precisely what an agency's purposes are and how the degree of achievement can be measured. (Of course the legislators are ambiguous about this. They want 'results' as well as financial integrity. Yet even 'results' are ambiguous. To the congressmen, in the area of public assistance it means a decreased case load and a decreased public expenditure; to the caseworker or program manager, it may mean that the need is being properly met if the caseload goes up.)

The building code analogy may be appropriate here. Traditionally, building codes have specified particular types and strengths of materials as the standard by which to insure proper construction. Recently, in order to get away from the anti-innovation implication of this approach, performance codes have been adopted. Under a performance code, all that is specified is that the construction meet certain tests of its ability, for example, to withstand fire, or to sustain certain weights, or to last for a certain length of time, etc. The builder then is free to choose whatever means—including new synthetic materials and new construction techniques—he finds capable of meeting the performance requirements. Thus the performance code stresses program rather than administrative means.

Accountability by performance versus accountability by detailed specification are also well illustrated as alternatives by the 'debate' that occurred in 1962 regarding the kind of accountability that the government should impose upon its R & D contractors.

At that time, a special Presidential committee headed by the then Director of the Budget, David Bell, concluded, after examining the federal government's major research and development program operations, that the most serious problem lay in the danger that the government might not have the in-house capacity (i.e., the managerial talent) to supervise and evaluate the work that had been contracted out. The Bell Report emphasized the need for programmatic accountability, the need most drastically to avoid situations in which the contractor's 'advice' became the government's 'decision' for lack of independent examination and evaluation of what was advised. At about that time also there occurred some 'flaps' over revelations of high salaries paid to the executives of contractor firms out of government funds and the charging off to the government contracting agency of a firm's expenses in connection with an evening at Disneyland for thousands of the firm's employees. A private management group concerned with defense contracting, headed by Helge Holst of the management consulting firm of Arthur D. Little, Inc., reviewed the same ground covered by the Bell Report and came up with a somewhat different view.

The accountability viewpoint of the Holst Report was that the government's only concern should be with results. If the substantive goal of the contract was achieved, then it was none of the government's business, to put it baldly, what the internal management arrangements of the contractor firm might be (e.g., with regard to executive compensation or employee benefits). The flavor of the Holst Report is indicated in these quotations from that Report's recommendations:

> The Government should direct its attention to results, but not to the methodology of contractors . . .

> The Government should concern itself with total price or overall cost, but not with components of costs or contractor's methods of cost allocation . . .

> The Government must subordinate the role of the audit function to selective verification of costs, but not to the control and direction of projects.

Since the government of the United States is an instrument of social action rather than a firm of CPAs, it makes sense to emphasize substantive rather than fiscal accountability, At the same time, public agencies do act with the people's money, and efficiency in the sense of getting the most program achievement for the least expenditure is an appropriate secondary objective. Thus, I could not accept the Holst Report's apparent position that the government should not be concerned at all with managerial efficiency, but only with the degree to which the programmatic goals have been reached.

Although there are exceptions, my own working rule of thumb (based both upon general impressions gained from studies of governmental programs and my own experience in bureaucratic organizations) would be that procedural efficiency and substantive effectiveness tend to go hand in hand. Certain publicized instances of community poverty programs indicate that when fiscal irregularities or sloppiness are found ineffectiveness in reaching substantive goals tends also to be found. To the extent that this rule of thumb holds up, it may be that the perhaps more easily measured indices of fiscal integrity and procedural efficiency can serve as indirect, short-hand measures of programmatic progress. At the least, one of the most crucial questions to be faced in thinking through the problem of accountability in grant or contract programs is that of the relative place to be given to direct versus indirect instruments of accountability.

(It might be noted parenthetically at this point that a movement away from the existing pattern of categorical grants toward revenue sharing would—no matter what other merits it might possess—make it much more difficult, if not impossible, to achieve any kind of accountability except fiscal auditing. By definition, revenue sharing is a system in which the granting government does not even inquire into the purposes for which the grantee government employs the funds, let alone whether the funds are effectively applied toward whatever purposes the grantee government decides upon.)

Because program goals, especially at the legislative level, tend to be stated in very broad terms, it is often difficult to operationalize them in such a way as to make direct measurement of substantive progress easy—or even possible. Unfortunately, it is also very difficult to devise indirect indices that are effectively linked to the substantive aspects one wants to hold the grantee accountable for.

These propositions are nicely illustrated by Gilbert Y. Steiner in his recent book, *The State of Welfare.*[8] Discussing a series of innovations in the public assistance programs in recent years, Steiner looks at the 1962 amendments to the Social Security Act of 1935 embodying the 'services concept.' It was the assumption behind those amendements that if a more intensive effort were made to provide social services to welfare families, then those families would be moved off the assistance roles entirely and others would attain higher degrees of confidence and independence. Offering three federal dollars for every state dollar, the 1962 legislation called for the Secretary of HEW to prescribe services 'essential to meeting the dual objectives of prevention and reduction

ency.' The legislation also required that states meet
se load standards, as a protection against low-quality
The primary standard was that caseworkers providing
red services not handle more than sixty cases each.
ices,' writes Steiner, 'is a fuzzy concept, not an exact one.'
Under AFDC (Aid to Families with Dependent Children), Steiner
writes, states could choose to provide one or more of the following for unwed mothers:

> Arranging for pre-natal, confinement, and post-natal care for
> the mother and child; planning with mother for her future and
> that of her child; help to mother in child care and training if
> child remains with mother or planning for placement elsewhere;
> help to mother with respect to legal problems affecting the
> rights of mother and child; work to change environmental
> conditions seriously contributing to illegitimacy; use of avail-
> able specialized agency and community resources for serious
> problems or needs.

After this quotation, Steiner remarks that the question of
whether the caseworker is actually doing something such as 'planning for mother for her future and that of her child' is 'highly
subjective and impossible to monitor.' Direct measurement being
impossible, indirect accountability was sought. The HEW Bureau
of Family Services seized upon the sixty-case maximum load as
presumptive evidence that a state was providing the required
services. That is, if a state's caseworkers did not handle more than
sixty cases, then they were presumed to have sufficient time to
provide the intensive services; and if they had sufficient time to
provide the services, it was further presumed that their supervisors
would make sure that they did so, apparently. But once one
accepts the quantitative measurement of the number of cases
handled by a social worker, one no longer is even looking at what
is in fact done. A rather large leap of faith is called for to believe
that this is adequate evidence of effective provision of services,
when one considers that the average public caseworker is an un-
trained or minimally trained person who constitutes part of a
rapidly rotating work force, rather than a stable, long-term professional employee.

The real joker in the deck concerning this mode of indirect
accountability of the services requirement, however, came when

the Bureau of Family Services completed its administrative review of all state social service programs in 1967. Because the sixty-case worker limit meant that many of the states had to try to find many more caseworkers than had previously been required, and because unattractive public salaries made it difficult to hire trained workers or to retain any workers, the Bureau of Family Services took an even larger leap away from direct evidence of compliance with federal requirements. Instead of actually proving that one had employed case workers on a sixty-case basis, good intentions were substitutable: all the states had to do was to show that they were trying to find the caseworkers! Writes Steiner:

> Active recruitment for and funding of the required positions became the standard for compliance with the case-load maximum, which in turn, was the principle test of whether services were being provided. Active recruitment and funding of positions may be indicative of a state's good faith, but non-existent workers can provide no services.

A story like that is sufficient to make one cautious about the accountability potential of indirect devices. At the same time, it cannot be denied that it will often be necessary to use indirect means. Among those are professionalism, personnel merit systems and a level-of-effort requirement on funding. In fact, it would appear that these indirect means of assuring high-quality programs have in the eyes of many federal administrators become autonomous goals in their own rights. Professional blinders are such, in our 'credentials society,' that no matter how effectively a program may be proceeding in terms of achieving its substantive goals, it is likely to be condemned by the professionally trained observer if it is managed by some means other than that contained within the boundaries of the 'operational code' of the professional schools in that field. The outstanding example, of course, is the assumption on the part of many medical doctors that group medical practice and governmentally subsidized medical care *cannot* be good—regardless of what the evidence may show—simply because professional norms specify individual practice for fee. Despite this danger of overdoing the professional bit, the shared values of professionals at federal, state and local levels and their genuine desire to achieve programmatic ends act as an important safeguard of programmatic integrity at the grantee

level. Shared professionalism, also, one might add, has the operational advantage of constituting a shortcut; that is, communications are much eased when the people at both levels speak the
same language.

Requirements for appointment and promotion through a merit
system, even though timidity and mediocrity will sometimes be
the price, are probably worth while in comparison with the price
paid by many states in other programs which are still run by
political appointees through the spoil system. A 'level of effort'
requirement (i.e., that one maintain the same level of funding
proportionate to a number of cases as in a base period) also is not
a fool-proof measure, but is a reasonably good one. If these major
indirect checks on quality are combined with as much direct programmatic review as is possible on a judgmental, if not a quantifiable, basis, then the grantor agency may have done as much as it
can to ensure appropriate accountability. At least, this may provide as much accountability in grant programs as is generally
obtained in direct operations.

One final means of attempting to achieve accountability in
grant-in-aid programs (perhaps it is more a precondition than a
means, actually) lies in the setting of clear and specific and un-
ambiguous objectives in the enabling statutes and administrative
regulations defining the more precise meaning of those statutes.
The political difficulty that Congress has in reaching sufficient
consensus to write into law such objectives constitutes a major
limitation upon the possibilities for administrative accountability.
Perhaps the classic example (certainly *a* classic example) is the
legislative mandate of the Federal Communications Commission,
which is charged with allocating broadcast frequencies for radio
and television stations according to 'the public interest, convenience, and necessity.' One can hardly evaluate whether a television
station is adequately promoting the public interest, convenience,
and necessity unless somebody spells out a more operational
meaning for content of those terms. And no one has done so.
Typically, Congress tends to be either vague or ambivalent.
Indeed, if Congress were very specific, the laws would probably
have to be changed too often. For example, if grants to improve
education for children from poverty backgrounds are the subject-
matter, it is appropriate that the legislative objective be to help
schools to compensate for the inadequate home backgrounds of

some of their students, in order to achieve more effective education, rather than for Congress to say that the objective is to raise the grade level of children's reading by one year.

In the setting of program goals, it is therefore necessary to operate at two levels: a legislative statement in rather broad terms, with operational implementation through administrative statement of goals contributing to the overall legislative goal. What seems to happen in the grant-in-aid programs, I would stress, however, is that the second stage is not performed by the federal grantor agency, but rather is left by congressional will to the grantee government. At the concrete level, the specification of objectives involves political value choices. For example, in public assistance the objective of maximum size of benefits per recipient may conflict with maximum breadth of eligibility. As Martha Derthick has remarked with regard to the setting of public assistance objectives.

> For the federal government to impose value choices on state government it must first arrive at such choices itself. It must formulate policies that are precise and internally consistent. In general this is very difficult to do, whether or not the policy applies to grant-in-aid programs, and grant programs may magnify the difficulty because the extremely diverse interests of all state governments are directly engaged in the programs' operation. . . . One of the functions the grant system performs is to enable the federal legislature to commit itself to serving very broad national purposes (such as 'more adequate' welfare) without assuming the burden of making all of the political choices it would have to make in a unitary system (how much welfare, for whom?). The difficult choices may be left to other governments.

The result, she then says, is that 'federal policy statements for grant-in-aid programs are likely to be inconsistent, ambiguous in what they do state, and altogether silent on much that is important.'

Until recently, public assistance was an excellent example of the federal government's 'passing the buck' to the state governments to make the hard political value choices. The federal government's role has been essentially that of supplementing state benefit levels through matching grants, and thus also encouraging the states to maintain assistance programs in the categories for which the matching grants are available. Substantive requirements have been minimal. For example, states were allowed to set their own minimal time limits of residence for eligibility, so long as those limits did not exceed five years. In recent years, federal legislation has permitted states to pay benefits in the dependent children category when there is an unemployed father in the household. Quite a few states, however, have chosen not to take advantage of this option. The federal government sets permissive goals; the states may op out of those goals.

Within the past five years, a curious thing has been happening: the federal government has been imposing its own standards more definitively than ever before, but through the courts rather than through legislation. Residency requirements have been struck down, and various state attempts to cut costs by eliminating certain types of eligibility or paying only a portion of their own standards of benefits requirements have been overruled by the courts as not consistent with accountability to federal standards. The curious thing is that as a result of these actions, which diminish the discretionary area of the states and generally cost them more money, the cry from the states for total federal assumption of welfare costs has considerably increased—which is contradictory to the generally assumed myth that he who pays the piper then calls the tune. Here the cry of the states is that since Uncle Sam is now calling the tune, he should pay the piper a larger share.

DIMENSIONS OF THE GRANT SYSTEM

Just as accountability is a word that hides a variety of conceptions and dimensions, so also with the phrase, 'the grant-in-aid system.' The various types of federal grants involve different kinds and degrees of intended federal supervision of the grantee units. The degrees of accountability and independence that are both appropriate and possible vary with the types of grant, both as regards their institutional characteristics and their purposes.

One cut into the grant system divides the grants into three types: categorical, block, and shared revenues. (In the current parlance of the Nixon Administration, the term 'special revenue sharing' appears to be a close equivalent to what the literature has for some time called block grants.) As regards fiscal auditing and accountability, there need be no difference among these three types. As regards substantive, programmatic accountability, there is (at least in theory) a very sharp difference. At one extreme, categorical grants (e.g., narrowly specific grants for such purposes as purchase of open land by a city for future park use; *or* purchase by a city of trees for its existing parks; *or* purchase by a city of a swimming pool for a public park), of which there were 160 different ones in 1962 but 379 as of 1967, are presumably much the easiest in which to hold the grantee accountable in the sense of insuring that he has spent the money on an approved federal purpose. Block grants—those which combine several specific programs within a general programmatic area, the outstanding current example being the Partnership in Health Act of 1966 or perhaps the Model Cities program—stand in the middle in this regard, since the function on which the money is to be spent is still sufficiently specific so that the grantor agency can be sure that its limits are not exceeded, but one can no longer insist that within that function the money be spent on one specific project rather than another. For instance, if the block grant is in the area of health care, then the local grantee may decide that its priorities call for spending all the money in an effort to eradicate VD, although the federal grantor might have preferred that some of it go into public health efforts at preventing youth drug abuse. At the other extreme stands the concept of general revenue sharing, as the Administration presently calls it. This so-called 'no-strings-attached' aid to state and local governments erases all possibility of programmatic accountability to the grantor government. In the eyes of its ideological sponsors, that is its primary objective, indeed its *raison d'être*. In their eyes, American federalism is being destroyed because the independence of state and local governments has been undermined by the system of federal categorical grants, which, it is claimed, substitute the goal choices of a far-away federal bureaucracy for those of the close-at-hand city council. In the eyes of the critics, this is the reason why general revenue sharing should not be enacted: it would permit waste of federal funds; it would be spent on purposes that may not be in accord with those of the national majority whose taxes are being spent; and there are no programmatic sanctions against misuse.[10]

Exactly because of the absence of programmatic accountability in a program of general revenue sharing, it is likely (ironically enough from the viewpoint of an Administration that is trying to decrease the federal 'presence' in the states) that an effort will be made to compensate by very extensive and stringent fiscal auditing. And exactly because the general revenue-sharing funds will be (so far as I can tell) melted in with the states' own revenues, then this fiscal accountability can only be attained if *all* of the states' expenditures are audited for the federal government —as opposed to the existing situation in which only programs clearly aided by federal grants are subject to such federal audits. A comment made by Duane Lockard is in point here:

> The fact that so many state programs receive grants-in-aid from the United States government has opened their books to federal auditors. In the opinion of some observers this may be the most significant effect of the widespread use of grant programs, for in the not too remote past state and local programs were often almost without audit and the opportunities for graft were rampant.[11]

Further, I suspect that fiscal auditing and programmatic direction are difficult to divorce entirely. While someone with greater detailed knowledge of the administration of fiscal controls than I possess would be needed to make a sound judgment in this regard, it does seem likely that controls that are on the surface only financial will end up being used by any smart program administrator as devices for getting at the substantive elements he wishes to control, too.

Let me note just parenthetically and in passing that one recent study of grant-in-aid controls argues that the proliferation of categorical grants-in-aid has produced a situation of *de facto* general aid, at least in the sphere of education. David O. Porter and David C. Warner argue that when there are many, many grants in a given area, the local prospective grantor agency can pick and choose among those for which it applies in such a manner as to make effective its own priority choices rather than those of the federal grantor.[12]

This leads us to a second distinction within the grant system, that between formula and project grants. Formula grants are those which are distributed automatically to all recipient governments in accordance with a formula written into the enacting law. The recipients receive the grants as a matter of 'right' within the limits of the amount of money appropriated. ESEA Title I money, for example, is allocated to the school districts on the basis of the number of poverty families in the district. Project grants, on the other hand, are not spread uniformly among all jurisdictions in a certain category, nor are they spread automatically. Rather, eligible jurisdictions must take an initiative and apply for the grant by writing a project proposal which is then reviewed and evaluated by the grantor agency, whose administrators must make judgmental decisions among competing applications. Urban renewal grants, community assistance program grants, and model cities grants are all examples of the project type. In dollar volume, for fiscal year 1966 projects, grants amounted to only $2.8 billion of a $12.6 total for federal grants. In terms of proportion of programs, however, 280 of the 379 programs in effect at the end of 1966 were of the project type. Clearly the trend is in the direction of project grants. An undersecretary of HEW testified at congressional hearings in 1966 that the main reason for the trend is the inflexibility of the formula approach in the face of great diversity of problems facing various local jurisdictions.

Whether formula grants or project grants are more conducive to accountability or independence seems to me a very important question, but one to which I do not yet see an answer. One can, however, see some parts of an answer. For one thing, the proposal that a local jurisdiction writes as a basis for receiving a project grant would seem to provide a handle for programmatic accountability that is apparently lacking under formula grants. At the same time, it might be said that the project system enhances local autonomy because the local jurisdiction can pick and choose among 280 project grant opportunities in deciding where it wants to place its matching funds, whereas under the formula system it does not have the choice of designing its own program. On the other hand again, because federal agency officials informally help local jurisdictions to work up their proposals, it may be that the close working relationship required by the proposal writing system enhances the leverage of federal administrators in the form of 'guidance.' Derthick's book on federal influence in the public assistance program in Massachusetts provides a detailed picture of the administrative sanctions available for enforcing accountability under a formula grant, and some of their limitations. We have, to my knowledge, no equivalent study of a project grant. We badly need one.

To discuss questions of accountability in federal grant-in-aid programs seems to imply that purposes of the programs are federal and the accountability is designed to insure compliance with nationally established objectives. Is this implicit assumption valid? Or, can we meaningfully speak of a division within grant-in-aid programs between those which are established to serve national purposes and those which are established simply to provide financial help for lower-level governments in pursuing *their own* purposes? If the latter (which, as we shall see, is argued occasionally in the literature), then the meaning of accountability has to be to insure that the recipient government is spending the money appropriately and/or effectively in pursuit of *its own* purposes, and that would seem to be a considerably more difficult matter for federal auditors or program executives to check up on than whether federal objectives are being complied with. That is, the federal administrators may have a hard time even finding out what the state-local objectives and requirements are. Or, perhaps that is not necessarily so. This is another area about which the present writer feels very uncertain, but the question apparently needs to be raised.

Sundquist has made the most explicit statement I have seen on the position that grant programs can be divided in the way indicated. His articulation merits quotation at length:

Characteristic of the legislation of the 1960's are forthright declarations of national purpose, experimental and flexible approaches to the achievement of those purposes, and close federal supervision and control to assure that the national purposes are served. Some earlier grant-in-aid programs are in this program too—urban renewal, for example—but typically the pre-1960 programs were cast in a different mold.

Before 1960 the typical federal assistance program did not involve an expressly stated *national* purpose. It was instituted, rather, as a means of helping state or local governments accomplish *their* objectives. It was the states that set the goal of 'getting the farmers out of the mud' through improved state highway networks; federal highway aid was made available simply to help them reach that goal sooner. Communities needed hospitals and sewage treatment plants and airports; the leading lobbyists for expansion of federal assistance for community activities were the national organizations of municipal officials, and they sought it for specific and accepted functions of local government.

Policy making for the established functions, in the older model, remained where it resided before the functions were assisted—in the state and local governments. Federal review and control, accordingly, sought primarily the objectives of efficiency and economy to safeguard the federal treasury, and did not extend effectively to the substance of the programs. Even controls for purposes of assuring efficiency could be loose because the programs called for a substantial state or local contribution—usually 50 percent—and it could be assumed that the sponsoring governments, in their vigilance against waste of their own money, would automatically protect the federal government too . . . where state plans had to have federal approval they were rarely rejected. The federal agencies saw their role as one of technical assistance rather than control. . . .

In the newer model the federal grant is conceived as a means of enabling the federal government to achieve *its* objectives— national policies defined, although often in very general terms, by the Congress. The program remains a *federal* program; as a matter of administrative convenience, the federal government executes the program through state or local governments rather than through its own field offices, but the motive force is federal, with the states and communities assisting—rather than the other way around. . . .

Achievement of a *national* objective requires close federal control over the content of the program. Projects are therefore individually approved; the state or community is not assured of money automatically through a formula apportionment. On the other hand, in order to accomplish the national objective the federal government must make certain—through one means or another—that sufficient and appropriate proposals are initiated. Accordingly, federal agencies aggressively promote the program, solicit applications, and provide extensive technical assistance, either directly or by federal contributions raised well above the 50 percent that was characteristic earlier. It commonly begins at 100 percent and often remains there. Since the states and communities have little or no financial stake in the undertaking, the expenditures must be closely supervised by the federal government from the standpoint of economy as well as substance.[13]

Sundquist concludes that the 'basic dilemma . . . is how to achieve the goals and objectives that are established by a national government, through the action of other governments, state and local, that are legally independent and politically maybe even hostile.'[14] He quotes the preambles and declarations of purpose from a number of statutes of the 1960s—Area Redevelopment Act, Demonstration Cities and Metropolitan Development Act, etc.— but is that any more than constitutional window dressing for the purpose of deflecting objections based on the premise that the problems dealt with are 'merely local'? I am really dubious that the difference lies in the question of whose objectives are being served. Take public assistance as an example again. The history of the Social Security Act of 1935 shows that the reasons why old age insurance was made a directly national program and public assistance was made a national-state program—meaning sharing of funds with most of the policy making done by the states—had little or nothing to do with considerations of the question of whether the objectives were state or national. The decision turned much more on the relative presence or absence of national political consensus on the desirability of national government action.

How does Sundquist determine that hospital construction and sewage treatment plants are matters in which federal aid can be said to be to assist in achievement of state purposes while aid for more general urban renewal was for national purposes? Even if the states originally did set the goal of 'getting the farmers out of the mud,' when the federal government enters the picture to supplement state financing, isn't it then making that goal a national goal also? Since the federal government does not aid every state and local purpose, in the process of selecting those purposes it will aid it is making, *de facto*, a determination of the state-local functions in which there is the greatest national interest. The concepts of national interest and local interest, as used in most discussions of American federalism, are, after all, quite squishy. In *realpolitik*, is it not the case that national purposes can only be defined tautologically: that embodies a national purpose which the national legislature has said to be a matter of sufficient national interest to warrant legislating about and providing funds for?

There is one sense in which I think Sundquist's distinction has some validity. I think the frame of mind within which grant programs are developed *has* changed. Prior to World War II, and especially before the constitutional revolution of 1937, we tended to assume that the national government could engage in domestic activities only where it could do so even-handedly, i.e., by offering its aid wherever persons of the category to be aided were located. That is, while not every program applied equally in every state the way, say, Crippled Children's Services (1935) might do because there were crippled children in each state, it would apply wherever the target population was located, for example, Indian Education and Welfare Services (1934) was available for all Indians, even though Indians were not available in every state. Sundquist is thus on the right track when he ties state-local purpose grants to formula grants and national purpose programs to project-type grants. Formula grants are by no means equally or proportionally distributed among the states in every case. Aid to impacted area schools (1950), for example, goes only to school districts in the immediate areas of federal installations, which are themselves geographically rather concentrated. But they are nation-wide in the sense that districts fitting the requirements need make no special case for themselves, need write no proposal, in order to establish their eligibility for aid.

Since World War II, we have accepted increasingly the notion that the national government may intervene in domestic affairs *selectively*. Project grants are an embodiment of that change in attitude, for they do *not* guarantee that every state or local jurisdiction possessing certain characteristics will be able to obtain federal aid even-handedly. Urban renewal (1949), which Sundquist cites as an early national purpose grant program, is simply one of the first major programs to fit this selective description. While there may be hardly a city incorporated more than thirty years ago that might not meet the characteristics of blight in some portion of its downtown area, the Urban Renewal Administration is committed to aiding only those cities that put forth the best proposals for renewing their blighted areas in a nation-wide competition, and within a fixed appropriation each year. The major difference between formula and project grants (and most of the new ones are the latter variety) may then be that the definition of focus and determination of eligibility shifts from a single legislative decision to a series of administrative decisions. *This* difference is, of course, quite relevant to the problem of accountability on project grants.

One other kind of variation among types of grants may substantially affect the question of accountability. That is the varying purposes for which grants are given. My hypothesis is that one does not look for the same degree of accountability (in the sense of recipient responsiveness to a grantor-determined objective or mode of operation) in programs of an intentionally innovative nature as one does when the grant is merely financial, i.e., when the intent is simply to ease the financial burden on a state or local government in continuing to carry on in the same way some function already in operation.

There would seem to be at least the following distinguishable purposes of federal grant-in-aid programs:

1. To relieve state-local financial pressures by having the national government pick up a share (or a larger share than before) of the cost of some on-going program. The widely heralded 'fiscal mis-match' situation stimulates calls for actions of this kind, most notably at the moment with regard to public assistance programs. (It is of course not accidental that the states are asking for the federal share to be increased on specifically that program which is least popular with state and local taxpayers.)

2. To establish national minimum standards with regard to some function or service already in existence, but at widely varying levels of adequacy. On the grounds that some states cannot afford to meet a professionally-defined minimum standard of service, the argument is made that the difference between state capacity and the minimum standard cost should be met by the national government.

3. Closely related, to affect the distribution of income among the states in order to improve generally the ability of the poorer

states to finance public services. This could be considered a subcategory of the previous one, but under the heading of 'equalization' it has become an important goal autonomously.

4. To encourage innovation; to get some new function going at the state-local level, or some new approach to an existing function. The anti-poverty program fits here. It is by no means the first or only attack on poverty or its symptoms, but does contain distinctly innovative approaches, for example the Community Action Programs and the maximum feasible participation clause. Highway beautification grants are offered to stimulate the states into doing something that most of them are not doing anything or much with. An important subcategory here is the demonstration program concept, under which some particular approach to a problem that has been successful in one jurisdiction and might be applicable to others, or that shows promise from an analysis even if it has not yet been tried, is funded as a way of demonstrating to all jurisdictions what can be done.

I think that to some extent these all fuse together. The federal program administrators, just because they are professionals and are interested, are going to think in terms of expansion, innovation, experimentation, better service, etc.—not just be satisfied with helping to finance what already exists. At the same time, it does appear likely that for purposes of accountability one could make distinctions along the lines indicated. And for purposes of independence, one should probably suppose that where the goal is explicitly experimental, and the entire grant program can be looked upon as a shared effort to find a better way of providing a given service, then more waste should be accepted and the local innovators who have come up with an imaginative proposal should be trusted farther than in the long-established programs. In the latter, accountability emphasis might be focused primarily upon administrative adequacy and financial integrity.

SANCTIONS AND CONSTRAINTS ON THEIR EXERCISE

When one is dependent for part of the performance of one's own task upon the efforts of another, one hesitates to apply very strong sanctions—or to apply any sanctions very strongly—to that other. Further, if the nature of the relationship is such that one's sanction has to be mostly of an all-or-nothing nature (i.e., cutting off the federal aid funds) then the difficulty of 'fitting the punishment to the crime' is a major constraint against the exercise of this drastic sanction. The cessation of funds is the obvious major sanction in grant-in-aid programs, but can rarely be used because in most instances that would mean the cessation also of the public service in question. Assuming that the service does well, the federal government doesn't want to see it stopped, and, politically, it doesn't want to share the blame for having it stopped. In the early days of the public assistance programs, for example, there were some effective threats about cutting off funds, but once the programs were in full operation and part of people's normal expectations, such threats were not continued because federal officials knew that they could never dare to carry them out.

Apart from the ultimate sanction of withholding funds, a major lesser sanction appears to consist of an implicit alliance between the state professionals running an aided program and their federal counterparts. Derthick reports, for example, that in the relationship between the Bureau of Public Assistance and Massachusetts welfare officials, the latter were able to gain state legislative reforms by using federal requirements as God-given and unalterable, as a kind of leverage.

Whatever the severity of the particular sanction, however, the federal government's need to obtain the states' cooperation considerably inhibits the application of sanctions. In a directly federal program, the obstreperous and uncooperative field employee who does not carry out headquarters policy may be dismissed and replaced. In our federal system, however, no national government official can dismiss a state government employee. Wheedling, cajoling, political pressures, endless meetings, etc., are all essential ingredients of a sanctions program on the part of the granting agencies. Counterbalancing the constraint, the major factor conducive to effective application of sanctions may lie in the professional pride of the officials at the receiving end of the grant. However, the professionals at the state level may themselves sometimes have their hands tied, as may well, for example, have been the case recently in California when the Governor tried to make what the federal government considered to be improper and illegal changes in the public assistance programs, apparently over the objections of the state professionals.

Another way in which the fact of federalism may make account-ability more difficult in our grant-in-aid programs is that the existence of a state-level role may diminish local government grantee responsibility to national agencies. A clear instance lies in the current California dispute over the California Rural Legal Assistance (CRLA) program. CRLA is funded by OEO and has rather clearly been doing what OEO intends. That is, it is programmatically accountable to its announced purposes The Governor, however, strongly disapproves of the whole concept, apparently, and has held up the program. Another kind of case is that in which state bureaucratic professionals may impede federal efforts to stimulate local innovation. In both education, where the state affiliates of the National Education Association represent stagnation through official doctrine, and in the law enforcement assistance program, this has happened.

American ideology also operates against effective national sanctions—although perhaps with declining impact. The states do have allies in Congress, for representatives as well as senators tend to see themselves as 'ambassadors' from their respective areas more than as members of a *national* legislature, and these ambassadors tend to accept unthinkingly state or local arguments against federal 'impositions,' 'arbitrariness,' 'dictation.'

Another whole area of concern from the viewpoint of sanctions and accountability consists of the problem of our seeming in-ability to define our program objectives in operationally measur-able terms in many instances. In educational aid programs, for instance, Porter and Warner have pointed out how the ambiguity of the goals sought and the inability of federal evaluators to assess —or even to define—the outputs of their inputs increase the dis-cretion of local grantee administrators or, conversely, decrease their accountability. Writing about Title I of the Elementary and Secondary Education Act of 1965 (ESEA), Porter and Warner summarize as follows:

> In ESEA I, the objective is to help poor children. The formula for distributing the funds is based on the number of children from poor and minority families and is distributed within districts to 'target schools' with the highest concentration of

eligible children. But what services or goods should be purchased with funds from ESEA I to help these children? How can the USOE be assured that the funds are being used effectively? How can choices be made among many alternative schemes for teaching poor children? What are the goals in teaching these children—giving them broader cultural experiences or narrowly preparing them for entry into the labor market after they leave school?

These questions were not answered when ESEA I funds entered the budgets of local schools in 1966. Administrators had great latitude in the pattern of allocation they chose because there were so many different programs which could reasonably be conceived of as assisting poor children. Programs ranged from attempts to expose ghetto children to culture by taking them on field trips to museums or bringing art exhibits and string quartets into the schools; the reduction of class size; hiring para-professionals to assist teachers; remedial reading, mathematics and speech programs; extended day programs with sessions after school to provide extra tutoring; summer programs; and many others. With so many choices, a district could choose a symbolic, catalytic or perfect pattern of allocation at will. For instance, one large district decided to use its ESEA I funds to reduce class size in the target schools. This required the hiring of more teachers and the building of 'temporary' classrooms; both of these objectives were objectives the district had been trying to fund for several years. Another district began a program of reading and mathematics remediation that rather quickly became much larger than could be funded through ESEA I funds alone.

As the program under ESEA I developed, there were growing pressures for concrete results. The goals were narrowed to increasing the reading and mathematics abilities of eligible children. With these more clearly defined goals, fewer programs could be proposed for support under ESEA I. However, because of the uncertain technology associated with teaching reading and mathematics to educationally deprived children, school districts are still able to adopt widely differing approaches to achieve the new objectives. Thus, the districts still have considerable choice in the programs they adopt and in the pattern of resource allocation they follow.[15]

The major difficulty indicated by Porter and Warner might be phrased as a dilemma: If the objectives are defined broadly—such as improving the education of disadvantaged children—then one has little initial guidance as to what would be permissible and what not. But one does have considerable flexibility and discretionary room for innovative efforts at the local level. Since we know little about the technology and processes of education in any case, innovative experimentation is very much worth while. On the other hand, only if one defines the objectives narrowly—such as improving the national reading test scores of children—can one readily assure that what is done conforms to the approved scope of the aided program through simple bureaucratic checks. But in doing so, one both inhibits most of the room for innovation and imposes one particular educational value at the expense of other, competing values that may be sought through the educational system.

An ancillary problem is that the measurable may drive out the meaningful. Overhead pressures may distort the grant recipient's efforts, forcing him into a 'numbers game' appropriate only to narrow sub-goal measurement. An example might consist of teaching specifically toward College Boards or other standard tests. In an employment program, one might emphasize the number of clients processed through an employment counseling service, and a large number processed might be taken as satisfactory despite the possibility that the number prevented effective counseling of any one individual. Obviously, one does need to measure results and input-output scores of comparative programs. The difficulty lies in finding the crucial thing to measure—the thing that most accurately reflects the underlying purpose. Careful programmatic analysis is surely the prerequisite to doing this job effectively.

In many circumstances and programs the most effective sanction working toward appropriate and effective use of granted funds by the recipient agency will consist of the norms of professional accountability embodied in the operating officials. However, political accountability may sometimes act as a constraint against professional accountability. When the norms of legislators and elected executives and their political appointees who are generalists (or the norms of the population which are being reflected through the elected officials regardless of the latter's personal beliefs) conflict with the norms of the professionals, be it in highway engineering, public assistance, health, or recreation, the professional norms are likely to suffer. As Adrian has pointed out, the major disputes in intergovernmental relations tend to be between the politicals and the professionals at each level, rather than between the levels of government.[16] The interaction between the two occurs when the politicians at one level try to ally with the politicians at a higher level to put down the professionals at the first level. Because school systems have traditionally been more isolated from the general political system than other categories of local activity, it would be interesting to examine the extent to which school system autonomy from city politics has made a difference in the kind of accountability obtained. While such a study would be interesting, I am not aware that it has been made, and therefore cannot press the point further.

Perhaps in our system the most effective sanction is sometimes the least formal: public information. In general, one can make a good case that public information—meaning both the legal availability of public records and decision-making processes and the accessibility of those records in fact through an alert press corps—has been an historic distinguishing mark of the American system of governmental accountability. For example, a researcher can gain access to State Department files that are almost current in the United States; a case study writer in England is not allowed access to Foreign Office files that are less than fifty years old. An example of public information as a sanction in a grant-in-aid program is provided by the instance of the Job Corps facility at Camp Kilmer in New Jersey. Federal Electric Corporation had the major contract for that Job Corps program, with an educational subcontract to some faculty members at Rutgers University. The latter group leaked their dissatisfaction with what they felt to be Federal Electric's educationally inappropriate program to the Press. Reporters were first turned away at the gate on the basis that Federal Electric was a private corporation and therefore not subject to reportorial snooping. Rather quickly, of course, Federal Electric had to back down, since it was simply acting as a governmental agent through its contract in this instance. The long arm of remorseless publicity has often been an effective sanction, and legislation for grant-in-aid programs should always make specific provision for the fullest possible disclosure of information.

Finally, we must point out the basic dilemma, that the goal of independence may itself constitute a major constraint on ability to achieve accountability (at least as regards accountability of means). In Smith's 'inevitable tension,' I assume the goal to be maximal freedom where innovation and experimentation are sought, and maximum performance in all cases. I assume that some independence is required to motivate for maximal performance, whether innovation is also sought or not.

Finding the most appropriate form of accountability may, happily, be a way of increasing independence at times, to the extent that he whom one knows to be accountable one can trust to act on his own more than one whose accountability is dubious.

The one general lesson we can draw, I think, is that the optimal mix of accountability and independence is likely to be achieved when the accountability is indirect—probably most often through professional standards—and when it emphasizes performance standards rather than adherence to prescribed means when the purpose is programmatic accountability. These modes need to be supplemented by fiscal accountability for efficiency's sake to the extent that one's purpose is to determine comparative cost-benefit ratios of different program approaches to the same objective.

CONCLUSION

The proliferation of grant programs and the vast expansion in grant funds that have taken place in recent years have already produced one new occupation, that of the grant expeditor—a man who advises local governments on the preparation of grant proposals and who develops expertise in that now well-known art of grantsmanship. This new occupational specialty arises spontaneously because state and local governments need help and have a strong financial incentive to hire a helper. They can look upon the grantsman's salary as an investment that is likely to pay off manifoldly on the first successful grant proposal. The grantor (i.e., the federal government) has an equal need for a new occupational skill—that of grant evaluator—but lacks the spontaneous incentive. The federal agency will not increase its revenue by hiring grant evaluators; rather, they will be one more personnel expense. Perhaps this difference in the 'market' at each end of the grant explains why an apparent need has been met at one end but not at the other. Whether the reasons be valid or not, the fact of the difference remains.

There is an evident need here for a new occupational skill. Perhaps program evaluation might even be looked upon as a subcategory of the rapidly developing field of policy analysis in which special programs have already arisen at Harvard, Berkeley, Buffalo, and other universities. So far, the main thrust of policy analysis has been in the direction of seeking better ways to compare alternative program proposals before a particular one is adopted. There is no reason, however, why this rational comparison approach cannot also be directed toward on-going programs. One of the main objectives of policy analysis as it has developed out of PPB (Programming-Planning-Budgeting) is on the clearer articulation of organizational objectives. That is also a crying need in the program evaluation area, and a governmental function that accounts for $27 billion annually can surely support the development of some special skills directed toward its effective utilization.

The need, in short, is for a system of program audits equivalent to financial audits. Our major goal and focus should be on effective programs run efficiently. We are probably much stronger in our ability to measure efficiency than program effectiveness, however. Since program auditing is very difficult and time consuming, it doubtless needs to be supplemented by indirect indices of quality (e.g., personnel standards and practices; reputation of the program in the eyes of clients and cooperating agencies, etc.) while developing operationally workable measures of direct program evaluation. Whether the emphasis be on indirect indices or on a more complex system of direct program evaluation, the most important contribution to accountability that one can suggest would be the development of an educational program for a new type of professional, the grant evaluator. Either the U.S. Civil Service Commission or a private foundation, acting in conjunction with one or more federal bureaus having active grant programs, should sponsor two or three experimental university programs aimed at the development of a targeted curriculum in program evaluation.

Notes

1. See Paul Appleby, *Big Democracy* (Knopf, New York, 1945), for a classic articulation of the myth that public agencies mean devotion to the public interest.
2. See Joseph P. Harris, *Congressional Control of Administration* (Brookings, Washington, 1964) ch. 8.
3. In *The Influence of Federal Grants* (Harvard University Press, Cambridge, 1970) p. 197.
4. James L. Sundquist, *Making Federalism Work* (Brookings, Washington, 1969) pp. 3–6.
5. Derthick, op. cit., p. 24.
6. Ibid., pp. 197–8.
7. These quotations, and larger excerpts from the Bell and Holst reports, may be found in Michael D. Reagan (ed.), *Politics, Economics and the General Welfare* (Scott, Foresman, Chicago, 1965) ch. 5.
8. (Brookings, Washington, D.C., 1971) pp. 37–8.
9. Derthick, op. cit., pp. 195–6.
10. For a full review of the revenue sharing-categorical grants issue, with some emphasis on program accountability aspects, see Michael D. Reagan *The New Federalism* (Oxford University Press, New York, 1972).
11. Duane Lockard, *Perverted Priorities of American Politics* (Macmillan, New York, 1971) p. 103.
12. David O. Porter and David C. Warner, 'How Effective are Grantor Controls?: The Case of Federal Aid to Education,' in Kenneth Boulding (ed.), *The Grants Economy* (Wadsworth, forthcoming). This evaluation rests upon the Porter-Warner conception of resource mobilization by grant recipients, as opposed to the more traditional notion of resource allocation by grantors.
13. James L. Sundquist (with David W. Davis), *Making Federalism Work* (Brookings, Washington, D.C.) pp. 3–5.
14. Ibid., p. 12.
15. Porter and Warner, op. cit., pp. 11–12.
16. See Charles R. Adrian, 'State and Local Government Participation in the Design and Administration of Intergovernmental Programs,' in *The Annals of the American Academy of Political and Social Science*, vol. 359 (May 1965) pp. 35–43.

8 Government Initiatives and Controls in American Medical Care

DAVID C. WARNER

The 'crisis' in medical care in the United States is not a crisis of supply and demand. Rather, it is a crisis of accountability. This crisis has been exacerbated by increases in voluntary insurance and in government expenditures. Ironically, the increases in the resources available to pay for health care have led to less consumer sovereignty as practitioners and health care institutions have become less dependent upon funds from the individual consumer's own resources. Accountability systems established by fiscal intermediaries have led to the proliferation of expenditure for lawyers, accountants, and experts by all participants with little increase in responsiveness to social needs. New methods must be developed to harness the energies and capabilities of the health care professions and institutions toward appropriate social goals.

The principal anomaly in American health care is the coexistence of a fee for service method of paying the physician and the hospital with widespread medical insurance. Medicare and Medicaid (government insurance for the aged and the poor, respectively) have been introduced into an entrepreneurial system of independent providers. Many difficulties in controlling costs, improving the quality of health care, and reorganizing the health care system can be traced to this asymmetry between the rationale for government finance and the incentives facing individual providers.

I. THE GOVERNMENT'S ROLE IN MEDICARE AND MEDICAID

Prior to the introduction of Medicare and Medicaid in 1965, federal health expenditures were principally for medical education, research, and hospital construction.[1] Local governments funded special hospitals for the poor, the infectious, the insane, and the senile.[2] Financing for 'mainstream' medical care was primarily out of the consumer's pocket or through private insurance schemes controlled in large part by regional associations of physicians and hospitals.

Two dominant characteristics of the American health system have been the ability of both physicians and hospitals to charge patients on a fee for service basis, and the freedom for hospitals and physicians to choose the role they find most attractive in the system.

American physicians have been remarkably free to choose their specialty and practice area, and to sub-specialize. Authority to choose a specialty has been decentralized to individuals, delineation of specialty training to relatively autonomous specialist associations. . . .[3]

This autonomy has had a significant impact upon the distribution and quality of services and the organization of hospitals. Any physician may decide to perform specialty functions or to specialize his practice irrespective of whether he has had appropriate or sufficient graduate training and experience as defined by the certifying agencies.[4] Many hospitals have been built and programs initiated to satisfy physicians who wish to provide specialized services but who have been excluded from existing facilities.[5]

Controls upon the costs, appropriateness, and quality of care were primarily developed by the medical profession and the hospitals themselves. Blue Shield, voluntary insurance for physician care, and Blue Cross, voluntary insurance for hospital care, were both controlled by those whom they paid.

The amount of money available for health care was determined largely by the amount individuals were prepared to spend and by the size of the premium that insurers were able to exact from unions, employers, and other large health insurance subscribers. This money was then distributed to providers of care based on the amount of business they did and the rates they were permitted to charge. Similarly, the push for accreditation of hospitals has been largely a result of the desire of various specialty boards and particular interests to protect and enhance the value of their credentials.[6] A hospital which allows uncredentialed physicians to perform certain services risks losing its accreditation.

2. GOVERNMENT INITIATIVE AND CONTROLS AFTER 1966

In the mid-1960s, with Medicaid, Medicare, and other specific programs, the federal government engaged in the business of subsidizing the capacity of groups to demand health care. The intended beneficiaries were the poor, the aged—especially the parents of the middle class—and a number of special target populations such as migrant workers, infants, and individuals requiring family planning assistance. Although there were some limited attempts to establish federally funded ambulatory care programs in poor areas, most of the increased funds were channelled through existing physicians, hospitals, and pharmacies who charged fees for services provided.

The administrators of the Medicare and Medicaid program were authorized to develop methods of controlling the appropriateness and quality of care provided under governmental funding. In practice much of this authority was delegated to state agencies or to fiscal intermediaries which had been established by the physicians and the hospitals on a state- or region-wide basis to control the allocation of private health insurance monies.

A. *Controlling Cost in a System of Cost-plus Reimbursement*

Medicare was developed as health insurance for persons over age sixty-five covered under the Social Security Program. The Medicare legislation contained a stipulation that only 'reasonable costs' would be reimbursed. In fact, this has amounted to the reimbursement of nearly any costs which are legitimately incurred and which can be said to be related to the covered population.[7] Salaries and rates of all providers have increased geometrically in the first eight years. The Social Security Administration requires that each hospital prepare elaborate accounting reports following a consistent method for allocating all of its indirect costs to billable units of service. This was instituted so that hospitals could be held accountable, and would not be reimbursed for costs associated with units of service like obstetrics or pediatrics which cannot be justified for a population over the age of sixty-five.

These regulations have unquestionably increased the financial sophistication of hospitals, but it is less clear that they have served to control redundant services or the levels of cost. Denied the opportunity to cover their costs fully in service areas such as obstetrics and forced to maintain rates for room rent, nursing care and the operating room at a level which third parties will accept, many hospitals have chosen to expand their services in laboratory, x-ray and pathology services.[8] Hospital charges for these services have commonly exceeded costs, so that these departments have generally produced a profit with a mark up from 33 to 100 percent.[9] These profits subsidize the losses incurred in other departments.

Medicare had the potential to require that pathologists, radiologists, and anesthesilogists be salaried employees of hospitals. Under intense lobbying, however, Part B of Medicare was developed in part to reimburse these physicians separately on the basis of services rendered.[10] Even when employed by the hospital, such specialists have often been reimbursed by the number of tests done. In the post Medicare and Medicaid era it has not been uncommon for many radiologists and pathologists to earn as much as $100,000 to $150,000 annually. Such incentives and the excessive tests and examinations resulting from this method of paying the physician may have negative effects on the quality of clinical decision-making.[11]

One initial criticism was that the Social Security Administration permitted insurance carriers to pay more under Medicare than under their own plans.[12] In an attempt to assure a kind of accountability, the Social Security Administration asked the fiscal intermediaries for Part B to report the names of those physicians who earned more than $25,000 a year through Medicare billings. Most of these carriers are Blue Shield plans organized and controlled by physicians. Initially, most of the Blue Shield plans refused to provide the Social Security Administration with information regarding payment of government money to physicians, saying that 'they had not been authorized to do so by the physicians involved.' The Social Security Administration was able to acquire this data by pointing out that the intermediaries were accountable as well to the provider of the funds.[13]

With Medicare and Medicaid covering the costs of what had formerly been the hospital's highest financial risks, less constraint remained upon hospital budgets or the amounts spent on care. An example was the extent to which capital expenditure and specialized facilities began to proliferate.

The cost of capital to the hospital became very low as debt repayment became a legitimate reimbursable item under Medicare and Medicaid.[14] Enormous capital commitments for expansion were made by hospitals all over the country with the expectation that most of the cost so incurred would be reimbursable under insurance. The most egregious cases are some of New York City's municipal hospitals which will cost in excess of $200,000 a bed. Even if these hospitals run at full capacity, $45 must be added to the daily bill for each patient for the next thirty years to cover debt service alone.

The purpose of much of this investment nationwide was to expand the capability of many hospitals to do specialized work so that most physicians could be associated with comprehensive and prestigious institutions.[15] In medical care such redundant facilities are not only expensive, they are technologically inefficient. Specialists are less likely to be able to do the amount of work of which they are capable or should do in order to maintain their skills.[16] The number of specialists and training programs has proliferated in this environment of freely available financing for expansion and specialized equipment. There are twice as many surgeons and twice as much surgery done in an average American city than in a comparable English city with no apparent additional benefits.[17] To fill the many specialty training programs that are unable to attract domestically trained medical students bars to immigration and licensure of foreign trained medical students have been substantially reduced.[18]

The intensifying 'doctor shortage' appears to have been a result of the decrease of generalists and family practitioners in the system rather than a shortage of doctors.[19] In fact, the regional maldistribution of physicians has probably worsened since Medicare and Medicaid. Medicaid appears to have redistributed funds for medical care from poorer states to richer ones. The four wealthiest states with 27 percent of the population and less than one fourth of the poverty population received 56 percent of total federal funds for health care in 1970. The ten states with lowest per capita income and with 15 percent of the population received less than 7 percent of total federal funds.[20] These extra federal resources were undoubtedly used to bid still more physicians and other resources away from poorer states to richer ones.

In terms of resource allocation, both Medicare and Medicaid to date have been relatively passive programs. The medical profession and institutions have mobilized resources to their own ends and with a large patient population with open-ended vouchers to pay for care their entrepreneurial objectives have been achieved.[21] Regulation of costs has been often at the behest of those being regulated who want to use the state to control competition.[22] The hospital cost regulatory Commissions established in Connecticut, Maryland, and several other states may in part have been established because the hospitals have begun to find it difficult to extract further rate increases from the insurance companies who must be responsive to the business and union interests who pay the premiums. New approaches to cost control include the encouragement of prepaid forms of group practices and new forms of contracting with regions and with institutions on the basis of a fixed prospective budget or rate per capita.

Prepaid group practice depends, as in part does the British system of reimbursing physicians, upon a capitation method of reimbursement for cost control. The difference between the incentives facing providers in the two countries is that American prepaid group practices usually bear hospitalization costs, while in Britain the individual practitioner does not. This might, given consumer ignorance concerning medical care, lead to under-hospitalization, investment in medically unnecessary amenities in the waiting-room to attract customers, or to more care than necessary.[23] Methods of controlling for quality will have to be developed in tandem with the cost controlling advantages of capitation.

The same criticism may be applied to an approach which would limit federal expenditure to a fixed per capita amount for each region. Instead of open-ended vouchers for 'deserving consumers' combined with fragmented special programs[24] some proposals advocate fixing the total amount of federal subsidy for health in each region.[25] This constraint would be combined with new methods of organization and provision in each region. Such a constraint on the total amount available from government to any particular area would be likely to cause some distress to particular areas. For example, in New York City where future Medicaid receipts have in effect been capitalized by an extensive building program, there would be accordingly fewer resources available for providing health care. Limiting funds by region and allocating funds to institutions and practitioners on a criterion other than fee for service does not automatically guarantee that services will be delivered equitably and that these services will be of uniformly high quality. Even though total costs may be controlled, the government will still have to develop effective methods of reviewing groups of peers in their practice of medicine.

B. *Emerging Methods of Improving the Quality of Health Services*

Both the conditions for participation in Medicare[26] and the new tendency of the courts to hold the hospital accountable for the quality and activities of their staffs[27] have intensified the search for effective methods of review of medical and hospital practice. Although hospitals have had to develop formal utilization review procedures, the review of office practice has never gone significantly beyond attempts to detect fraud. In both the hospital and in the private office settings the selection of criteria for determining quality of care, the designation of the appropriate groups responsible for carrying out the evaluation, and the design of new institutional arrangements to provide incentives for high quality care, are all important unresolved issues.

Forms of evaluation

Approaches to assessing the quality of care include attempts to assess the adequacy of the structure of care, the process of care, and the outcome of care.[28] The structure of care includes the availability and organization of facilities and services, the qualifications of physicians and others, and the cost and other rationing devices in the system. Most evaluations of structure tend to be evaluations of credentials, completeness of facilities, and cleanliness. Such evaluations often require only automatic applications of predetermined standards. The structure of care is evaluated and, in part, controlled by state level accrediting groups, regional hospital planning groups, public regulations, and private insurance companies.

The process of care is judged by examining the appropriateness of clinical decision-making and treatment of patients. At the most superficial level, evaluation of process examines relatively public information such as the length of stay by diagnosis of patients in a particular facility. Such evaluation may be quite important in order to control costs since almost nothing in a health delivery system based on cost reimbursement selects automatically the least costly treatment amongst medically indifferent alternatives. There have been some limited attempts to approach the activities of hospitals as if they are firms with output to which costs can be assigned through extremely complex procedures. Those espousing this managerial approach would assign managers to departments —a form of discipline probably anathema to physicians and, if carried too far, destructive of high quality medical care. The physician in the hospital most properly functions as an ombudsman or patient advocate who may demand nearly anything from the hospital bureaucracy in order to accommodate the particular needs of each of his patients.

A more sophisticated method of evaluating the process of care is the examination of the particular medical decisions or treatments applied to each patient or to selected groups of patients. Problems arise in determining what criteria to use for choosing cases for review,[29] and what criteria to use for evaluation.[30] The false concreteness and homogeneity which would be generated under a system of process review which is too punitive must be avoided. Peers must be given the privilege of free discourse and discretion without permitting them complete license.

The outcome of the care which patients receive can only really be evaluated over time. Outcome evaluation is not currently used to make comparisons between physicians and hospitals, but would in theory be possible. General comparisons of morbidity and mortality between nations or large populations are available. It is ironic that the American medical establishment makes a major point of the fact that white mortality and morbidity statistics in the United States are comparable to those of most European countries. The substantial differences between black and white mortality and morbidity in the United States would seem to indict the health care system on equity grounds.

Who will do the evaluating?

An adjunct to effective evaluation might be to give the consumer of care more information. The Insurance Commissioner of Pennsylvania has issued shoppers' guides to hospitals, life insurance, and surgeons.[31] Another proposal would make it a matter of law for patients to receive copies of their medical records from physicians and hospitals as soon as each service is completed. Patients would understand their medical problems better and would be able to have consulting opinions regarding both their own medical problems and the quality of the care they have received.[32] Physicians would improve the quality of the care they provide since *decentralized peer review* could always be initiated by the patient. Consequently, the physician's legitimate authority would be enhanced since it would be based upon auditable expert judgment. Improved physician-patient relationships will likely yield increased satisfaction. Similarly, with records circulating, physicians would be less isolated from one another and the decision-making process would be improved.

As pressures have grown for review of medical practice, the profession itself has sought methods of controlling evaluation. The most recent manifestation of this is the 1972 Bennet Amendment to HRI (the omnibus Social Security Act legislation of 1972). The Bennet Amendment requires that the Secretary of Health Education and Welfare 1.) divide the country into areas and at the earliest practicable date and 2.) designate a qualified organization as the Professional Standards Review Organization (PSRO) for each area.[33] Each PSRO will include as its membership a substantial number of physicians in the area and will serve at the pleasure of a majority of the physicians in the area. Indeed, if 10 percent of the physicians in the area wish to reconstitute the membership and procedures of the PSRO they may force a referendum of the physicians in the area.

The PSRO will have the responsibility for evaluating care in the region; but it will be largely controlled by the medical establishment in the region. The medical community will have to find a way of evaluating and guaranteeing quality without causing too much direct conflict. One emerging development in this direction has been the increased affiliations of municipal and community hospitals with medical schools or prestigious voluntary hospitals.

New forms of contracting

The affiliation of municipal and community hospitals with medical schools has been designed to provide highly-qualified specialized talents to a large number of service institutions. In addition, medical schools gain access to larger numbers of clinical subjects for their teaching and research objectives while the municipal and community hospitals gain increased status and implicitly a warrant of higher quality with the affiliation. In the early sixties, New York City entered into a contract arrangement with a group of medical schools and prestigious voluntary hospitals to provide physicians and other professional services in sixteen of the eighteen municipal hospitals. The rationale for these contracts was that the city would be able to attract higher quality physicians in the municipal hospitals, attract more American-trained interns and residents, and avoid burdensome line item controls over procurement and equipment purchases.[34]

The municipal administration has in general retained broad control of programs and such activities in the hospital as housekeeping, dietary, and maintenance services. The $160 million a year which the affiliates receive includes about $10 million in management contracts, and also provides them with a 'farm system' of extra beds and teaching material where they can send new doctors, train specialized interns and residents, and even employ doctors who for political or technical reasons they no longer wish to employ in their own institution.

Inevitably, as with most new fiscal arrangements, there were scandals and irregularities. Equipment purchased for the municipal hospitals, for example, was found in the voluntary institutions. Several municipal hospital administrators were found to be receiving salaries from the affiliated voluntary institution as well as their own hospitals. There were also occasions on which an affiliated institution, perhaps unwisely, persuaded the city to build municipal hospitals on their grounds. This has made it easier for the voluntary hospital affiliates to direct either the uninteresting or uninsured patients to the municipal hospital while keeping the more attractive patients, either medically or socially.[35]

Neither the New York City Health Services Administration nor the New York City Health and Hospitals Corporation has developed effective methods of monitoring these contracts for quality and of assuring themselves that the affiliated medical schools are indeed providing the services which they have agreed to provide. The City could hire a blue ribbon panel of expert clinicians, mandate a thorough medical audit of each of the hospitals, or work out some sort of intramural accreditation process. The fact that they do none of these implies that the public sector in New York City has permitted their contractors to usurp authority which should be legitimately retained by public officials.

Similar problems exist in microcosm in all hospitals in the country which treat some private and some public patients. The rights of the publicly supported patients frequently are subordinated to those of private patients who pay their physicians individually. Although Medicaid patients represent the same financial asset to the institution as private patients, they generally go to the clinic for care and stay in wards. Private patients, on the other hand, go to their physician's office, enter the hospital through a private entrance, and stay in private or semi-private rooms.

3. CONCLUSION

Government expenditures for health care have escalated from $3.6 billion annually in 1950 to over $30 billion a year in 1972.[36] Some observers predict that by 1980 the government share of annual health expenditure will become $60 or $70 billion out of a total expenditure for health of approximately $150 billion. At that point Congress could decide to install a National Health Service without raising taxes, saving most people the expense of buying any private health insurance.[37] Such an outcome, however, does not seem likely.

Major interest groups appear to have too much political power and the government insufficient will and discipline for the development of a system in which the government could take command of the major hospitals and control of the wages paid most physicians as in England. New forms of contracting through regions and large institutions seem to be the form by which medical care costs will be contained and quality assured. Whether these new forms of payment and organization on the regional level will serve to control costs, increase equity of treatment, and reduce risk of catastrophic expense will depend largely upon the criteria of accountability and authority which are operational within regions and institutions.

The challenge facing the government in the 1970s will be to introduce public wants into the calculations of those who determine the supply of medical care. Rather than permitting open vouchers and free choice by suppliers to guide resource decisions, the more idealistic and helping attributes of the medical profession must be encouraged.[38] It may be that just as uncertainty characterizes the consumer's views of medical care,[39] the physician in an entrepreneurial and status-dominated system also is very insecure. Perhaps only by finding means of reducing the insecurity of physicians may real change in American medical care take place.

Notes

1. This was in the face of earlier proposals for a system of comprehensive health care. The outstanding example is *Medical Care for the American People, Final Report of the Committee on the Costs of Medical Care* (Chicago, 1932).

2. Indeed in 1952 the Chairman of the President's Committee on the Health Needs of the Nation stated explicitly that 'The building up of our health resources in terms of training more health personnel and providing more physical facilities must start from the ground up. We have recommended federal grants-in-aid to these and other necessary activities because we believe that the role of the federal government is to stimulate them, not to control them. Government must take the leadership in the promotion of good health; its major energies should go there rather than in extensive direct operation of health services.' Odin Anderson, *Health Care Can There Be Equity?* (John Wiley & Sons, New York, 1972) p. 72.

3. Rosemary Stevens, 'Trends in Medical Specialization in the United States,' *Inquiry*, VIII, 1 (March 1971) p. 10. For an exhaustive discussion of the subject see her *American Medicine and the Public Interest* (Yale University Press, New Haven, 1971).

4. Ibid., p. 12.

5. M. Pauly and M. Redisch, 'The Not for Profit Hospital as a Physicians' Cooperative,' *American Economic Review* (March 1973) pp. 87–99, carry

the assumption of physician control of the voluntary hospital to its logical limit. Maw Lin Lee, 'A Conspicuous Production Theory of Hospital Behavior,' *Southern Economic Journal* (July 1971), holds that status competition with very few cost constraints explains most hospital behavior.

6. Anne Somers, *Hospital Regulation: The Dilemma of Public Policy* (Industrial Relations Section, Princeton University, 1969). There is an additional reason for specialists and other physicians to escalate standards and lengthen training time and that is so that supply can be constrained and those already in the system can charge more.

7. For an elaboration see John D. Thompson, 'On Reasonable Costs of Hospital Services,' *Milbank Memorial Fund Quarterly* (Jan. 1968) Part 2, pp. 33–51.

8. Elton Tekobste, 'Medicare Strains Hospital-Payer Relations,' *Modern Hospital* (1971) 65–7.

9. Anne Somers and Herman Somers, *Medicare and the Hospitals* (Brookings Institution, Washington D.C., 1967).

10. Ibid., pp. 132–53.

11. Paul F. Griner and Benjamin Liptzin, 'Use of the Laboratory in a Teaching Hospital: Implications for Patient Care, Education, and Hospital Costs,' *Annals of Internal Medicine*, vol. 75, no. 2 (Aug. 1971).

12. *Medicare and Medicaid: Problems, Issues, and Alternatives*, Report to the staff to the Committee on Finance United States Senate, Feb. 9, 1970, p. 61.

13. Ibid., pp. 117–20.

14. For a discussion of the sorts of investment that take place in medicine and defense when the cost of capital becomes low or even negative see Richard R. Nelson, 'Issues and Suggestions for Study of Industrial Organization in a Regime of Rapid Technical Change,' in Victor Fuchs (ed.), *Policy Issues and Research Opportunities in Industrial Organization* (National Bureau of Economic Research, 1972).

15. Anthony R. Kovner, 'The Hospital Administrator and Organizational Effectiveness,' in Basil Georgeopoulos, *Organizational Research on Health Institutions* (Institute for Social Research, University of Michigan, 1972) pp. 355–76. Each hospital could aspire to be a medical center.

16. F. C. Spencer and B. Eismman, '*The Occasional Open Heart Surgeon*,' *Circulation* (Feb. 1965) 161–2, showed in 1961 even before Medicare and Medicaid that well under 15 percent of the 1,100 hospitals with open or closed heart surgical facilities did more than fifty operations annually.

17. Stevens, op. cit., p. 13. See also Bunker, 'Surgical Manpower: A Comparison of Operations and Surgeons in the U.S. and in England and Wales,' *282 New England Journal of Medicine* (1970) 137.

18. James Haug and Rosemary Stevens, 'Foreign Medical Graduates in United States in 1963 and 1971: A Cohort Study,' *Inquiry* 10:1 (1973) 26–32.

19. Anderson, op. cit., shows that the U.S. has substantially more physicians per capita than either Sweden or England and Wales, p. 231.

20. Bruce C. Stuart and Lee A. Blair, 'Health Care and Income, the

Distributional Impacts of Medicaid and Medicare Nationally and in the State of Michigan,' Research Paper No. 5, p. 42 (Michigan Department of Social Services, Research and Analysis Division, Lansing, Jan. 1971).

21. For a description of mobilizing behavior in a regime of public provision see David O. Porter and David C. Warner, 'How Effective are Grantor Controls?' in Kenneth Boulding, Martin Pfaff and Anita Pfaff (eds.), *Transfers in an Urbanized Economy* (Wadsworth, 1973).

22. For a generalization of this view to all regulation see George Stigler, 'The Theory of Economic Regulation,' *Bell Journal of Economics and Management Science* (Spring 1971).

23. Jeff Brown, 'Public Utility Regulation of Health Maintenance Organizations in Connecticut,' Yale Legislative Services, New Haven, Conn., 1974.

24. See Secretary Richardson's testimony, Hearings before the U.S. Senate Committee on Appropriations, Dept. of Labor, and Health, Education, and Welfare Appropriations, Fiscal Year 1971, HR 18515, 91st Congress, 2nd Session, Part 4 (Washington, D.C., 1970) p. 1944. He points out that, if there were discussions of family planning and vocational rehabilitation referrals, at the clinic, the government will reimburse at 75 percent rather than the usual 50 percent. Providers with more sophisticated accountants are more prosperous.

25. The Kennedy-Griffiths Bill for National Health Insurance contains such a provision. The Nixon administration's revenue sharing provisions would reduce the fragmentation of many programs while not dealing with the cost escalation in the Medicare and Medicaid programs.

26. Conditions of Participation of Hospitals, Federal Health Insurance for the Aged Regulations: Section 405:1035. Conditions of Participation— Utilization Review Plan, Baltimore, Maryland, Social Security Administration, 1966. This stipulation was extended to Medicaid in 1972.

27. For a discussion of the Darling case and other cases extending the hospital's liability see Anne Somers, *Hospital Regulation: The Dilemma of Public Policy* (Industrial Relations Section, Princeton University, 1969).

28. See, for instance, Donald Riedel, Lee Brauer, Harvey Brenner, Phillip Goldblatt, Carol Schwartz, Jerome Myers, and Gerald Klerman, 'Developing a System for Utilization Review and Evaluation in Community Mental Health Centers,' *Hospital and Community Psychiatry*, vol. 22, no. 8 (Aug. 1971) pp. 17–20.

29. See, for example, John McClain and Donald Riedel, 'Screening for Utilization Review: On the Use of Explicit Criteria and Non-Physicians in Case Selection,' *American Journal of Public Health* (March 1973) pp. 247–251.

30. Robert Brook and Francis Appel, 'Quality of Care Assessment: Choosing a Method for Peer Review,' *New England Journal of Medicine*, vol. 288, no. 25 (June 21, 1973) pp. 1323-9. They show that using different criteria from 1.4 to 63.2 percent of the care examined is judged acceptable.

31. See Herbert Dennenberg, 'Shoppers Guide to Hospitals,' 'Shoppers Guide to Surgeons,' and 'Shoppers Guide to Life Insurance,' available from the Pennsylvania Insurance Department, Harrisburg, Pennsylvania.

32. Budd Shenkin and David Warner, 'Giving the Patient His Medical

Record: A Proposal to Improve the System,' 289 *New England Journal of Medicine* (September 27, 1973), 688–92.

33. See Amendment No. 476, HR 1, *To Amend the Social Security Act*, 1972. See also House of Representatives Report No. 92–1605 and Senate Report No. 92–1230.

34. Robb Burlage, *New York City's Municipal Hospital: A Policy Review* (Institute for Policy Studies, Washington, D.C., 1967) pp. 69–70.

35. See the survey article by Erik G. Furabotn and Suetozar Pejovich, 'Poverty Rights and Economic Theory,' *Journal of Economic Literature* (Dec. 1972) pp. 1137–62. They point out 'that privately owned resources will always tend to be allocated to the highest valued uses (in a mixed private-public organization).'

36. Odin Anderson, op. cit., pp. 116, 219 and 225.

37. I am indebted to Rosemary Stevens for this insight.

38. Ser Sandor Kelman, 'Toward the Political Economics of Medical Care,' *Inquiry*, VIII, 3 (Sept. 1971), believes that physicians have already lost effective control to the insurance companies and that their chances of regaining it are slight.

39. Kenneth Arrow, 'Uncertainty and the Welfare Economics of Medical Care,' *American Economic Review*, LII, 5 (Dec. 1963).

9 Public Accountability and Reporting Systems in Medicare and other Health Programs

PAUL M. DENSEN

The concept of public accountability is essentially the concept of democracy. It embodies the principle that government should be responsible to the people. The discharge of that responsibility requires that government have information about the operation and effectiveness of the programs brought into being by federal, state, or local legislators in response, presumably, to the wishes of their constituency.

There is little quarrel with these statements. The problem is how much and what kind of information is needed for the proper rendering of an accounting, how is the information to be collected, who is responsible for what in the collection system, and how to make the information available in the most useful manner. It is my task to address these questions as they apply to Medicare and similar types of health care programs.

WHAT KIND OF INFORMATION IS NEEDED?

The primary purpose of Medicare is to provide the financial means to help older people pay a major portion of their bills for hospital and medical care. Does it do this?

At a minimum the information needed to answer this question is the percent of the total expenditures by people sixty-five and over for hospital and medical care paid for by Medicare and their out-of-pocket expenditures. This information is obtainable from the aggregate income accounts and from the aggregate expenditures under the program. Is this sufficient for purposes of public accountability? Let's examine the data.

In fiscal 1971 the average expenditure for an aged person was $861 as contrasted with $528 in 1967, the first year of the program. In 1971 Medicare and Medicaid picked up a little more than two-thirds of this bill, while only a little more than half was paid for by public funds in the earlier year. However, the out-of-pocket expenditures from 1966 (before Medicare and Medicaid) to 1971 remained almost the same—$234 and 225 respectively.[1]

These figures point up a fundamental aspect of the accountability issue, namely, that there are several 'publics' to whom Medicare and Medicaid must account for these rising costs. There is the beneficiary who is not satisfied with the knowledge that these programs are covering an increasingly greater proportion of his medical bill if he can see no improvement in his own personal expenditures for medical services. There is the taxpayer who, since he must ultimately pay the bill, has a deep and growing concern with rising costs. There is the population of patients of all ages who are concerned with the demands on the delivery system and how this may affect the availability of medical care to meet their own needs, and, finally, of course, there is Congress.

Although the aggregate data reveal the mounting costs, they are not sufficient to pinpoint efforts to control these costs, nor to assess the effectiveness of these efforts or to indicate the way in which the delivery system is being utilized. Is the length of stay in the hospital longer than is necessary? Does the recertification program have any effect on length of stay and costs? Is there a shift from public hospitals to voluntary or proprietary hospitals, and what does this do to costs? What is the relation between allowable charges and total charges? Is there 'unnecessary surgery'?

Questions like these require information on the patterns of utilization and on the individual components of costs. It is this kind of information which is needed to provide a rational basis for regulating and adjusting the operation of the system and for making recommendations for legislative changes to Congress. But if one deals only with averages for the entire system and takes no account of the fact that there is enormous variation in costs and utilization among different parts of the system, then the regulatory process may work undue hardship on some parts of the system while rewarding others.

In general, the analysis of variation among the elements of the system is one of the most powerful tools available to the Social Security Administration to improve the system. To use this tool effectively requires an ability to classify utilization and costs not only in regard to size of claim and to the kind of use made of the delivery system, but also in regard to the socio-demographic characteristics of the beneficiary and, at times, of the provider. For instance, as we have seen, on the average the aged person incurred an out-of-pocket expense of $225 in fiscal 1971. Even if this average prevailed among all socio-economic groups, it would be a heavier burden among the poorer than the richer groups of the population. But if the distribution around the average is heavily skewed toward the poorer economic groups, the problem is even more serious than it at first appears. The possible implications of such information for the financing of the system as a whole or for the financing of national health insurance bear consideration.

The desirability of socio-economic and demographic data to assess the distributional impact of Medicare is also brought out by the recent report of Scitovsky and Snyder[2] on the experience in the Palo Alto clinic which showed that the deductible and co-insurance features of the program do have an impact on utilization and, therefore, on costs—at least, in the first year after they are put into effect. This impact was greater among the less economically advantaged group of the Palo Alto study population than among the more affluent groups. But this is the very group likely to be most in need of medical care. It does not follow, therefore, that deductibles and co-insurance are, *ipso facto*, socially desirable devices to control utilization even should the effect persist over time.

In the effort to render a useful public accounting, we have progressed from aggregate to distributional data on utilization and costs and to the desirability of classifying this information by soci-economic status. There are, undoubtedly, other important determinants of utilization and costs such as size of family, living arrangements, attitudes of the consumer, attitudes of the provider, and so on. How far do we go with this process? How much detail is to be collected? How is the decision to be made as to what is collected in the normal course of the operation of the system and what should be obtained through special studies?

The answer to these questions invokes the principle that only that information should be collected *routinely* which is needed for the day-to-day operation of the system. Medicare is primarily a bill-paying mechanism, and the payment depends upon the nature of the service provided. It follows that the bills submitted must have sufficient information to make a decision on eligibility for payment and on the amount of the payment under the rules of the game. This information is needed to operate the program, not for statistical purposes. But given the information on the bills or claims forms, a great deal of the data required public account-ability on utilization and costs can be developed.

Unless there are overwhelming, compelling reasons, all other information not directly required to operate the program should be obtained through special studies. The special study approach for this class of information is cheaper, more reliable, and more likely to be specifically aimed at answering a useful question. Socio-economic status is a case in point. There is no need for this information to pay the bills; therefore I would not collect it routinely. As has been noted, however, socio-economic information is important for purposes of public accountability. The fact that it is not collected routinely does not absolve management from the necessity for obtaining it. It only changes the method of collection.

THE PERFORMANCE OF THE SYSTEM

To my knowledge, Medicare is the first large-scale program in the health field combining the resources of both the public and private sectors of the economy. At least one of the factors in reaching the decision to enter into such a cooperative arrangement was the belief that the private sector already had experience in administering programs of this kind and could do so economically and efficiently. What criteria shall be used to judge whether this belief is justified?

It seems to me that there are two measures which have particu-lar relevance: One is the administrative expense of the program expressed as a percentage of total expenditures; the other is the length of time it takes for the bills to get paid.

In regard to the first of these measures, administrative expenses in 1971 for the hospital insurance program, Part A, ran at the level of about 3 percent and for Supplementary Medical Insurance, Part B, at roughly 13 percent, with an overall figure of approximately 5 percent to 6 percent. These are remarkably low figures for a program of this magnitude.[3]

The record with regard to the time required to pay the bills once they are received by the intermediary is also good. For hospital bills this period, on the average is eight days, for ECFs it is fifteen days, and for out-of-hospital care (Part B) it is twenty-one days.[4]

On the whole, the overall performance of the system seems very good indeed.

In spite of this excellent overall record, there seems to be no other area which arouses quite so much irritation, controversy, and mistrust as the monitoring of carrier performance. What appear to be some of the reasons for this?

1. While there does not seem to be any quarrel with the measures as such, there is resentment over the way the measures are used to compare one carrier's performance with another. The crux of this argument is that like is not being compared with like. It is as though one compared the death rate of two cities with totally different age distributions and concluded that the one with the lower crude death rate was healthier. Is it fair, for example, to compare the performance of a large carrier dealing with large numbers of providers in urban areas with another carrier having a much smaller total of claims and dealing with a relatively small number of providers? In essence, what seems to be called for is a comparison of agreed-upon measures in somewhat the following fashion:

Carrier A's Performance	Peer Group Performance	National Average
_____	_____	_____

But if one is going to do this, then there has to be a definition of peer group, that is—what kinds of groupings of the carriers will result in comparing like with like, rather than lumping all carriers together? Such a definition is best arrived at through joint discussion.

2. There are areas where definition and agreement on

classification procedures are needed. For instance, how does one count claims? If a claim is sent back for further information, is it one or two claims? What is a pending claim? What shall be included in the cost of processing claims? In regard to this last question, I am puzzled. On the one hand, I hear the intermediaries say their costs are not covered, and on the other hand, I hear Social Security say that if this is so, it is because the carriers have not asked to be reimbursed for total costs incurred. I conclude that there is a difference in definition of costs which can only be resolved by joint discussion.

3. The philosophy of monitoring is in terms of detail rather than in terms of end results. Given an overall performance as good as it seems to be, there seems little to be gained by monitoring the *processes* by which an efficient and economical operation is obtained. Indeed, to do tends to stifle initiative, adds to cost, and arouses resentment. Moreover, the potential to review carrier performance in detail is always present since, if the statistical distribution shows a carrier to be out of line in comparison with his peers, the reason can always be sought more closely.

A quote from Don Price's book, *The Scientific Estate*, is particularly relevant to this question. 'The surest way for the top administrator . . . to lose control over his essential purposes is to try to tell his professional subordinates exactly what to do and make them stick to it.'[5] If this is true for professional subordinates, how much more so for professional colleagues!

MAINTAINING QUALITY

We have repeatedly pointed out that Medicare as originally conceived was primarily a mechanism for paying the medical bills of the elderly. Does this mean that there need be no concern with the quality of the product being purchased? I scarcely think so. The fact that certification of facilities is required is one indication of concern with quality. Another is the discussion before the Senate Finance Committee which suggests that the failure to include any mention of quality in the original bill was a legislative oversight.

Be that as it may, even if we confine the discussion to the issue of control of costs, we inevitably become concerned with the kind of health care being delivered. The problem is to see that appropriate payment is made for appropriate care, that the patient who needs Cadillac care gets it, but if only Volkswagon care is required, this, too, is readily available. This requires that there be standards of some kind for determining the appropriateness of care in relation to the patient's needs.

As yet there is little agreement on what standards should be used to judge services received in health care programs. Since, according to the agenda, Dr Breslow will specifically discuss this question, I shall not attempt to deal with it in detail. However, whatever standards are set will require some form of peer review. Peer review of every case is unworkable unless it is coupled with a statistical mechanism for flagging the high-risk cases. Indeed, the process of reviewing the length of stay in the hospital is an example of the working of this process, the statistical distribution of length of stay being used to decide on the point at which review should take place. The procedures used by the San Joaquin Foundation are another example of coupling the statistical system with case review. Once standards are set, there is no reason why the statistical system cannot be extended to include these standards.

Any set of standards must be reviewed periodically as knowledge changes. What is good medical care today is not the same as it was a generation ago. If we are to insure that appropriate payment is made for appropriate care, we must be prepared to finance research into methods of measuring the quality of care —particularly research which is concerned with end result measurements—that is measurement of the patient's clinical and functional status, because only by knowing which processes of care influence the patient's health can we determine what is appropriate care and insure that the standards are meaningful. The process is never-ending and constantly changing, and the system must be prepared to change with it.

RESPONSIBILITY

Up to this point I have discussed public accountability as it relates to: (1) meeting the costs of medical care for the aged; (2) the efficiency of the cooperative arrangement between the public and private sectors of the economy; and (3) the maintenance of quality of care in the system. I have discussed all of these from the standpoint of the kinds of information required to render a meaningful accounting to the beneficiary, the taxpayer, the users of the health care delivery system generally, and the Congress. In this discussion I have pointed out that there are several areas which warrant joint discussion by the interested parties. Among these are the following: what is to be collected routinely and what is to be collected through special studies, the areas which require special study, the criteria for judging carrier performance and for classifying carriers into like groups for comparative purposes, the definition of terms, the development of standards by which to judge quality, the criteria to be used to select high-risk cases for review, and, most important, the philosophy underlying the monitoring of carrier performance.

In these joint discussions I suggest that the first order of business should be the fixing of areas of responsibility rather than the technical details, for I have no doubt that the latter can be ironed out with good will and plenty of honest sweat once the former is decided upon. Who is responsible for what? Whose responsibility is it to control costs? To maintain standards of quality? Are the carriers simply to act as pass-through mechanisms for handling pieces of paper, or do they have wider responsibilities? What is expected of them by the government? What do the carriers expect of the government?

Undoubtedly these questions have been discussed before, and there have been numerous committees concerned with them. I would like to suggest, however, since the health delivery system is not a static entity and is rapidly undergoing change at the present time, that there be an on-going advisory group meeting regularly, say twice a year, to discuss these matters. The composition of this group should consist of representatives of the Social Security Administration, the carriers, the providers, and the consumers. Its charge should be to make recommendations to the Administrator regarding the areas of responsibility of the various participants in the system, to consider and make recommendations regarding such matters as those mentioned above and regarding changes to be made in the system. Some mechanism for handling emergency situations arising between meetings should be developed, but I am sure that this can be done. At the very least, such an approach to the issues of public accountability would introduce the possibility of more orderly planned change in the regulations governing the system.

In this matter of who is responsible for what, there is one other area I wish to discuss. This is the area of consumer education. Medicare is a complicated system. The consumer doesn't understand it. Words like 'deductibles' and 'co-insurance' mean nothing to him. He is upset and angry when he finds that he has to pay something from his own pocket for the medical care of either himself or his aged parent. This anger is likely to be indiscriminate, directed alike at the private and public sectors. Moreover, he is never quite sure where to turn to get information about the working of the system. Whose responsibility is it to educate the consumer and to act as a source of information for him? A more effective ombudsman system is needed which preserves the warmth and dignity of human relationships. There is room for experimentation here. For example, what about developing training programs for medical secretaries, clinic and hospital receptionists, etc.—the people the public is most likely to come in contact with when they are in need of care?

THE REPORTING MECHANISM

Having dealt with the kinds of information to be collected, I should like now to turn to the specific collection mechanisms. Clearly, most of the information must come off a form which is generated at the time the patient enters the hospital, or is seen by a provider in the case of ambulatory care. The form should meet certain requirements. It should be simple to understand and to fill out. It should minimize paper work and contribute to the ease of processing, and, in general, to the efficiency of the operation. It should lend itself to some degree of standardization and, whenever possible, it should be of use to the consumer, the provider, the intermediary, and the government in their daily work; that is, it should not be an extra piece of paper which the system requires for some mysterious purpose, but has no meaning to the person filling it out.

In general, the present system conforms very well to these criteria. There are really only three basic forms, the admission and billing record for Part A, and the 1490 form for Part B. Nevertheless one hears complaints about the system. It is too complicated, it is clumsy, etc.

The majority of these complaints about the mechanics of the

reporting system seem to relate to the lack of any standardization of the billing forms on which claims are sent in and attached to the 1490 form. The situation has been likened to that which would arise if every business and individual used his own income tax form. Under such circumstances, the Internal Revenue Service would have a very difficult time in collecting taxes efficiently. Some may argue that this is not necessarily bad. Be that as it may, if one remembers that the purpose of the income tax program is essentially a social purpose, it is clear that the procedures for collecting the taxes must be practical.

There is another point of analogy here; that is that over the years, a great deal of thought has gone into making the mechanics of the tax collection system as simple and understandable as possible for the general taxpayer. On the whole the system works very well indeed. It may well be worth while to spend the equivalent amount of time and thought in experimenting with the mechanism by which the information comes from the individual provider to the intermediary in the Medicare program.

Specifically, I suggest that we consider further the implications of the criterion that the reporting forms should be meaningful to each user in his daily work. If one could design a form which would be useful to the individual provider in taking care of his patient, such as a uniform encounter record, and this encounter record became the basis for the reporting system one would not only improve the basic medical record keeping of the country, but would also give the provider something which he feels is useful to him in taking care of his patients and is not just another piece of paper which he is required to fill out.

There is some experience with this kind of an idea developing at the present time. For instance, in one situation of which I am aware, the encounter form becomes part of the medical record, but at the same time the form is so organized as to give the kinds of information that is needed for the 1490 form. The latter is made automatically from the encounter record through the use of a computer. Experience with this type of reporting is still too slim to judge its pros and cons, but the concept deserves watching and encouragement.

The practice of medicine is changing sufficiently at the present time to warrant thinking further about this kind of an approach. More and more, physicians are practicing in association with other physicians. The young physician coming out of medical school is anxious to practice in this way, because he feels such association makes it easier for him to practice the kind of medicine he learned in medical school. So the possibility of developing a more uniform type of medical record which might also serve for billing purposes should not be taken lightly.

Efforts to implement these ideas are already under way on a number of fronts. Under the auspices of the National Center for Health Services Research and Development, a Conference on Ambulatory Care Records was held in Chicago earlier this year. As a result a Technical Panel on Medical Care Records of the National Committee on Health and Vital Statistics has been organized to try to design the minimal set of data which should be on any ambulatory care record. At the same time, a Policy Committee on Ambulatory Care Records is being organized in the Secretary's Office to consider policy issues in incorporating such a form in the workings of programs such as Medicare, Medicaid, the insurance industry in general, and the Blue Cross and Blue Shield programs.

It is worthy of note that the British National Health Service offers an incentive to good record keeping by paying for the services of a secretary to do the necessary paper work when several physicians work together. Moreover, the current efforts to re-organize the entire Scottish health system are based upon making the medical record the cornerstone of the system.[6] Perhaps we should take a leaf from notebooks of our British and Scottish friends.

Another area in which there are complaints about the mechanics of the reporting system relates to the feedback of information about the operation of the system. The complaints generally fall into two categories: the kind of information which becomes available and the timeliness with which it is provided. On the first of these points, the usefulness of the 5 percent sample is not clear to many of those working with the system. But, as I have tried to show earlier in the discussion of the kinds of information to be collected for purposes of public accountability, it is important to be able to look at the distribution of the various pieces of inform-ation as well as at the average figures. Much of this distributional information derives from the 5 percent sample, since it can only come from the detailed bills themselves. There is the feeling on the part of some that 'more useful information' could be derived from the 5 percent sample, but when pressed a bit on the kinds of information desired, the answers are slow in forthcoming. I suggest that the whole question of feedback of information to intermediaries, providers, and the public be placed on the agenda of the advisory group previously recommended.

The timeliness of reports is a serious problem. The report on Medicare for 1967 was not issued until 1971. The Division of Research and Statistics of the Social Security Administration is well aware of this situation. There are several reasons for this, but perhaps the most overriding one is the question of priorities in the computer processing. The entire computer operation of the Social Security Administration is in one place and has to process literally billions of jobs. The primary task is to see that the checks for recipients of Social Security benefits go out on time. This takes precedence over everything else and properly so. But it does raise the question as to whether this degree of centralization of the computer operation is desirable.

There is another aspect of the current computer operation which affects the timeliness of reports. Basically, the use of the computer for mailing out the checks in the Social Security program is non-statistical, requiring primarily listing and up-dating. This calls for relatively simple programming. The programming procedures of a statisical operation are considerably more complex. The technology in this area is in its infancy and needs a great deal more improvement. This may be another reason why it may be desirable to separate the computer aspects of the Medicare program from that of the other aspects of the Social Security program.

In any event, the whole question of timeliness and of presenting reports in an interesting, readable fashion is one that should be given a great deal more attention.

THE CHARACTERISTICS OF THE MEDICARE PROGRAM PER SE:
IMPLICATIONS FOR PUBLIC ACCOUNTABILITY

Although there are problems with the reporting system which provides the basic information for public accountability, as we have seen, on the whole the system works reasonably well. The basic problem is not really the characteristics of the data collection system but rather the characteristics of the program. It is the way the program is set up that creates some of these problems. For example, the fact that there is a deductible and co-insurance feature in the program presumably designed to control utilization and costs means that the eligibility for benefits must be checked on an individual basis. Each individual's claims have to be examined to see if he satisfies the deductible and co-insurance feature. This all takes time and is often a source of irritation, but it is inherent in the system and would be present whether there were a statistical reporting system or not.

Then there is the whole question of allowable charges. If one is going to have a system of allowable charges, then each bill has to be checked to be sure the charges are within the allowable limits. Again, the focus must be the individual, and the procedures would be present whether there was a statistical reporting system or not.

Along with allowable charges there is the problem of allowable services. This, too, focuses on the individual and is an area which is often a source of considerable irritation to the conscientious provider and to the patient. It is an area in which there is relatively little information about what happens to the patient. What is best for the patient in situations in which there is a difference between the allowable services and the services requested?

Consider, for example, the following situation. An elderly patient breaks her hip and after it is mended in the hospital is ready for discharge. Because of the patient's family circumstances, the physician feels that rather than place the patient in an ECF or in a nursing home, the patient is better taken care of in the home of her relatives which is some miles away. If the patient were placed in an ECF or in a nursing home, the ambulance would be paid for under the Medicare program and so would the cost of care in the ECF or nursing home up to the allowable limit. But since the patient decides to go home and her family decides that they would like to have her in their home and the physician decides that this is best for the patient, the family incurs the expense of the ambulance and the expense of taking care of the patient without any further reimbursement.

Now consider the opposite kind of situation. An elderly woman lives with her daughter. The daughter is a conscientious lady who feels obligated to take care of her mother. The mother is getting along very well, but the daughter is extremely tired and becoming ill because of the additional care of her parent. The doctor in his routine checkup notices this and advises the daughter to take two weeks off to get back on her feet. He attempts to place the mother in a nursing home for this period, but cannot do this without first placing the patient in the hospital, resulting in an expense that is charged to the Medicare system.

These particular examples are highly selected ones and may be isolated instances. I do not present them as representative of the system, but simply to make the following points: (1) that the constraints of the system itself result in the complicated checking which is required and that these constraints are not necessarily a part of the statistical reporting system; (2) that if the orientation of the system is on the prevention of cheating rather than what is best for the patient, there may often be times when rather than costs being kept down these costs increase. The system should operate so that in terms of eligibility for service it is sufficiently flexible so that the people get what they need in a dignified manner. This whole area deserves special study.

THE FUTURE

The likelihood that we will have some form of national health insurance at some time in the near future seems very high. The question is not whether, but when. I will leave the answer to that question to others more politically acute than I. But if the statement is correct, then the experience with Medicare should prove invaluable in planning for the future. The opportunity is present to do this planning well in advance of the legislation, and, indeed, even to guide the legislation particularly as it relates to the operating characteristics of the program. What, for instance, should be the administrative structure within which the national health insurance program is administered? Should it be part of the general Social Security program or should it be a separate unit? Clearly, any general program of national health insurance will be a huge operation, and the administrative arrangements will need to be thought through very carefully. We have seen some of the difficulties in Medicare which arise out of conflicting priorities with other aspects of the Social Security system.

If the population of the country as a whole comes under a national health insurance program, then the question of checking for enrollment in the program no longer becomes a question. However, if the concept of deductibles and co-insurance is part of the program, then one will have to check for eligibility with all of the accompanying difficulties. The report of Scitovsky and Snyder raises the question of the social desirability of such devices. The follow-up of those studies over the next year or two should be watched with considerable interest, and it is to the credit of the Social Security Administration that they have funded the original as well as a follow-up study.

There is also the question of the cost of checking on eligibility and co-insurance. One has to ask, is it really worth it? At this point we don't know, but in making plans for a national health insurance program, we should know something about this.

In planning the procedures for the reporting system required in any national health insurance program to provide the information needed for public accountability and to make it possible to draw samples for purposes of special study, planning should go forward jointly as a cooperative endeavor of the government, the providers, representatives of the public, and the intermediaries. In this connection, the possibility of developing a national health insurance system around the basic encounter form as the cornerstone of the reporting system should be seriously considered.

The record of Medicare to date has been very good. With this experience to guide us, it should be possible to organize a national health insurance program, both from the financial standpoint and from the delivery standpoint which is a workable system generally satisfactory to the consumer, the provider, the intermediary, and the government.

Notes

1. B. S. Cooper and N. L. Worthington, 'Medical Care Spending for Three Age Groups,' *Social Security Bulletin*, vol. 35, no. 5 (May 1972).
2. Anne A. Scitovsky and Nelda M. Snyder, 'Effect of Coinsurance on Use of Physician Services,' *Social Security Bulletin*, vol. 35, no. 6 (June 1972).
3. Howard West, 'Five Years of Medicare—A Statistical Review,' *Social Security Bulletin*, vol. 34, no. 12 (Dec. 1971).
4. Aaron Krute, personal communication.

5. Don K. Price, *The Scientific Estate* (Harvard University Press, Cambridge, Mass., 1967).

6. K. E. Bodenham and F. Willman, 'Foundation for Health Service Management,' *Nuffield Provincial Hospitals Trust* (Oxford University Press, 1972).

10 Trends in General Accounting Office Audits

JOSEPH POIS

The metamorphosis which General Accounting Office audits have undergone is reflected in the fact that the term 'audit' has become increasingly deceptive as a designation for many of the reviews conducted by the GAO. There has been a widening gulf between the products of the GAO's efforts and what typically flows out of the audit work in the private sector. The latter ordinarily takes the form of examinations made to enable the auditor to express an opinion as to the fairness of financial statements, 'their compliance with generally accepted accounting principles, and the consistency of the application of those principles with that of the preceding period.'[1] The Comptroller General has established a much broader frame of reference for the reviews conducted by the GAO.

EARLY BACKGROUND OF GAO AUDITS

What has evolved is a complete departure from the type of audit that characterized the GAO from its inception in 1921 until the early 1940s. During that period, the audit function was performed through a highly centralized examination of documents submitted to the GAO. Engulfed with a mountain of paper work, the Comptroller General made no pretense of applying the audit approach and standards of the public accounting profession. What was done was basically of a clerical character, the only professional element being that injected by the legal staff, which concerned itself with the resolution of legal questions arising in connection with particular transactions. The process had an insularity to it that precluded any first-hand insight into, and understanding of, operations that gave rise to the transactions being scrutinized. The GAO did have an investigation unit whose inquiries could impinge on the kind of financial examination made by a professional auditor.

It is only fair to point out that the Budget and Accounting Act, 1921, made no reference to the term 'audit.' The Act provides for the settlement of accounts of accountable officers as well as claims and demands by or against the government. It also states that the Comptroller General shall investigate 'all matters relating to the receipt, disbursement, and application of public funds. . . .' The reference to the word 'investigation' undoubtedly impelled the establishment of the investigative facility and was conducive to the development of a strong sleuthlike motif within the GAO.

Under the pressures engendered by emergency programs initiated by President Roosevelt and World War II spending, the GAO began to abandon its separatist approach and started to conduct reviews at the so-called audit sites. This development meant a major change in GAO-agency relationships since it brought the audit process to the agencies and dispelled the image of GAO cloistered in its Washington headquarters and passing on transactions in vacuo. But, even with this development, GAO continued, until some time in the 1950s, to pre-audit vouchers that had been administratively approved but were voluntarily submitted by agencies for GAO examination prior to payment. The fact that agencies availed themselves of such pre-audits reflected, at least initially, their fear of the Comptroller General's tight-fisted and faultfinding attitudes with respect to public spending. The eagerness of Comptroller General McCarl to assume this responsibility was still another manifestation of the untenable manner in which the GAO at first conceptualized its audit responsibilities.

EFFECTS OF GOVERNMENT CORPORATION CONTROL ACT

The enactment of the Government Corporation Control Act (1945) was one of the most significant factors which made for a recasting of the audit philosophy of the GAO. This statute not only required that the GAO audit corporations coming within the purview of this legislation but stated explicitly that such audits should be made 'in accordance with the principles and procedures applicable to commercial corporate transactions.' The Act also provided that the required audits should be 'conducted at the place or places where the acounts of the respective corporations are normally kept.' These provisions afforded clear-cut congressional recognition of the auditing practices employed by the public accounting profession. Although the requirements applied to only those GAO audits involving government corporations, they had important 'spillover' effects that had a profound impact throughout the GAO. The staffing of the Corporation Audits Division, established to implement the responsibilities imposed by the Government Corporation Control Act, resulted in the ascendancy of the certified public accountant. The GAO's auditing assumed a professional character, and the trained accountant began to occupy key positions within the organization.

COMPREHENSIVE AUDIT CONCEPT

Those concerned with reshaping the audit posture of the GAO so as to enhance its vitality and professional stature evolved the concept of a 'comprehensive audit.' Varying interpretations were given to the term, which proved to be a source of continuing confusion. Comptrollers General Warren and Campbell strove valiantly, albeit unsuccessfully, to clarify the concept. The pretentiousness of the term even impelled a staff recommendation for its discontinuance. But the very ambiguity was a source of strength. Those who might have been prone to challenge it could not really come to grips with such an elusive concept. However amorphous, the comprehensive audit concept afforded the GAO a vehicle for articulating the idea that GAO was striving for breadth in its reviews.

At first, breadth—following the pattern established in the private sector—was conceived in terms of the financial aspects of agency operations. In fact, the initial pronouncements stressed application of the comprehensive audit concept to agencies whose activities were of a commercial character. Then 'comprehensive' was construed as looking into the operations that ultimately find expression in the form of financial transactions. The proponents of this approach apparently sought to articulate dimensions and encompass managerial implications. This reaching out was rationalized by citing the phrase 'application of public funds' in the statutory provision—previously mentioned—for the Comptroller General making investigations. The word 'application' was the nexus for couping up the Budget and Accounting Act with audits having significant breadth and depth.

Even the 'Accounting and Auditing Act of 1950,' which was Part 2 of the Budget and Accounting Procedures Act of 1950, made no reference to the 'comprehensive audit.' The Act specifically recognized the auditing responsibilities of the Comptroller General but reflected a perspective that was entirely financial in character. Faced with the dilemma posed by the apparent incompatibility between the statutory wording and the broad dimensions envisaged by the comprehensive audit concept, the GAO worked out a novel line of reasoning. This started off with the disarming postulate that the primary purpose of GAO audits 'is to make for the Congress independent examinations into the manner in which Government agencies discharge their financial responsibilities.'[2] But 'financial responsibilities' were construed very broadly so as to encompass not only 'the administration of funds and the utilization of property and personnel only for authorized programs, activities, and purposes' but also 'the conduct of programs or activities in an effective, efficient, and economical manner.'

Seeking to avoid any doubt that GAO audits can extend far beyond the accounting realm, the Comprehensive Audit Manual stated: '. . . our audits are not restricted to accounting matters or to books, records, and documents. The scope of these audits is much broader and may extend into all significant aspects of an agency's operations.[3] Manifestly, the thrust for the broad-based reviews which the GAO has been emphasizing in recent years did not come from the language of the Office's statutory charter, but from within the GAO itself. At the same time, the extent to which this thrust could be translated into the audit program was very much dependent upon the responsiveness of committees and individual members of the Congress.

PROGRAM REVIEWS

The term 'comprehensive audit' was discarded in favor of 'program review.' This represents the third stage in the progression which began with the financial examinations and then expanded into analyses of the managerial adequacy reflected in the particular operations. While pointing out the limitations that staff resources place upon the extent to which program reviews can be made by the GAO, Comptroller General Staats told a House Appropriations Subcommittee that the GAO had increased its capability to 'examine the adequacy of program management and evaluate the effectiveness or results of those programs of heavy dollar impact and Congressional interest.'[4] Staats made it clear that, in his thinking, program reviews and managerial examinations are not mutually exclusive but rather that program reviews, building on evaluation of managerial processes, analyze the results that are actually being achieved.[5]

The Legislative Reorganization Act of 1970 for the first time provided a specific statutory basis for the type of broader review such as the GAO had already been conducting. Section 204(a) of the Act reads as follows:

> The Comptroller General shall review and analyze the results of Government programs, and activities carried on under existing law, including the making of cost benefit studies, when ordered by either House of Congress, or upon his own initiative, or when requested by any committee of the House of Representatives or the Senate, or any joint committee of the two Houses, having jurisdiction over such programs and activities.

In its explanation of this provision, the House Committee on Rules stated that the intent was that the Comptroller General 'shall review and analyze program results in a manner which will assist the Congress to determine whether those programs and activities are achieving the objectives of the law.'[6] The Act's emphasis upon cost-benefit studies will undoubtedly stimulate more intensive use of this approach in connection with program reviews.

COMPTROLLER GENERAL'S POSITION ON
REVIEWS OF LEGISLATIVE PROPOSALS

The Comptroller General has sought to 'draw a sharp line between a matter which is pending before the Congress, where it is before a committee with assigned responsibility as contrasted with a GAO review of a program that is on-going where we attempt to make assessments as to the effectiveness of that program, as to whether it is being administered economically, efficiently and in accordance with the intent of Congress.'[7] Staats' rationale for this position is that GAO's objectivity in reviewing the implementation of programs might be questioned if it made recommendations for the adoption of particular programs.[8]

The Legislative Reorganization Act of 1970 is basically consistent with the dichotomy drawn by the Comptroller General. It contains the rather innocuous provision that the Comptroller General shall, upon the request of any congressional committee, explain to, and discuss with, the committee or its staff any GAO report which would assist the committee in connection with 'its consideration of proposed legislation, including requests for appropriations. . . .' (Sec. 231.) The Act vests the Legislative Reference Service of the Library of Congress, redesigned as the Congressional Research Service, with responsibility for assisting congressional committees 'in the analysis, appraisal, and evaluation of legislative proposals. . . .' (Sec. 321 (d).)

The demarcation between reviews of on-going programs and studies directed to the formulation or evaluation of proposals for new programs may in some instances be fuzzy. The earnestness with which the Comptroller General has articulated the distinction may strike some as puzzling, especially in light of the fact that the GAO submits numerous reports on legislative proposals to congressional committees.[9] The GAO also provides advisory assistance in developing legislative proposals, and the Comptroller General has pointed out that his Office is 'in a unique position to provide advisory assistance of real value to the Members of Congress because of the wide range of knowledge of governmental activities gained through our audits and the broad scope of questions our legal staff is called upon for decisions.'[10]

But it should be observed that what Staats was apparently striving to eschew in connection with proposed legislation was having the GAO being placed in the position of saying, to use his words, 'We think this is the alternative that Congress should buy with respect to a program or a matter of policy.'[11] He specifically stated that GAO could analyze alternatives, present the cost implications of alternatives, and examine the reasonableness of cost estimates.[12]

A major thrust of the proposed Budget and Accounting Improvement Act,[13] which passed the Senate twice but was not acted upon by the House, is that of involving the Comptroller

General in committee consideration of legislative proposals. It would authorize him to make analyses and reviews of such proposals and alternatives thereto, 'including those available to the departments and agencies, the long-term costs and benefits thereof, the analytical processes involved in the justification of such proposals and the validity of the data supporting them, when ordered by either House of Congress or requested by the chairman of any committee' having jurisdiction over the proposal (Sec. 101). The bill even provides for individual members of Congress initiating requests for having the Comptroller General make analyses or reviews of legislative proposals.

The Senate Committee on Government Operations report on this bill was careful to point out: 'The Comptroller General will not be involved in making basic policy. His functions will be confined to the objective review and analysis, on request, of the program proposal to Congress and reporting the findings. The decisions are left to Congress.'[14] There is definite overlap between the program analysis role the Committee envisages for the Comptroller General and the duties which the Legislative Reorganization Act places upon the Congressional Research Service to assist committees 'in determining the advisability of enacting such proposals; estimating the probable results of such proposals and alternatives thereto; and evaluating alternative methods for accomplishing those results.'[15] Entirely apart from the legislation recommended by the Senate Committee on Government Operations, the provisions of the Legislative Reorganization Act had impelled the House Committee on Rules to recognize the possibility of 'overlapping activities.'[16]

The overlap anticipated by the Committee on Rules would obviously be aggravated by the enactment of the Senate proposal. However, the fact that GAO finds other Congressionally-established agencies 'competing' with it in certain facets of the review function is not in itself undesirable. The workability of such an arrangement depends in large measure upon the manner in which committees and members of Congress utilize the agencies and the relations between the different resources available to Congress.

REVIEW OF ECONOMIC PROGRAMS

The stellar example of a program review was that made of the Economic Opportunity Programs. This review was carried out in response to a congressional mandate included in the 1967 Amendments to the Economic Opportunity Act of 1964. The Comptroller General, who had been declaiming on a broader type of GAO audit, must have been taken aback when he found himself confronted with the congressional directive calling upon the GAO 'to make an investigation in sufficient depth of programs and activities financed in whole or in part by funds authorized under section 2 of this Act, in order to determine—

(1) the efficiency of the administration of such programs and activities by the Office of Economic Opportunity and by local public and private agencies carrying out such programs and activities; and

(2) the extent to which such programs and activities achieve the objectives set forth in the relevant part or title of the Economic Opportunity Act of 1964 authorizing such programs or activities.

The inception and prosecution of this study was one of the most significant milestones in GAO's history. The GAO suddenly found itself with the herculean task of not only evaluating the management of the complex of Economic Opportunity Programs but also assaying their effectiveness. The programs patently are of the type that is distinctly elusive so far as measurement of results is concerned. Equally, if not more, discomfiting was the controversial nature of the programs. Such an assignment inevitably catapulted the GAO into the political firing line. Venturing into a frontier area, the Office found it necessary not only to mobilize a large segment of its regular staff resources but also to supplement them with substantial help by contractors and consultants. A comprehensive report on the study was issued early in 1969,[17] which was followed by the outpouring of more than fifty reports on the reviews or examinations made at various program sites throughout the country.

Congressional reaction to the Comptroller General's report on the Economic Opportunity Programs was understandably mixed, and feelings of individual members were influenced by their attitudes with respect to the OEO and specific facets of its programs. The Comptroller General was subjected to grueling, intensive, and even hostile questioning by committees of both Houses. During the course of such interrogation, some of the members of Congress took the opportunity to question the propriety of the GAO getting into such matters.

Even before the completion of the study, the House Appropriations Committee had observed:

> As a general proposition, it strikes the committee that there may be a valid question whether the Congress in future consideration of program authorization legislation, ought to follow the precedent established in the OEO amendments of placing, by statute, specific responsibilities on the Comptroller General for evaluating the efficiency and effectiveness of entire major programs with statutory reporting deadlines.[18]

It was the Committee's feeling that, if Congress followed this precedent, it would tend to diminish the flexibility of the GAO in examining all the programs and expenditures of the government. The Committee also expressed concern that such projects by the GAO would, if carried too far, 'considerably duplicate the expensive staffs and special 'investigative' Committee expenditures.'

Following the submission of the OEO report, the House Appropriations Committee commented even more strongly and at greater length concerning the implications of such a congressional assignment. It pointed out that the GAO did not have the in-house capability for this kind of policy examination and, therefore, found it necessary to retain outside firms on a contractual basis at a substantial cost. A still more compelling criticism made by the Committee was that the project 'brought the GAO into the business of making recommendations in controversial legislative policy areas.'[19]

In retrospect, it appears that the OEO study came at a point of time when GAO was not yet 'tooled-up' to conduct such a project. It, therefore, entailed not only excessive costs[20] but undue organizational stress. But the fact that GAO was able to produce a study which stood up despite very searching and adverse scrutiny strengthened immeasurably GAO's credentials as a program review agency. The OEO review established that professional personnel whose primary expertise was in accounting could adapt themselves to the needs of a project that essentially called for the talents of the social scientist. The assignment was something of an acid test of GAO's capability to make a program effectiveness review in a very sensitive and complex area.

DIVERSITY OF GAO REVIEWS

The reports which the GAO prepared on the effectiveness of the construction grant program for abating, controlling, and preventing water pollution reflects the Comptroller General's willingness to undertake program reviews involving technical subject-matter. GAO did not hesitate to state in its report to the Congress that the program had been using a 'shotgun approach' and to express the belief that the existing level of federal funding would not be sufficient to enable a significant increase in the effectiveness of the program.[21] The Comptroller General was able to state that the Office of Science and Technology in the Executive Office of the President had not only viewed the report but stated that it was excellent and that its conclusions and recommendations were sound. GAO made the most of the opportunity these studies afforded it to demonstrate its competence to assay a technical program that seeks to be responsive to the public concern over the nation's environment.

Although it might not strictly be considered a program review, the GAO report on the status of the acquisition of selected major weapon systems exemplifies the trend for GAO to analyze, and report on, an increasingly broad spectrum of subject-matter.[22] GAO evaluated the Department of Defense's own system of reporting on acquisitions and also reported to the Congress on the status of fifty-seven individual programs. The report dealt with both time lags in completion of the programs and deviations from original cost estimates. In undertaking this project, the GAO was responsive to the mounting congressional demand for more complete information on the status of military procurement, with particular reference to the incurring of costs far in excess of those estimated at the time that procurement was initiated.

The information so furnished the Congress, as well as the GAO's continuing review of the acquisition of weapon systems, reflects the Office's increasing involvement in the substantive aspects of Defense procurement. GAO is seeking not only to furnish Congress data on the status of major weapon acquisitions but also to provide data that will 'determine if the fundamental concepts and processes utilized by DOD in determing the need for and in selecting and acquiring major weapon systems, are capable of and are producing the desired results.'

Still another study illustrative of the diversity of GAO studies was that concerned with the feasibility of applying uniform cost-accounting standards to negotiated Defense contracts.[23] Although originally loath to make such a study, the GAO was directed to do so by a 1968 amendment to the Defense Production Act of 1950. The resolution of the question posed by the Congress called for accounting expertise; and the GAO could reasonably be expected to have the technical talent essential to deal with the matter in a professional manner. But the controversial nature of the issue and the need to explore this particular aspect of accounting in considerable depth impelled the Comptroller General to make extensive use of outside consultants in conducting this study. The resultant evoked both congressional and public support and led to the enactment of the statute establishing a Cost-Accounting Standards Board.

The wide range of subject-matter covered by GAO audits is reflected in the report entitled *Federal Assistance For Presidential Transitions.*[24] The report states that its basic purpose is 'to provide information on the transitional process, which may be of interest to the Congress and the executive branch.' Mention is made of the fact that the Office of Management and Budget supported the conclusions of the report. Within the same month, the Comptroller had released reports dealing with the audit of a government corporation, elimination of duplicate stocks in the Marine Corps, medical screening of selective service registrants, effectiveness of on-the-job training in Appalachian Tennessee, transfer of regional activities to local post offices, the reporting of excess land by the Veterans Administration, adverse effects of large-scale production of major weapons before completion of development and testing, and more effective use by the Forest Service of funds appropriated for roads and trails.

The Comptroller General has stated that he is mindful of the need to maintain a proper balance between program reviews, audits concerned with financial accountability, and managerial anlysis. Yet there is the danger that the challenge and interest afforded by the broader-based reviews may gradually erode the resources available for other types of GAO audits, which—although narrower in scope—are nevertheless essential elements of a complete audit program. This leads into consideration of the emphasis the Comptroller General should be expected to place upon financial audits.

APPROPRIATE RECOGNITION OF FINANCIAL AUDITS

Audits directed at the more strictly financial aspects of government may seem pedestrian in light of the challenge and allure of the broader-based reviews that have evoked marked interest within both Congress and the GAO. Even when the GAO was expounding vigorously the comprehensive audit concept as applied to the fiscal aspects of the federal government, there was in reality no all-embracing financial audit program. It was not surprising, therefore, that the Committee for Economic Development, some years ago, concluded that GAO's operations 'provide no government-wide view of agency financial operations.'[25]

The Committee raised a pertinent issue as to the lack of periodic financial examination coverage encompassing all agencies. The settlement of the accounts of accountable officers can hardly be equated with the type of audit envisaged by the Committee. For that matter, as is pointed out elsewhere in this paper, such settlement work has been de-emphasized by the GAO.

The CED criticism was followed, two years later, by the Budget Bureau suggesting to the Comptroller General that the GAO audit reports 'systematically include financial statements for the various agencies and present your opinion with regard to the degree to which the figures therein fairly and consistently reflect the financial position and operating results of the agency in accord with the accounting principles and standards which you have promulgated.'[26] Staats' response to the Budget Bureau proposal was that the professional audit staff of GAO is not large enough to make annual systematic examinations of agency financial statements. However, the GAO did not cavalierly brush aside this facet of its audit responsibilities, and an internal memorandum issued as an aftermath of the Budget Bureau-Staats exchange of letters had this closing paragraph:

We are not recommending any broad-scale audit
examining financial statements but we do need
that we have a responsibility in this area under
audit responsibilities and that we should be regis
evaluation of the fairness, reliability, and credibilit
financial reports.[27]

GAO AUDIT RESPONSIBILITIES VIS-À-VIS
GRANTEES AND CONTRACTORS

The large number of grant-in-aid programs involving increasingly
large federal expenditures together with the widespread use of
government contracts totaling many billions of dollars mean that
GAO's audit responsibilities need to be viewed not only in relation
to government agencies proper but also from the standpoint of
these outside recipients of federal funds. The Office of the General
Counsel of the GAO had observed that GAO audit authority
under the Budget and Accounting Act, 1921, as well as the
Budget and Accounting Procedures Act of 1950 does not extend
to funds granted to states, local governments, and other grantees.
This was based upon a United States Supreme Court ruling that
federal funds turned over to grantees cease to be federal funds
and, therefore, do not come within the purview of general statutes
with respect to accountability for federal funds. Hence, the extension of GAO audit authority to recipients of such grants has
necessitated enactment of special legislation. This has generally
been piecemeal with the outstanding exception of the Inter-
governmental Cooperation Act of 1968 which gave broad
authority to the Comptroller General insofar as state governments
receiving grants-in-aid are concerned. But, even if the GAO had
sweeping authority to conduct audits of governmental units and
other agencies receiving funds under federal grant programs,
there would still remain the basic question as to how extensively
the GAO could conduct such audits. The practical limitations
upon GAO's capabilities to conduct audits in connection with this
aspect of governmental spending was brought out in testimony of
the Deputy Director of the GAO Civil Division before the House
Subcommittee:

As a matter of policy, Mr. Chairman, in view of the very
limited resources which we have in relation to the magnitude of

the problem in the grants-in-aid area and in all other areas, for that matter, any time we undertake to take a look at a particular program or a particular agency's operation, our first step is to take a look at what kind of audit effort has been brought to bear in that area either by the Federal Agency involved or by the State agency involved or the State auditor general or an outside auditing firm, or, at the local level, by any local audit organization that might have taken a look at the area.[28]

Staats recognized the increasing relevance of state and local governmental audits to the GAO's underlying responsibilities. But he was also mindful of the importance of not appearing to intrude upon the prerogatives of these other levels in the federal structure. Hence, the statement of audit standards he issued in 1972[29] was adroitly described as 'intended to be applicable to all levels of government in the United States.' Regardless of these semantics, it was obvious that the basic purpose sought to be achieved was that of strengthening the audit activities of state and local units of government.

The Comptroller General's efforts in this area are all the more meaningful in light of the revenue sharing legislation enacted only a few months after the audit standards were published. The Secretary of the Treasury is responsible for providing the 'accounting and auditing procedures, evaluations, and reviews' necessary to insure compliance with the requirements applicable to the expenditure of funds which states and units of local government receive under the Act. The Secretary may accept audits which state governments make of such expenditures. However, the legislation requires the Comptroller General to 'make such reviews of the work as done by the Secretary, the State governments, and the units of local government as may be necessary for the Congress to evaluate compliance and operations under this title.'[30]

Audits of defense contractors involve a more delicate issue than grants-in-aid. Not only the magnitude of contracts but also congressional and public apprehension of possible abuses in connection with such transactions result in significant pressure upon the GAO to play an increasingly active role in the monitoring of such contracts, particularly in the defense area. The fact that governmental departments may have extensive facilities for conducting contract audits does not completely satisfy the Congress. There is a strong insistence upon GAO maintaining a relatively close surveillance of the manner in which contractors discharge their obligations to the government. The very sensitivity of the procurement area precludes the GAO from sharply cutting back its activities in connection with government contracts. In fact, the reduction in contract audit work that was the aftermath of the Holifield Committee hearings—described subsequently—made GAO vulnerable to criticism when contract overruns such as those in connection with the C-5A plane were disclosed.

ACCESS TO INFORMATION

The Comptroller General's audit activities need to be perceived in light of how readily he can obtain information that he deems to be essential for his analyses. Access to relevant data is manifestly a *sine qua non* to the meaningful functioning of any monitoring agency. Despite the broad statutory provisions for the Comptroller General having access to the records of agencies and those of government contractors who have been awarded negotiated contracts, there have been perennial impasses.[31]

Rebuffs by government establishments are not surprising, in light of the fact that Congress itself has had sharp confrontations with executive agencies that have invoked 'executive privilege' as the rationale for refusing information requested by the Legislative Branch. This concept has also been the basis for denying access to the GAO. In 1960 and 1971, the Comptroller General was drawn into two bitter controversies arising from Presidential rejections of requests that congressional committees had made for specific information with respect to the Foreign Aid Program.[32]

The Comptroller General may also be denied access, sometimes only temporarily, on the grounds that certain documents are of a strictly internal character and, therefore, do not fall within the ambit of the GAO's inquiries. The term 'temporarily' reflects the fact that often what is involved is delaying action rather than outright refusal. Still, an agency can, through procrastination, subject the GAO to a process of attrition that makes the ultimate obtaining of the information an empty victory. The Defense Department's refusal of access to Inspector General reports is an example of an agency being adamant in the position it has taken concerning documents it considers to be strictly internal.

A Budget circular has been used by agencies to fend off GAO requests for projected costs of programs. Staats, who spent much of his professional career in the Bureau of the Budget, maintains that the agencies have misunderstood or misinterpreted this circular.[33]

In other instances, agencies have relied on their interpretation of special statutory provisions applicable to them to justify refusal of GAO access.[34] Two such cases about which the Comptroller General has been very much exercised are the firm refusal of the Federal Deposit Insurance Corporation to make available the information flowing from the examinations of individual banks, and the unwillingness of the Internal Revenue Service to permit the GAO to examine the returns of individual taxpayers.

A U.S. Circuit Court of Appeals ruling, which the Supreme Court refused to review, gave a broad interpretation to the access authority granted the Comptroller General in connection with negotiated contracts. But this has not afforded a complete solution to the Comptroller General's problems with respect to obtaining information from contractors. Staats contends that much time and effort can still be lost in obtaining access to pertinent contractor records.[35] :

The proposed Budget and Accounting Improvement Act sought to strengthen the Comptroller General's position with respect to obtaining necessary information. The Bill provided for the Comptroller General bringing to the attention of a member requesting the study and also the chairman of the appropriate committee any instances in which he has been refused information or documents. The Bill contemplated that the chairman would 'endeavor to resolve the dispute with officials of the department or agency involved.' Furthermore, the Comptroller General would specify in his reports any information or documents to which he was denied access or any questions that the department or agency would not answer, and the reasons given for such action.

The Bill would vest the Comptroller General with the power to issue subpoenas 'requiring the production of negotiated contract and subcontract records and records of other non-Federal persons or organizations to which he has a right of access by law or agreement.' This provision ils responsive to Staat's recitals of the access difficulties GAO has experienced in its dealings with defense contractors. However, the wording goes beyond contractors and is applicable to other individuals and organizations that are outside the federal government. Hence, this subpoena authority would buttress the Comptroller General's capability to conduct reviews of contractual and other activities financed out of federal funds and not conducted within the regular governmental framework.

INITIATION OF GAO AUDITS

The Comptroller General reported that, during the fiscal year 1971, the GAO had issued a total of 975 audit reports, of which 173 were presented to the Congress, 287 had been submitted to committees or individual members of the Congress, and 515 had been transmitted to agencies.[36] These figures can be deceptive because of the heterogeneous character of the subject-matter covered by these reports as well as the varying types of examinations or analyses required for their preparation. The several categories of reports are explained in the discussion of GAO's reporting practices.

The outpouring of reports impels one to speculate on how the Comptroller General determines what audits should be undertaken and the relative priorities they should be accorded. The audits mandated by statute impose a relatively light burden upon the GAO. An increasingly larger proportion of the Office's audit work load consists of analyses made in response to requests of committees and individual members of Congress. The Budget and Accounting Act, 1921, had not envisaged the widespread congressional utilization of GAO. Section 312(b) of that Act provides that the Comptroller General 'shall make such investigations and reports as shall be ordered by either House of Congress or by any committee of either House having jurisdiction over revenue, appropriations, or expenditures.' But, over the years, this narrow concept of the Comptroller General's congressional constituency was abandoned in favor of making GAO's resources generally available to congressional committees and members.[37]

With Staats' assumption of the Comptroller Generalship, still greater emphasis was placed on responding to congressional requests regardless of the particular committees from which they emanated. Similarly, Staats, while stating that he was not 'looking for more business,' indicated strong receptivity to requests of individual members. His posture has been one of maximizing the assistance that GAO renders the Congress through examining and reporting on issues or problems which are referred to the Office by committees and members.

Section 204(a) of the Legislative Reorganization Act of 1970, to which reference has already been made, provides a statutory mandate for the Comptroller General to make reviews when ordered by any committee or joint committee having jurisdiction over the programs and activities that are involved. The provision, which legitimatizes what had become the prevailing practice, does not encompass requests of individual members; but it is apparent that the Comptroller General is not contemplating any change on that score. The saving grace is that many members of Congress —either because of lack of interest or unfamiliarity with the GAO—do not avail themselves of the services which the Comptroller General has so lavishly placed at their disposal.

GAO's eagnerness to respond to congressional requests is reflected in the policy of generally giving them a top priority regardless of their real merit and their relative significance as compared with audits that are initiated by the Comptroller General. The result could be disruptive of the GAO's work program. However, the Comptroller General's maintenance of close liaison with the Congress has, up to this juncture, averted the need to seriously compromise GAO's audit program in order to respond to Congressional demands. Requests from committees and members are often modified and, in some instances, even deferred or withdrawn as a result of suggestions made by GAO's representatives. Furthermore, a report that is labeled as having been initiated by a committee or member may have, in fact, been stimulated by the Comptroller General's emissaries, who might have even helped to phrase the letter requesting the particular study.

It is entirely appropriate for the Comptroller General to keep closely attuned to the informational needs and the interests of the Congress. Such rapport can afford added assurance that GAO's audit efforts will be productive. But there is an underlying issue as to what balance should be maintained between the Comptroller General's responding to congressional demands and the conduct of audits which he independently determines to be necessary to the discharge of his responsibilities.

APPROACH OF AUDITS

Implicit in the changing nature of GAO's audits is the approach they reflect. The alleged emphasis on the identification of deficiencies was for many years the underlying criticism directed at the GAO's reviews. In fact, it had been felt that the degree to which staff members were able to come up with agency shortcomings had a significant bearing upon their advancement within the organization. In the 1960s, the reports which the Comptroller General prepared on the basis of his contract audits aroused a welter of criticism by contractors and Defense Department officials. The protestations reached such a crescendo that the Military Operations Subcommittee of the House Committee on Government Operations held extensive hearings in 1965 on the audit of Defense contracts. The Subcommittee was chaired by Congressman Chet Holifield; and the hearings are, therefore, more popularly known as the Holifield Hearings.[38]

Although the criticisms were directed primarily at Defense contract audits, they had implications that extended to the totality of the GAO's audit activities, As a result, the Subcommittee's deliberations crystallized issues as to: the manner in which the GAO conducted its reviews generally, the approach reflected in its analyses, and the practices employed in reporting findings and recommendations on the basis of its audits. The outpouring of criticisms reflected pent-up resentment for which the hearings served as something of a release. The sharp and repeated strictures expressed during the hearings placed the GAO in a relatively submissive and placatory mood, particularly since matters came to a zenith just about the time Comptroller General Campbell was relinquishing his office.

The Acting Comptroller General conceded that many of the GAO audit reports had not 'included enough information about the overall aspects of the areas of operation discussed, or their size and nature, to provide an adequate perspective against which the significance of reported weaknesses could be fairly judged.' GAO undertook to effect the necessary corrective action. Another change which was promised was that the detailed comments in the reports would be presented 'in as constructive a vein as possible.' The letter to Congressman Holifield in which these commitments were made also set forth other revisions in the GAO reporting practices, all of which added up to an ostensibly marked overhauling of GAO's approach to the discharge of its audit responsibilities.[39]

However sincere the GAO executives might have been in their intention to de-emphasize the faultfinding approach, the stress on the uncovering of deficiencies was deeply inbred and resistant to significant change. Yet, there is evidenced a growing effort to view agency inadequacies in perspective and to avoid deficiency findings as the *raison d'être* of audits. The very breadth of program reviews in itself constrains a more balanced point of view. However, the GAO staff members are not unmindful of the fact that congressional and public interest in audit reports may generally be stimulated by 'the derogatory element of our reports.'

In a report on the construction program in Vietnam, GAO avoided the appearance of a carping critic by setting forth, very early in its report, the contractor accomplishments cited by the Navy and summarized some of the obstacles which the Navy said were encountered in the build-up of the construction force and the execution of major projects.[40]

The Comptroller General regularly apprises Congress in his annual report of 'collections and other measurable savings' effected by the GAO. In his 1971 Report, Staats informed the Congress that refunds of $24.9 million and other savings of $243.0 million were attributable to the work of the GAO.[41] Although supposedly reluctant to emphasize the saving aspect of GAO operations, the Comptroller General has not been completely averse to exploiting the potentialities of such figures in winning congressional goodwill, particularly when the GAO appropriation requests are under consideration. At the same time, he has cautioned against permitting GAO's audit efforts to be channeled on the basis of chalking up dollar savings figures.

REPORTING PRACTICES

A major concern of any agency or contractor undergoing review by the GAO is how the results of the review will be reported. Obviously, if the review such as that of the Economic Opportunity Program is one mandated by statute, the Comptroller General has no choice but to submit his report to the Congress. Similarly, reviews having their inception in requests by committees or individual members of the Congress culminate in reports to the initiating committee or congressman. Yet, in the case of reviews initiated by the Comptroller General, that official determines whether the report shall be submitted to the Congress or only be transmitted to the particular agency. The congressional reports, which are ordinarily blue-covered, have assumed considerable importance in the eyes of GAO staff, who are prone to look upon the production of such reports as a far more significant professional accomplishment than reports going to agencies or even the gray-covered reports that are submitted to members and committees of the Congress. In fact, the congressional report involves a morale element since personnel tend to be disappointed if reports they hope to have submitted to the Congress are 'downgraded.'

A critical issue with respect to GAO's reporting is whether a report should be issued to the Congress if the agency and the GAO are in agreement and the agency undertakes to effect the corrective action that is indicated. Agencies assert that submitting reports to Congress under these circumstances serves no constructive purpose and merely produces irritation and resentment. Referring to this line of reasoning, a GAO executive pointed out that, when an agency says it has corrected an inadequacy, it frequently has not actually dealt, or come to grips with, the basic cause or difficulty.

There apparently developed over the years a presumption in favor of reporting to the Congress. The criteria set forth in the GAO Report Manual[42] still leave considerable leeway in the exercise of judgment as to whether a congressional report will be submitted on the basis of study initiated by the Comptroller General. In some instances, the decision to prepare a congressional report may be made when the study is initially undertaken. On the other hand, developments since the inception of the project may be the determining factor.

The Far East Supply System Responsiveness Study, which was begun shortly after Staats assumed the office of Comptroller General, is an outstanding instance of GAO not submitting a formal report to Congress although the review was of far-reaching significance. In undertaking the study, the Comptroller General expressed a desire that the review be carried out insofar as practicable on a cooperative basis. The Comptroller General reassured Secretary McNamara that, aside from possibly reporting to a subcommittee of the Joint Economic Committee on improvements made in defense supply systems since his last appearance before the Subcommittee, 'there is no request from the Congress or commitment on my part to report to Congress on the present study.'

As the audit program of the GAO, following the present trend, becomes even more responsive to the interests and specific wishes of committees and members, it will be increasingly difficult for the Comptroller General to avoid reporting to the Congress upon reviews made by his Office. It is true that reports submitted to committees and individual members are in a different category from those transmitted to the Congress itself, but often the distinction may not be a meaningful one so far as an agency is concerned.

REPORTING DELAYS

Any realistic consideration of GAO audit trends would be truncated unless there were taken into account the period of time that is required from the initiation of the study until the issuance of a report. Reporting delays have bedeviled the GAO for many years. In fact, they became 'institutionalized' so that the extended lag between completion of analytical work and the availability of a finished report had become something of an accepted norm rather than a shortfall from established standards. One element in the perturbing delay in the report preparation process is the GAO policy of requesting agency comments on draft reports except those which are prepared in response to specific congressional requests and where the GAO feels that it is precluded from clearing with the agency. GAO personnel have been free to admit that the purpose of the clearance policy 'is not to be just nice to the agency but also to protect the GAO.'

This leads into the more fundamental cause of report delays, and that is what this writer has termed GAO's 'quest for infallibility.' The preparation of reports has been characterized by what appears to be almost a phobia with respect to possible errors or weaknesses that might make the report vulnerable to criticism or attack. The draft reports undergo a tortuous process of review by multiple checkpoints within the GAO. The result is an institutional product which may differ considerably from what was initially prepared by those immediately concerned with the analysis. This checking exacts a heavy price in terms of reporting delays and internal stress and strain.

Both agencies and congressional committees have been critical of the slowness of the GAO reporting process. What has saved the GAO from serious censure by Congress on this score is the fact that audits made in response to congressional requests receive top priority and hence are completed more expeditiously than reviews initiated by the Comptroller General. The usefulness of the GAO reports, whether for the guidance and assistance of those concerned with management of programs or for Congress in connection with the discharge of its oversight function, can be seriously undermined if a report is issued long after the fact. As GAO engages in more program reviews, there may be an even greater propensity for intensive checking of draft reports because of the broad scope, depth, and complexity of the subject-matter encompassed by such reviews. The present Comptroller General has recognized what a formidable obstacle the present reporting situation can be to effective utilization of GAO's resources. It is very significant that one of the purposes which Staats sought to achieve through the GAO reorganization effected in 1972 was that of accelerating the report production process.

IMPACT OF INTERNAL AUDITS UPON GAO REVIEWS

The Budget and Accounting Procedures Act of 1950 clearly envisaged that the Comptroller General would, insofar as practicable, consider 'internal audit and control' as complementary to his own reviews. The Act mandates establishment of 'appropriate internal audit within agencies.' At least equally significant has been the strong and continuing pressure by the House Committee on Government Operations, which has been very supportive of GAO's efforts for the establishment of agency internal audit units. The Committee, following through on recommendations made by Comptroller General Campbell, formulated specifications for internal audit operations. Prodded by Congressman Jack Brooks, the GAO undertook reviews of the internal audit activities in each of the major government agencies. The GAO enunciated a broad role for internal audit and stated that its scope of operations should not be restricted to accounting and fiscal matters.

Apropos of the coordination of internal audits and its own reviews, the GAO states that it does 'give particular consideration to the internal audit work which has been done in the areas under audit. To the extent feasible, we utilize the internal audit work rather than performing work directly ourselves.'

Even if one assumes that the GAO has been doing its utmost to make maximum utilization of internal audit efforts, this does not afford adequate assurance that there is an optimal integration between GAO reviews and internal evaluations. The internal audit units, as GAO itself has ascertained, are not always envisaged by their respective agencies as having very broad areas of concern. Internal audits may not get into substantive program areas and, therefore, not be equipped to make significant contributions to the program type of review to which the GAO is giving increasing emphasis. The GAO is faced with the problem of establishing firmer relations with internal evaluation units of agencies that do not carry the internal audit label. This can involve delicate problems of relationship; these units may be closely tied in with the top administrative and decision-making processes, and there may be reluctance to make full disclosure of these analyses to the GAO.

The GAO has become more circumspect as to its role in program reviews. In a letter addressed in the summer of 1972 to Congressional Committee Chairman, the Comptroller General expressed the view that 'program evaluation is a fundamental part of effective program administration' and that the responsibility for such evaluations rests initially upon the respective agencies. Staats urged that 'the Congress give careful consideration in authorizing new programs, or in reauthorizing existing programs, to including in the authorizing legislation specific statutory requirements for a systematic evaluation by the department or agency involved of the results of programs in operation.'[43]

GAO'S CHANGING PERSONNEL NEEDS

Reference has already been made to the ascendancy of the trained accountant as GAO auditing work assumed a true professional quality. As previously intimated, those not familiar with the range of subject-matter encompassed by GAO reports might be misled by the use of the term 'audit' to describe the GAO reviews.

Accounting expertise may appear to be the sole skill essential to the effective discharge of the Comptroller General's audit responsibilities. However, there is increasing awareness within the GAO that accounting talent by itself no longer suffices to meet the needs of the GAO's audit program, which has gone so deeply into the evaluation of managerial efficiency and program effectiveness. But, even with the broader type of review, the usefulness of accounting as an analytical tool should not be minimized, particularly as the horizons of the profession expand and as there is attendant rethinking of the training for this field. Furthermore, there are particular facets of the GAO's audit program such as financial examinations of government corporations, contract reviews, and audits of in-house industrial activities that require accounting skill.

But it will not suffice for the GAO to recruit specialists from such areas as economics, systems analysis, statistics, and computer science. It will have to be on the alert to assure that the talents of the non-accountants are utilized effectively and that these individuals are afforded adequate career opportunities within the GAO. Effecting a blend between persons coming from these varied disciplines and the accountants who presently occupy a predominant role poses problems requiring perceptive leadership.

The capability to perform program reviews in depth will necessitate having specialists in functional areas such as defense, education, health, and housing. Furthermore, the GAO cannot rely exclusively on technical or analytical talent in performing program reviews but must have on its staff persons who have had actual experience at relatively high levels in program formulation and administration.

GAO can, of course, supplement its in-house personnel resources through the use of consultants and contractors. The OEO study was an example of extensive resort to outside talent. However, there cannot be excessive dependence upon the availability of the outside expert lest the Comptroller General become more of a 'broker' for the mobilization of talents for conducting a review rather than being the instrumentality really responsible for the ultimate findings and recommendations.

INTERACTION BETWEEN GAO AUDITS
AND ITS OTHER RESPONSIBILITIES

One cannot rigidly compartmentalize the GAO's activities and view its audit work entirely apart from other facets of the GAO's operations. Unlike such countries as Britain, in which the central monitoring agency functions entirely through the medium of audits, the GAO has other responsibilities and powers which inevitably interact with the audit function. One needs to recognize that an auditor who can exercise significant authority over the agency he audits is functioning in a frame of reference that sets him apart from his counterparts in other countries whose tasks are confined entirely to the post-audit function. Trends in the conceptualization and implementation of the GAO's audit role should be viewed against the backdrop of the authority vested in the Comptroller General to intervene directly in the day-to-day management of government programs. The essentiality of relating the audit activities to the totality of GAO functions is underlined by congressional action, either already effected or under active consideration, to expand still further the Comptroller General's powers.

The Comptroller General's authority to settle the accounts of accountable officers, which settlements are final and conclusive upon the executive branch, gives the Comptroller General a sanction which makes his activities more than the ascertaining and disclosure of facts. Staats has made significant strides in shifting much of the settlement work over to agencies, but he has been careful to still retain the ultimate authority to make disallowances. Hence, an agency being reviewed by the GAO cannot be unmindful of the fact that such review could bring to light items to which the GAO may take exception in settlement of accounts.

The original draft of the Budget and Accounting Improvement Act of 1970 (S. 4432) would have eliminated the Comptroller General's dependence upon the Department of Justice for litigating claims against accountable officers and payees arising from the GAO's settlement of accounts. The Comptroller General would have been authorized to institute civil proceedings and be represented by counsel he designated for this purpose. This provision, which was subsequently deleted, had the full support of the

Comptroller General. There is some incompatibility between giving the GAO this additional muscle and establishing Comptroller General-agency rapport that is optimal from the standpoint of not only facilitating in-depth reviews but also gaining agency receptivity to findings and recommendations.

In the background of the control which the Comptroller General exercises with respect to the executive branch is the authority vested in him to rule on questions which accountable officers or department heads present to him with respect to expenditures for which they are responsible. The law provides that these decisions shall govern the GAO in passing upon the account containing the disbursement in question. The Comptrollers General have been prone to be assertive, if not aggressive, as to the area encompassed by their decision-rendering authority and as to the legal standing of such decisions.

The range of subjects covered by these rulings run the gamut from decisions on highly specialized matters, including many of relatively limited significance, to those having important policy implications. The Comptrollers General either overtly or tacitly have claimed that their decisions are 'final and conclusive upon the Executive Branch,' although this statutory wording relates to account settlements rather than decisions. The law clearly stipulates that decisions shall be responsive to questions raised by accountable officers and department heads. Yet the Comptroller General has recognized a broader constituency for these rulings so that the first ruling with respect to the landmark Philadelphia Plan was submitted to a member of Congress and the final ruling —although addressed to the Secretary of Labor—was never requested by that official, who denounced it roundly.

The issue as to the compatibility between the Comptroller General's role as auditor in the broadest sense of that term and the authority vested in him vis-à-vis executive agencies is underlined by the provision in the proposed Budget and Accounting Improvement Act authorizing the Comptroller General to institute civil actions for declaratory and injunctive relief whenever, in the performance of his statutory functions, he 'has reasonable cause to believe that any officer or employee of the executive branch is about to expend, obligate, or authorize the expenditure or obligations of public funds in an illegal or erroneous manner or amount.' The Attorney General would be authorized to represent the defendant in such action if he certifies that he is in disagreement with the Comptroller General. This provision not only has the blessing of the Comptroller General but reflects a suggestion made by President Nixon at the time he injected himself into the Philadelphia Plan controversy, i.e., 'to permit court review of any differences between the Comptroller General and those of the Executive and to permit the Comptroller General to have his own counsel (rather than the Attorney General) to represent him in such cases.' Before the Bill got out of the Senate, this proposed grant of authority was circumscribed by the addition of a provision that no such actions could be instituted by the Comptroller General until the expiration of sixty calendar days following the date in which the Comptroller General has furnished the House and Senate Government Operations Committees explanations of the circumstances giving rise to the actions contemplated by him. During this sixty-day period, the action proposed by the Comptroller General could be stopped by a concurrent resolution.

Although, as the Senate Committee intimated, the authority proposed by it would probably be invoked infrequently, this would be a significant addition to the aggregate of power vested in the Comptroller General and would place him in an even more strategic position to control Executive Branch operations. The possibility of finding himself a defendant in judicial proceedings initiated by the Comptroller General might impel an official to regard GAO reviews of his agency with a jaundiced eye and even suspicion.

The Comptroller General's responsibility for approving the accounting systems of executive agencies is still another factor that distinguishes him from monitoring agencies whose sole concern is that of conducting audits. The expansion of GAO's audit activities may reopen the question as to whether the approval of accounting systems of executive agencies should not be a responsibility of the executive branch. One can reasonably contend that the demands imposed by the more broadly conceived audit responsibilties of the GAO are such as to make it highly desirable, if not essential, that the GAO shed those tasks that are clearly not indispensable to its effective functioning. Also, it could be argued that the Comptroller General might make a better contribution to the improvement of agency accounting systems if he dealt with this aspect of financial management entirely through his review activities. For that matter, the Comptroller General, in seeking to simplify the process for approval of accounting systems, has placed greater emphasis upon evaluations made when agencies are audited.

The 1970 statute[44] establishing the Cost-Accounting Standards Board has drawn the Comptroller General—despite his initial protestations—still more deeply into executive branch operations and has saddled him with a responsibility clearly at odds with the task of monitoring agency performance. This Board, which legally is separate from the GAO, is responsible for promulgating cost-accounting standards 'designed to achieve uniformity and consistency in the cost-accounting principles followed by defense contractors and subcontractors under Federal contracts.' It patently has vital implications for the procurement activities of departments and other executive establishments—an aspect that was pointed out by President Nixon at the time the legislation was submitted for his action. Yet the Board was not only made independent of the executive branch but consists of the Comptroller General as chairman and four members appointed by him. The commingling of audit and operational responsibilities cannot but impair the type of arms-length, objective relationships that should characterize the frame of reference within which the Comptroller General's reviews are conducted.

Congressional proclivity for dumping responsibility upon the GAO regardless of their relevance to the fundamental mission of the government's central monitoring agency is evidenced in the important role which the Office was given in the administration of the recently enacted federal election laws.[45] The Office's enforcement activities in connection with the Federal Election Campaign Act of 1971 gave it unwonted publicity of a headline nature and did much to dispel—at least temporarily—the anonymity that has more typically characterized GAO operations. The fact that these new tasks made for much greater public awareness of the Office does not dispose of questions as to the propriety of vesting them in the Comptroller General.

GAO POSTURE VIS-À-VIS AGENCIES AND THE CONGRESS

The Legislative Reorganization Act of 1970 manifestly affords the GAO a sounder statutory basis for the program reviews which the

Comptroller General had espoused with such zeal. The Act also increases the pressure upon agencies to give appropriate consideration to GAO reports since it requires each agency to report to the House and Senate Government Operations and Appropriations Committees on the action it has taken with respect to any recommendations which the GAO makes, in its report, to the head of the agency (Sec. 236). Such expressions of congressional confidence and support are helpful, but they do not obviate the need for the GAO to be most judicious in its dealings with agencies, particularly as it penetrates more deeply into programs of a technical, specialized, or professional nature. For many agencies and even members of Congress, the GAO still has the image of the financial auditor, and this engenders skepticism as to its competence to conduct reviews having the breadth and depth which the GAO is increasingly seeking to achieve.

A NASA official questioned the tenability of GAO attempting to evaluate management decisions with respect to his program on the basis of a documentary study made through the audit approach: 'Sure as hell, the GAO's staff are not engineers or scientists. . . . I do not object to them one damn bit as auditors.' More recently, Deputy Secretary of Defense Packard, referring to problems in connection with Defense procurement, remarked: 'Nor will it help to put the General Accounting Office in the process of making management decisions. The GAO deserves the highest marks for auditing, but the talents of a good auditor are not identical with those of a good manager.'

One can discount, but not dismiss in their entirety, such reactions as reflecting the defensive attitude which an organization is prone to manifest toward any independent evaluator of its operations or programs. At the same time, the Comptroller General must aproach the more broadly conceived audit function with restraint, tact, and a realistic appraisal of GAO's own capabilities. The multidisciplinary approach which Staats is developing should make for a better dialogue between the GAO and agencies and evoke greater confidence in the Office's capacity to respond effectively to the demands created by far-reaching program reviews.

The present thrust of GAO's audit efforts, with its emphasis on responsiveness to the Congress, raises a crucial question as to the extent to which the Comptroller General should be deemed to have an overriding responsibility to the public that transcends his obligations to the Congress. The usefulness of the government's 'watchdog' as an instrumentality for protecting the public interest through effective accountability can be seriously attenuated if the allocation of its audit resources is unduly dependent upon congressional wishes. In his eagerness to be of the fullest assistance to the Congress, the Comptroller General may unduly circumscribe his own freedom of action to determine what audits should be made and the priorities to be accorded them. There is patently a need for balancing GAO's utility as a congressional resource with the independence which a central monitoring agency should have to initiate audits and schedule their completion.

Notes

1. American Institute of Certified Public Accountants, *Codification of Statements on Auditing Procedures* (1962) p. 11.
2. United States General Accounting Office, *Comprehensive Audit Manual*, Part 1, pp. 1–2.
3. Ibid., pp. 2–9.
4. House, Committee on Appropriations, Hearings before Subcommittee, *Legislative Branch Appropriations for 1970*, 90th Congress, 2nd Session, 1969, p. 533.
5. Senate, Committee on Government Operations, Hearings before the Subcommittee on Executive Organization, *Capability of GAO to Analyze and Audit Defense Expenditures*, 91st Cong., 1st Sess., 1969, pp. 33–4.
6. House, House Committee on Rules, *Report of the House Committee on Rules on H.R. 17654*, 91st Cong., 2nd Sess., 1970, p. 82.
7. Hearings on *Capability of GAO to Analyze and Audit Defense Expenditures*, op. cit., p. 21.
8. Ibid., p. 7.
9. *1969 Annual Report of the Comptroller General* states that 469 reports on legislative proposals were submitted during the fiscal year 1969.
10. Iibd., pp. 32–3.
11. Hearings on *Capability of GAO to Analyze and Audit Defense Expenditures*, op. cit., p. 21.
12. Ibid.
13. See S.1022, 92nd Cong., 1st Sess. (1971). The same bill had been previously introduced as S.4432, 91st Cong., 2nd Sess., 1970.
14. Senate Report No. 91–1264, 91st Cong., 2nd Sess., 1970, p. 8.
15. Legislative Reorganization Act of 1970, Section 321.
16. *Report of the House Committee on Rules on H.R. 17654*, op. cit., p. 18.
17. Report of Comptroller General of the United States, *Review of Economic Opportunity Programs*, B-130515 (March 18, 1969).

18. House, Committee on Appropriations Report, *Legislative Branch Appropriations Bill, 1969,* 90th Congr., 2nd Sess., p. 18.

19. House, Committee on Appropriations Report, *Legislative Branch Appropriations Bill, 1970,* 91st Cong., 1st Sess., 1969, p. 31.

20. See House, Committee on Appropriations, Hearings before Sub-committee, *Legislative Branch Appropriations for 1970,* op. cit., p. 566.

21. Report of Comptroller General of the United States, *Examination into the Effectiveness of the Construction Grant Program for Abating, Controlling, and Preventing Water Pollution,* B-166506 (Nov. 3, 1969).

22. Report of Comptroller General of the United States, *Status of the Acquisition of Major Weapon Systems,* B-163058 (Feb. 6, 1970). See also the reports dated March 18, 1971 and July 17, 1972.

23. Report of Comptroller General of the United States, *Feasibility of Applying Uniform Cost-Accounting Standards to Negotiated Defense Contracts,* B-39995(1) (Jan. 19, 1970).

24. B-149372 and B-158195, Nov. 16, 1970.

25. *Budgeting for National Objectives* (New York: Committee for Economic Development, 1966) p. 56.

26. See Joint Financial Management Improvement Program, *Annual Report Fiscal Year 1967,* p. 79.

27. Memorandum from Director, Office of Policy and Special Studies to the Directors of the Civil, Defense, and International Divisions, Aug. 2, 1968.

28. House, Committee on Government Operations, Hearings before Inter-governmental Relations Subcommittee, *Grant Consolidation and Inter-governmental Cooperation,* 91st Cong., 1st Sess., 1970, Part 2, p. 275.

29. Comptroller General of the United States, *Standards for Audit of Governmental Organizations, Programs, Activities and Functions* (1972).

30. State and Local Fiscal Assistance Act of 1972. PL 92–512 Sec. 123(C).

31. See Staat's testimony on GAO access problem. Hearings on *Capability of GAO to Analyze and Audit Defense Expenditures,* op. cit., p. 35. The Comptroller General's 1971 Annual Report discusses GAO's 'increased difficulty in obtaining access to information and documents needed to carry out its responsibilities, principally in relation to international matters,' p. 13.

32. The 1971 dispute impelled the Chairman of the Senate Foreign Relations Committee to request the GAO that it compile a list of recent access denials encountered in making audits of foreign operations and assistance programs. See letter from Acting Comptroller General R. F. Keller to Senator J. W. Fulbright, Sept. 10, 1971.

33. Budget Bureau Circular A-10 (Revised 1–18–64).

34. Hearings on *Capability of GAO to Analyze and Audit Defense Expenditures,* op. cit., p. 35.

35. Ibid., p. 36.

36. *1971 Annual Report of the Comptroller General,* p. 5.

37. *Hearings before the Joint Committee on the Organization of the Congress,* 89th Cong., 1st Sess., 1965, Part 9, p. 1364.

38. House, Committee on Government Operations, Hearings before Sub-

committee, *Comptroller General Reports to Congress on Audits of Defense Contracts*, 89th Cong., 1st Sess., 1965.

39. House, Committee on Government Operations, Twenty-Fourth Report by the Committee on Government Operations, *Defense Contract Audits*, 89th Cong., 2nd Sess., 1966.

40. Report of Comptroller General of the United States, *United States Construction Activities in the Republic of Viet Nam*, B-159451 (May 15, 1967), p. 13.

41. Comptroller General of the United States, *Appendix to the 1971 Annual Report*, p. 144.

42. General Accounting Office, *Report Manual*, p. 1.

43. Letter from Comptroller General Elmer B. Staats to congressional committee chairmen, Aug. 11, 1972.

44. Public Law 97-379.

45. Public Law 92-178 and Public Law 92-225.

11   The Politics of Auditing

IRA SHARKANSKY

INTRODUCTION

The auditor is a little-known actor with great importance in the American political system. To journalists and political scientists —and thus to much of the population—the auditor arouses far less interest than members of the legislature, heads of administrative agencies, the chief executive and his staff, candidates for public office, and functionaries of the major political parties. Only a small handfull of political science scholarship or auditing has appeared since 1939.[1] Among the great functions in the political process, auditing is the least well-known among the scholars who specialize in government and politics. Senator William Proxmire has written about the principal audit unit of the United States government: 'Few people have heard of the General Accounting Office. Few know what it does. Fewer still know that it is an arm of the United States Congress.'[2]

The range of the auditor's work and his impact on other parts of the political process depends on how broadly he defines his task. There is much dispute about the breadth of this task among auditors themselves and other actors in the political system. At one extreme, some advocates urge that auditors limit themselves to reviewing and certifying the reliability of the financial accounts that are compiled by administrative departments. To the extent that the auditor remains within this sphere he deserves little more attention than he has received since 1939. Yet, at another extreme, some would have the auditor perform important tasks in the expenditure process, program planning, evaluation, and implementation. One's view of the auditing function varies with both intellectual perspective and political interest. Some of the grand issues of political theory are relevant to the definition of the auditor's role. Also relevant are one's expectations about what the auditor would do—if he had the authority—about certain programs of current interest. The likelihood of the auditor goring a favored ox has much to do with the authority that one prefers to assign his office.

What powers of the auditor put him in contention with the great actors in American politics? His clout comes from a central position in the expenditure process. But although it starts with money, his status goes from there to many features of program evaluation that are tied only indirectly to financial issues.

The most elementary feature of the auditor's work in the United States government is the verification that expenditures are made within the scope of existing legislation. Typically this occurs a long time after the legislative and executive branch have passed upon a program, and even after the working administrators have begun to operate. Despite the lateness of his entry, the auditor can throw a large monkey wrench into a program's machinery. Without his approval the Treasury will not pay for goods ordered or services rendered. With no payments forthcoming, any subsequent operations are unlikely. The importance of this function, of course, is that it allow the auditor to determine just what kinds of activities are within—and outside—the realm of current statutes. This is not always a simple task. Administrators often develop programs that differ in detail from those described in the statutes. Various statutes may apply to the same program, and some inconsistencies may appear in their language. For clues to legislative 'intent,' an auditor may go beneath formal enactments to debates on the floor of Congress or to statements in committee hearings or committee *Reports*. This kind of a search increases the alternative standards open to the auditor and broadens his discretion with respect to the activities he will allow. When an auditor says a department cannot operate in a certain way, he may be charged with usurping the powers assigned by the Constitution to other branches of government. When this charge is made—and we shall see it below in connection with programs of significant importance—we know that the auditor has become a major actor.

When auditors move out from a narrow consideration of the 'legality' of expenditures to a consideration of their 'efficiency,' there opens additional opportunities for involvement in policymaking. Auditors in the national government do not have the authority to stop expenditure they find to be inefficient. Yet they do inform administrators, Congress and the Press about major inefficiencies they find, and thus become a persuasive force that program administrators must recognize. Moreover, along the way to judging the efficiency of expenditures the auditor acquires the skills and information of a systems analyst; these provide him with other powers. On the basis of his own systems analysis, the auditor may quarrel with the decisions made in the executive branch about the activities that will accomplish certain goals for certain costs and under certain conditions. When the auditor can take this kind of a posture, he is a long way from the accountant's green eyeshade and into the thick of program debate.

With the skills of a systems analyst, an auditor may define the standards of program accomplishment that become fixed in the decision-processes of the executive or legislative branches. These standards of accomplishment identify which projects are producing more or less of the desired output. When it is time to assign funds for the next go-around of program implementation (and that time is always imminent in a government that works on an annual budget cycle) the personnel who set the standards for evaluating earlier activities may have a telling impact on subsequent funding.

Systems analysis has increasing importance in a government that operates complex programs that require escalation in stages from program *conception* to *research and development*, to *production*, *operations*, and *reassessment*. At each stage there are opportunities for reassessment that allows the systems analyst to have an influence on the 'go,' 'no go,' or 'how much' decisions. The General Accounting Office has acquired systems analysts within its own staff and is willing to employ outside consultants for special tasks. To the extent that legislators see themselves in need of an 'in-house' expert who can help them cope with the details of proposals that come from the executive branch, the auditor will enjoy an escalation of his significance.

The role of the auditor in the national government is not without its problems. With power over the ingredients of public programs comes criticism and attack from competing centers of power. It is unnecessary to elaborate that it is easy to enter the political fray and compete for power, but difficult for any one unit to prevail in imposing its wishes on others. The principles of separation of powers and checks and balances warrant some attention in this discussion of auditing: they remind us that competition and conflict are major ingredients in our governmental process, and that an 'uppity' auditor is likely to find numerous antagonists who wish he would stay with the high desk and green eyeshade of the accountant. Before we can understand how the auditor got where he is, or his opportunities for further development, we must view him in the context of other factors.

This essay explores the function of auditing in the national government as conducted by the General Accounting Office (GAO). It is not a final statement on the topic. It is written with the hope of making the topic interesting to political scientists and outlining some features of auditing that political scientists might study with profit. As we shall see below, auditing seems to be entering a phase of role expansion. The auditing agency is doing more than ever before that pertains to program evaluation and program planning. As expected, this expansion of its role is placing the auditor into sharp conflict with other actors. The auditor's status is thus subject to both increasing prominence and dramatic change. It is the best time since 1939 for political scientists to look at auditing in the national government.

We start by examining the numerous elements of the auditor's job. As we have seen already, this job has many components and the choice of those which are 'proper' is a subject of endless dispute. To help us understand the dispute insofar as it has raged to the present, we next consider the political environment that surrounds the GAO. Finally, we explore the opportunities, problems and prospects of the GAO in light of its political surroundings. One of the major impressions that comes to an outsider is that the GAO is a dynamic organization. Its current status and its immediate future appear to be more flexible than at any other time in its history If we can understand this flexibility—even if we cannot predict accurately the outcome—then we may understand better how programs are designed, selected and implemented in the national government.

THE AMBIGUOUS NATURE OF THE AUDITOR'S JOB

In order to understand why the role of the GAO is currently in a state of flux, it is necessary to explore the ambiguities in the nature of government auditing. The auditor's job is different things to different people. Because the outlines of the job are not clear, they provide the basis for expansion. The auditor can enlarge his participation in program evaluation and modification without departing from the boundaries that some actors assign to his task.

There are several features that feed the ambiguity of the auditor's job. 'Auditing' is not a term that conjures up a clear meaning. For many people, auditing centers on the assessment of accuracy in the financial statements assembled by administrative agencies about their own operations. This is related to the processes of 'administrative control,' 'oversight,' and 'accountability.' The outer boundaries of these concepts, however, range far beyond the verification of financial accounts. The GAO has the power to stop expenditures it holds to be 'illegal.' This power departs from the most simple conceptions of auditing. Yet it is not so different or inconsistent with 'administrative control' that it is widely considered to be an improper acquisition for the government's auditor. Another source of ambiguity comes from the expanding conception of government. From the perspective of the GAO, the outer borders of the 'national government' include the numerous business firms, social agencies and universities that receive public funds on a contract basis, plus agencies of state and local governments, plus international organizations that receive United States grants or loans. The Comptroller General has listed eight categories of 'external organizations' that should be considered within the 'accountability system.'

1. Private enterprise.
2. Not-for-profit organizations.
3. Universities.
4. Government-sponsored research centers.
5. Mixed Government-private organizations (COMSAT or Corporation for Public Broadcasting, etc.).
6. State and local governments.
7. International organizations.
8. Quasi-independent corporations (TVA, FNMA, Port of New York Authority, etc.).[3]

One figure is that $71.5 billion in federal money was allocated to state and local governments and government contractors during fiscal 1968.[4] Additional funds go to the United Nations and other international organizations, and to governments that participate in bilateral agreements with the United States to receive financial and technical assistance. Each of these activities provides some access of GAO auditors to the records—and perhaps the decision-making processes—of the recipients. Yet the Comptroller General recognizes the ambiguity of his own boundaries. In reference to international organizations, he has written: 'We must start by recognizing that membership in international organizations presumes a willingness on the part of member nations to rely heavily upon the management of these organizations, an agreement which severely limits action that can be taken unilaterally.'[5] The Comptroller General also sees a difference in the authority of his auditors within the agencies of the national government, and within the agencies of state and local governments. The respect for federalism, with its implications for state and local discretion, appear in the GAO as it does elsewhere in the legislative branch. With the onset of 'revenue-sharing' and its increased respect for state and local discretion, there may be new problems in defining what GAO auditors should do in the states.[6]

Some boundary problems of the GAO concern its own proper functions as opposed to those of competing units. The GAO is a creature of the legislative branch. The Comptroller General is appointed by the President, but makes his reports to the presiding officers of the House and Senate. Within the limits of his fifteen-year term, he is subject to removal only by joint resolution of the Congress. Yet Congress has other instruments to assist the members in their supervision and control of the administration: the professional staffs of the committees and the staffs of individual Senators and Representatives; personnel of administrative agencies who are 'loaned' to the committees to bolster their own staffs; and the Congressional Research Service (formerly the Legislative Reference Service) of the Library of Congress. The activities of the General Accounting Office overlap with the work of each oversight institution. There is considerable dispute that some of the functions assumed by the GAO belong more properly in the exclusive domain of other units. Although 'auditing,' 'accountability,' and 'oversight' are loose and ambiguous concepts, there are some who allege that 'real auditing' does not include some of the accountability and control functions that should be left to congressional committees or to the Congressional Research Service.

The Comptroller General defines three types of accountability: (1) *fiscal* accountability that focuses on the quality of accounting practices maintained by the operating agencies; (2) *management* accountability that inquires into the efficiency with which resources are used; and (3) *program* accountability that deals with the effectiveness of program operations. Fiscal accountability is the most traditional of GAO concerns and program accountability represents its frontier. The program audit asks whether—and how well—administrative activities are accomplishing their stated objectives. It may ask whether alternative procedures would improve the present rates of accomplishment.[7] How far the frontier of program auditing will expand—perhaps to include the assessment and original design of programs to accomplish major social goals—is currently the subject of dispute among those who would expand and those who would constrain the activities of the GAO.

The three types of accountability mentioned by the Comptroller General are less controversial in themselves than in the operations they may support. It is not so much the GAO's involvement with fiscal management or program analysis that is upsetting, as the tasks the GAO does—or might do—in relation to particular programs that have their own constituencies of legislators, administrators, and citizens. Again it is the question of who's ox and how much is he gored?

The following list portrays the range of operations that are included in—and related to—various conceptions of auditing. It is arranged from the narrowest to the most inclusive set of activities. It parallels the three types of accountability cited by the Comptroller General. The move from 'fiscal' to 'management' and 'program' accountability involves increasing emphasis on the operations at the far end of this scale. This array also coincides with the range of antagonists aroused by each activity. The broader the function—and the more it differs from the narrowest meaning of 'fiscal audit'—the more actors feel that the auditor is stepping over his proper function.

1. Verifying financial reports made by administrative units;
2. approving the accounting procedures used by administrative units;
3. identifying expenditures that exceed or lie outside of statutory authorizations;

4. preventing payments for illegal purchases or pursuing repayment to the Treasury of payments made for illegal purchases;
5. assessing administrative accomplishments of program goals;
6. defining of program goals for purposes of systems analysis and assessment of accomplishments;
7. advising legislature about administrative program accomplishments as part of the legislature's concern with program review, reauthorization and reappropriation;
8. advising the legislature with respect to initial program planning;
9. assuming broad responsibility to report to the legislature and the public with respect to the 'social accountability' of government programs.

While these functions differ in the controversy they arouse, there are no clear lines of demarcation between functions. The skills required for each function are related. One feeds off the other. It is difficult to argue that a government unit that has acquired the resources necessary for one of these functions should be halted from exploiting its resources for others. It is a case of the auditor having 'surplus capital.' He could limit himself to a simple financial review, but the kind of review he is expected to perform brings him close to the status of a systems analysis. Why should he avoid the larger assignments in a legislative arena where sophisticated information is highly prized and in short supply?

Functions 1–4 are squarely within the traditional activities of the GAO. To some observers, however function 4 (preventing or recouping improper payments) compromises the proper role of the auditor. From this point of view, auditing is rightly limited to the *disclosure* of financial activity. When the auditor has the authority to curtail certain financial practices, administrative agencies have an incentive to be less than candid in their dealings with the auditor

With the possible exception of function 1 (verifying financial reports), each of these 'traditional' roles of the General Accounting Office (i.e., roles 1–4) provide some opportunity to affect the design or modification of programs. By means of its control over departmental accounting procedures (2), the GAO can shape the information that is given prominence in the financial records of each unit. Accounting records can highlight or submerge various kinds of financial data. They may be coupled with data on agency workload and service production. The records can be bland with respect to the statutory goals of an agency, or formulated in a way to emphasize items of controversy. Insofar as agency accounts play a role in the review of accomplishments and subsequent appropriations for each program, they can affect the design and modification of agency operations. For the most part, government auditors seem to pass up the opportunity to affect program assessments by the kinds of accounting procedures they approve. Yet this does not lessen the potential of their function.

Operations 5 through 7 (the assessment of existing programs) represent the current frontier of auditing activities for the GAO. For many years, GAO reports have dealt with agency purchases and procedures that are 'legal' (and so escape any immediate threat of nonpayment), but 'inefficient.' Items uncovered in this category include: duplication of efforts by different programs; the use of commodities which have lower initial cost but costly maintenance and a lesser life-span than competing products; inefficient use of skilled personnel; the failure of agencies to buy in bulk; and the failure of administrators to enforce in a stringent manner the obligations of contractors. This work is on the 'frontier' of GAO activities, however, because efforts in this direction have recently escalated in scope and increased in their command of GAO resources.

By expressing GAO's historic concern with the 'efficiency' of government operations in terms familiar to a systems analyst (i.e., 'goal accomplishment'), we can emphasize the small step involved in the extension of this effort to other functions assumed by the systems analyst. Once an auditor seeks to define the efficiency of an activity, he must first decide what the activity is designed to produce. This is not easy at the level of multi-goal complexity that marks all but the simplest of federal programs. If the auditor has aspirations of measuring in precise—rather than judging in general—terms the efficiency of operations, he has further opportunities to exercise his judgment. He must choose from among numerous program goals those he will measure and use as the standards for his quantitative analysis. He must also select the indices that will measure goal accomplishment. For some programs, the auditor may attempt to sort out the impact on a target population from the clients' experiences with other government programs and their experiences in the private sector. How much of students' learning comes from each of the many programs in a school, for example, or from their out-of-school contacts with parents, friends, books, and the mass media? With the need to be creative in his analyses comes further opportunities for the auditor to imprint his own work on procedures that shape program activities.[8]

It is only a small step in terms of GAO activities, and no step at all in terms of its technology, to move from an assessment of efficiency in goal accomplishment to providing this information in a way the legislature can use it in formulating reauthorization or reappropriation for an existing program. The step from functions 5 and 6 to function 7 may only be a matter of timing on the part of GAO or perceptiveness on the part of legislators. Yet program advice (7) opens the GAO to more controversy than does its lesser functions. According to one view, the auditor loses his credibility for reports about the legality or efficiency of expenditures if he had earlier identified himself with program design. The GAO itself is aware of the possible conflict, and does not wish to compromise its credibility in the narrower range of auditing by taking too prominent a role in program design:

> The GAO does not have the authority nor should it seek to become a congressional Bureau of the Budget with responsibility for the review of departmental appropriation request; i.e., to assess the needs for particular funding levels based upon program needs or the priorities among different programs. . . .
>
> We believe that as a general proposition, the GAO should refrain from making recommendations for the adoption of a particular program or policy under legislative consideration, in view of its responsibility for subsequent independent reviews of the implementation of programs which may be authorized.[9]

Despite this disclaimer by the Comptroller General, the *Annual Report of the General Accounting Office* for 1971 includes a section entitled 'Reports on Pending Legislation':

> The GAO professional staff is well acquainted with the programs and activities of most Government agencies through on-site review and observation of agency operations. Consequently, the Office can provide the committee with independent advice

and information on proposed legislation; often there may be no other available source for such well-informed comment. During the past year GAO responded to 632 committee requests for comments on bills. The significant increase from 438 such reports in fiscal year 1970 is a measure of the increasing congressional reliance on GAO's legislative analysis expertise.[10]

The point where the role of the auditor may broaden appreciably comes in relation to functions 8 and 9. Function 8 (advice on initial program design) is already operational in GAO. Function 9 (supervision of social accountability) is the open-ended item that represents the possible (perhaps improbable) future of GAO. 'Social accountability' refers to activities that 'inspire general confidence and serve what (are) widely regarded as desirable social ends.'[11] An auditor who employs this standard has a broad mission in the policy-making process. The skills of the systems analyst can be coupled with the tools of survey research to provide a continuing reading of public wants. Technologically, it is small from program auditing to the establishment of continuing referenda. Private researchers have developed the basic arts. Why not bring it into government and assign the responsibility to a body that is already protected from too direct control by the chief executive or individual members of the legislature? The work could feed back into long established programs of the GAO. Instead of selecting for itself the goals of on-going programs that are tested for the efficiency of their outputs, why not survey the population to see which of a program's numerous goals are to be considered? This is not an advocacy of a desirable enlargement of GAO's functions. It is, rather, an illustration of the thin border that surrounds the notion of 'auditing,' or rather separates one function of the auditor from others that he might acquire. The term 'auditing' is not precise. Like other features of the political process, it can be expanded when the advocates have enough votes in the appropriate decision-making arena.

The GAO has acquired some functions that stretch the Comptroller General's notions of fiscal, management, or program accountability, or any item on the longer list of nine operations just reviewed. The GAO received several assignments as part of the Federal Election Campaign Act of 1971 and the Presidential Election Campaign Fund Act that suggest a congressional view of a reliable aide, useful in matters considerably removed from the supervision of the Administration's expenditures and program activities. Under these Acts, the GAO is empowered to prescribe regulations dealing with the use of communications media in campaigns for federal elective office; to serve as a clearing house for information on the administration of elections; to award contracts for special studies of elections; to prescribe regulations and to supervise the recording of contributions and expenditures for Presidential campaigns; and to administer the program whereby taxpayers can designate $1 of their federal tax payment for a political party.[12]

THE POLITICAL ENVIRONMENT OF THE GAO

No important actor in the national government of the United States exists in a benign environment. Perhaps nowhere in the world is there a guarantee of smooth, pleasant relations for a government official who is charged with making decisions that will please some and be a source of discomfort to others. In the United States we have taken special steps to insure difficult surroundings for officials charged with important tasks. Framers of the Constitution established a mode of government self-protected against undue expansion of its powers. They separated its institutions into executive, legislative, and judicial branches, and gave to each certain powers over the others. 'Separation of powers' and 'checks and balances' are simple labels memorized by generations of school children. What they represent, however, is anything but simple: different elections for the chief executive and members of the legislature; life tenure for judges; a bicameral legislature; provisions for an executive veto and legislative review of the veto; elaborate—if seldom used—procedures for impeachment; and constitutional enumerations of certain powers that are granted and others that are denied to the national government. James Madison summarized the case for this kind of government in an often-quoted passage of Federalist 51: '. . . the great security against a gradual concentration of the several powers in the same department consists in giving to those who administer each department the necessary constitutional means and personal motives to resist encroachment of the others. . . . Ambition must be made to counteract ambition. . . .'

Despite the vast economic, social and political changes we have experienced since the eighteenth century, the separation of powers and checks and balances still prevail. They are more complex today. Members of each branch—still motivated by Madison's principle to 'resist encroachment of the others'—have added various institutions to strengthen their own intelligence and their control over constitutional responsibilities. Congress now deals with an executive-administrative establishment that has formidable resources of information and is capable of operating complex programs beyond the range of most legislators' understanding. Yet Congress has not surrendered. It has developed specialized committees, staff aides for individual legislators and the committees, and additional units under its direction (the Congressional Research Service and the General Accounting Office) to aid in the development and supervision of government programs. On the President's side there is an extensive Executive Office. The shape and extent of this institution varies with the wishes of each President, but its general growth is upward in size and in the sophistication needed to maintain executive control over program development and operation. We now have many more units in each branch of government, plus concerns for sophistication and specialization that were not present in Madison's day. However, we still have the institutional loyalties that he helped to create and set against each other in 1787.

THE MEANING OF CONFLICT FOR THE GAO

What does this fractured and jealous system of government mean for the GAO? The GAO is widely identified by its parent branch. As a creature of the legislature, the GAO is seen by members of the House and Senate as one of the units to be strengthened and employed in their frequent efforts to understand and to control activities in the executive branch. The GAO is not the only institution to receive the legislators' attention. The Congressional Research Service and the staffs of individual members and committees also benefit from the legislators' need for help. Yet the GAO is the most prominent of the legislative institutions that seems capable of filling important assignments in the assessment of on-going programs and new proposals from the executive. Even if the GAO wanted to concentrate on 'traditional' auditing, it is unlikely that Congress would be content with its inhibitions.

While the GAO receives resources and prominence from Congress by virtue of its identification with the legislative branch, it also pays a price in its rapport with the executive branch. Relations between the GAO and administrative departments are typically cooperative. The reports of illegal or inefficient operations are often welcomed by the President, Office of Management and Budget, and administrative superiors interested in credible information about their subordinates' activities. Yet there are times when the GAO runs into the barrier of strict formality on the part of administrators. Some information about agency programs is denied to the GAO by officials who cite 'executive privileges' and the need to keep certain affairs within the Administration. To the administrators who cite these protections, the GAO is an arm of Congress that—with certain information at its disposal—would help legislators to gain undesirable advantages. When administrators deny information to the GAO, they exhibit those 'constitutional means' which Madison *et al.* gave them to 'resist encroachment' from the legislature.

It is overly simple to think of GAO as an institution which serves—or is supported by—a united legislature. Perish the thought. Recall that the framers created a bicameral legislature and established each House with a different set of constituencies. To be sure, the Senate is no longer the exclusive body of the eighteenth or even the nineteenth century. But despite its popular base, the Senators' constituencies are not coincidental with those of the House. The viable nature of the bicameral arrangement makes itself evident each time the House and Senate fail to agree on major items of legislation. And it is not only bicameralism that assures occasional dissonance in relations between the GAO and the Congress. Perhaps even more important are the internal differences in opinion that characterize the members of each House. There are sharp differences on policy that affect the views of various congressional factions toward the GAO. On some occasions when the GAO has involved itself in a prominent controversy, the legislators who speak out for and against the benefits of an active auditor are the legislators who favor or oppose the substantive position that is favored by GAO's action. When the GAO held up government contracts that included certain clauses supporting the recruitment of minority group members (the Philadelphia Plan), the most prominent legislative supporter of the GAO was a southern Senator with a conservative voting record. The antagonists of the GAO were liberal Republicans and Democrats from outside the South who have characteristically provided leadership in civil rights causes. On another occasion when the GAO collided with the Defense Department over the use of certain information that figured into DOD planning for a major weapons system, it was a group of liberal opponents of military procurement who provided the major support for the GAO. There are also differences among legislators about abstract issues of governmental theory that pertain to the functions of the auditor. When Alan Cranston came to the Senate, he had experience as Comptroller of the State of California. In that position he developed strong ideas about the proper role of the government auditor. As he expressed these ideas at a subcommittee of the Government Operations Committee, they would keep the GAO from moving further into program analysis:

> (The auditor) should not be permitted, and customarily is not permitted in California, to lead the way in eliminating or paring back educational or public works programs except for reasons of efficiency and cost. Whenever the legislature allows him to go beyond that, it abdicates its own responsibilities . . .
>
> I fear that a number of proposals that we have seen in the Senate in recent weeks threaten to assign to the GAO duties that would undermine its ability to make sound, independent fiscal decisions. Its involvement in policy judgments and in programing matters would impair the credibility of its financial judgment. The proposals would ask the GAO to undertake tasks it is not competent to undertake, thereby putting the Congress in the unwise and untenable position of looking in the wrong direction for advice, counsel, and expertise.[13]

There are disputes in Congress about the proper limits of a 'legislative bureaucracy' that affect the resources given to the GAO as well as to other institutions attached to the legislative branch. A popular argument is that the bureaucracy of congressional staffs, the Library of Congress and the GAO should not become so unwieldly as to challenge the legislators' personal control. There are strong pressures in Congress to 'keep things about as they are' so the members can employ their customary procedures in dealing with employees. With too much growth in these staff units, Congress may reach the point where the personnel employed to help control the Administration's bureaucrats are themselves beyond congressional supervision.

At times GAO seems beset with legislators who want to expand its functions beyond the desires of GAO leaders. Some members want a congressional agency to range widely in evaluating the actual and potential goals of the nation, and making recommendations to the Congress with respect to goals. This would resemble the 'social accountability' function described above. In 1969 Senators Case and Mondale introduced an amendment to the Defense Procurement Authorization bill that would have the GAO consider a series of high policy questions about the proposed carrier fleet. In the words of the Comptroller General—who was successful in having the senators modify their amendment— the assignments were 'beyond the scope of our competence to make independent studies and render judgments. . . . They concern, for the most part, matters such as military strategy, threat assessment, and foreign policy.'[14] Certain members want the GAO to be more hardnosed in its dealings with the executive branch. They would have more victories for the legislative branch by minimizing fraternization between GAO and the Departments and by keeping GAO's draft reports away from program administrators until the Congress could use the reports to discipline the bureaucrats.

The congressional environment of the GAO is sufficiently fractured so that different kettles may brew at the same time with a surprising lack of communication among the cooks. In September 1969 the Subcommittee on Executive Reorganization chaired by Senator Abraham Ribicoff (D., Conn.) of the Government Operations Committee heard testimony concerned with the capacity of the GAO to audit expenditures of the Defense Department. The hearings ranged outward from that topic and prompted the drafting of a bill to enhance the GAO's statutory powers. Yet the Ribicoff hearings did not range so wide as to take account of the massive clash then going on between the Comptroller General on the one side, and the Labor Department and the Attorney General on the other side. As we shall see below in our discussion of the Philadelphia Plan, that clash came to an unprecedented constitutional crisis between the legislative and executive branches. The Philadelphia Plan was an effort of the Labor Department to encourage the employment of minorities in federally funded construction projects. It was ruled an improper subject of government funding by the GAO; and the Administration challenged GAO's ruling. The Plan became the subject of hearings conducted in October 1969 by the Subcommittee of Senator Sam J. Ervin, Jr. (D., N.C.) on the Separation of Powers (of the Judiciary Committee). Why didn't the Ribicoff Subcommittee broaden its inquiry to consider the Philadelphia Plan? Government Operations is the legislative committee for the GAO, and the bill drafted for Ribicoff did take account of the testimony before the Ervin Subcommittee. The suspicion is irrepressible that Senator Ribicoff and his liberal colleagues did not want to conduct a forum that would support GAO's ruling against a major civil rights program. Participants in the hearings play down such motivations. They cite the timing of the Ribicoff hearings and the decision to focus narrowly on GAO's review of military procurement. Yet the Ribicoff Subcommittee did broaden its agenda to include other features of GAO's work. Also, the chairman of the Government Operations Committee—John McClellan (D., Ark.)—cooperated with Senator Ervin in getting the GAO involved in the Philadelphia Plan, and in placing the resulting controversy on the agenda of Ervin's Subcommittee, on which he also has a seat. The Subcommittee that would be led by Senators Ervin, McClellan and Roman Hruska (R., Neb.) was far more hospitable to the GAO's case on the Philadelphia Plan than would a subcommittee where a majority of five could be drawn from Senators Ribicoff, Fred Harris (D., Okla.), Lee Metcalf (D., Mont.), Jacob K. Javits (R., New York), Charles H. Percy (R., Ill.), and Charles Mathias, Jr. (R., Md.).

At times the political environment surrounding the GAO includes supporters and antagonists among the nation's prominent interest groups. The GAO is not often on the shopping list of Washington lobbyists. There is usually more excitement, from their perspective, on Capital Hill or the administrative departments. When the GAO renders a decision about a controversial issue, however, those groups who perceive themselves to be threatened—and some who recognize GAO's beneficence— surface to express their views. During the hearings of the Ervin

Subcommittee on the Philadelphia Plan the position of the GAO (against the plan) was supported by spokesmen from the AFL-CIO, the Southern States Industrial Council, the General Building Contractors Association of Philadelphia and Associated General Contractors of America. In contrast, statements in support of the Philadelphia Plan came from the NAACP, the Urban Coalition Action Council, and the Philadelphia Urban Coalition. The Philadelphia Urban Coalition opened its statement with an expression of government theory:

> The United States Attorney General has reviewed the question of the separation of powers raised by the opposition to the Philadelphia Plan by the Comptroller General and support of the Plan by the Executive Branch of Government and he has concluded that the Philadelphia Plan is a statement of policy which is clearly within the province of the President. The Comptroller General has no policy-making role for the country and his opinions are only relevant when they relate to specific contractual and other fact situations.[15]

THE INDEPENDENCE OF GAO

It would be a mistake to leave the impression that the GAO is a passive receptor of stimuli from its environment. Any discussion of the demands, desires, and constraints that affect the activities of the GAO must take account of those coming from the Office itself. The Comptroller General has certain notions about the proper functions for his unit. He has dissuaded legislators who want him to provide services that are outside those he considers proper. The limits of 'proper functions' lie somewhere between the analysis of proposals that are initiated in the Congress or the Administration, and the independent initiation of new program proposals. The Comptroller General would keep away from questions of 'policy.' By this, he seems to mean the original design of major programs meant to deal with newly recognized social, economic, or technological problems. Within his borders are the analysis of programs already in operation, and the analysis of proposals made by others. On occasion, the information obtained in such inquiries will lead the GAO to recommend a change in existing legislation.

Our reviews of programs from the standpoint of achievement of objectives can and often do result in providing information which suggests the need to revise or strengthen a program or its administration to improve its effectiveness. In some cases this information leads us to recommend a change in the governing legislation itself. . . .

We do not believe that the Congress intended that the GAO initiate or be called upon to initiate new program proposals to deal with technological, social, economic, or other problems or needs. Nor do we believe it was intended that we initiate recommendations with respect of funding levels or budget priorities.

It is clear, however, that the GAO can and should direct its work in a way which will provide information concerning the results of authorized programs and activities which will be useful to the Congress and its committees in making judgments on these matters. Also, GAO can and should be available to assist committees on a case by case basis in analyzing information relating to alternatives considered by executive agencies to propose specific research programs or other courses of action.[16]

It is not easy to define the borderline between what the GAO would—and would not—prefer. The extent of involvement with program review and recommendation may vary on a case to case basis. The Comptroller General guards the independence of his Office, and asserts his capacity to assign manpower and set priorities with respect to the requests that he receives.

One issue that legislators have presented to the Comptroller General concerns his responsiveness to requests from individuals. The Comptroller General prefers to honor the requests of committees or the Congress as a whole.[17] This preference coincides with that of personnel in the administrative departments, who feel that requests from the committees would be less threatening to their own interests than requests from individual legislators. The individual who suffers from such an arrangement, or course, is the maverick congressman or senator who is on the outs with his committee leadership and feels unable, for the lack of staff assistance, to press his antagonism with a department. To some observers who are outside of the GAO, but within the orbit of legislative and executive personnel who deal regularly with the Office, the Comptroller General's network of relationships rely heavily on his ability to maintain rapport with committee chairmen. That committees are central to the decision-making of Congress has been evident since Woodrow Wilson penned his famous treatise.[18] More than any other individuals, the committee chairmen control the votes needed to support GAO rulings or recommendations within the range of their committee's jurisdiction. The Comptroller General must be wary in following the lead of some junior legislator who could not—or would not—support the GAO when its recommendation faced the wrath of an important committee chairman. Talking about the GAO's involvement in defense expenditures, one legislative staff man said the GAO cannot 'follow some Johnny-come-lately liberal who will not be around with the votes when it comes time to stare down Richard Russell.' Senator Proxmire is one senator who has made extensive use of the GAO. He has earned the label of 'maverick' for himself, and values his kind of individual prodding of the bureaucracy.

> I would resist strongly any attempt to limit the services of the GAO merely to the committees of the Congress. The individual House or Senate member must have access to them. The tendency to act as though the committees were the Congress, rather than the creatures of the House or Senate and subordinate to them, is a practice which has gone too far.[19]

Several senators saw the Ribicoff bill as the opportunity to enhance the use of GAO by individual legislators. When the Bill came out of the subcommittee (after being marked up in consultation with the GAO), however, it left the control of GAO resources with the Comptroller General and committee chairman. Any member could ask the GAO to review an existing program or pending legislation. The Comptroller General would then advise the member and the chairman of the appropriate committee which issues are within the competence and available resources of the Office. And finally, 'the Comptroller General shall determine the relative priority of all studies and reviews undertaken.'[20]

This is not to imply that the GAO is a rigid organization that spends much of its resources resisting efforts to involve it in areas of potential controversy. Within the limits described above (i.e., avoiding original proposals for major new programs and avoiding direct conflict with committee chairmen), the GAO demonstrates a capacity for innovation and expansion. The signals of this innovation and expansion include the Comptroller General's efforts to recruit a broad range of professional expertise; the scope of the program reviews he undertakes; and his willingness to publish findings and proposals that are certain to invite strong opposition from key people in Congress, the Administration and interest groups. The Ribicoff Bill would have changed the name of the GAO to the 'Office of the Comptroller General of the United States.' The present label, 'General Accounting Office,' does not accommodate the wide range of operations beyond the field of accounting. The Comptroller General would replace the term 'audit' for his operation to 'review.' These semantic alterations may appear minor to an outsider. In a world that is moved at least partly by slogans, however, the message is made clear that the GAO no longer is concerned only with the financial activities of government agencies. The assessment of program effectiveness ranges widely into administrative practices and the capacity of those practices to accomplish the stated goals of major programs.

Possible changes in the terminology surrounding the GAO are mirrored in its recruitment of new personnel. No longer are the professionals in the Office limited to accountants and auditors. Increasingly, it is hiring persons with advanced training in statistics, actuarial science, computer technology, sociology, economics, political science, public administration, mathematics, engineering, and systems analysis. At the beginning of the 1969 fiscal year about 300 of GAO's professional staff (totaling then about 2,600) had educational or experience backgrounds in areas other than accounting and auditing.[21] Over the preceding four years the GAO's annual recruiting from outside the accounting-auditing fields had increased at the levels of 22–45–200–250.

The Comptroller General also accommodates some desires of individual senators and congressmen, even while he respects the primacy of committees. Recent *Annual Reports* of the GAO have featured a section entitled, 'Reports to Individual Members of Congress.' The *Report* for 1971 notes that 'the Office furnished 143 audit reports to individual Members covering the activities of nearly all of the departments and agencies,' and lists several inquiries made by the GAO as a result of special requests by Senators Proxmire, Joseph M. Montoya (D., N.M.), Gordon

Allot (R., Colo.), Margaret Chase Smith (R., Me.), and Congress-men H. R. Gross (R., Ia.) and Henry Reuss (D., Wis.).[22]

There is one image in Washington that the activities of the GAO are 'Dullsville' from the perspective of the activist. Accord-ing to this view, the work of the Office consists of probing into established programs, and complicating bureaucrats' lives with challenges of financial transactions that occurred months or years ago. Another image, however (that seems to be more accurate), is that the GAO is moving increasingly into areas of relevance and controversy. Perhaps an indicator of this move lies in the com-ments that program administrators make in connection with the GAO:

Sure you can come and talk about the GAO—if you can stand a torrent of four-letter words.

(The GAO) is beholden to the sympathies of reactionary con-gressmen kept in power by the rotten borough system.

Just a sample of recent activities and recommendations of GAO suggests the range and intensity of issues aroused by its activities:

1. finding certain features of the Jobs Corps program 'dis-appointing,' and doubting they justified the use of re-sources;
2. finding less accomplishment than was reasonable to expect in Community Action Programs to focus attentions and action on the problems of the poor;
3. finding that the Agricultural Research Service has been remiss in responding to the findings of the Public Health Service and the Food and Drug Administration concerning the use of certain pesticides;
4. finding that the Department of Labor was pursuing an illegal course of action in conducting a program to increase the number of minority-group members hired by building con-tractors working on federal projects;
5. finding that the Farmers Home Administration was partici-pating in loans to private clubs that were discriminating on the basis of race in accepting members.

The environment of the GAO is only occasionally combative. Its involvement in controversy and its notice by the public does not approach that of congressional committees or major administrative agencies. From his side, the Comptroller General pursues rapport between his Office and the Administration with a series of inter-agency lunches and discussions about potential or actual problems. A high-ranking official in one department with a long record of GAO-administered discomforts conceded that the auditors and other investigators were cordial and smooth in their dealings, and—despite the potential for role clash—did not add any increment of friction to the situation by their own behavior. In the vast majority of cases, GAO's rulings about the legality of expenditures appear to be accepted—although sometimes with regret—by the heads of the departments involved. Its findings and recommendations on the efficiency of government operations likewise are often welcome by increased members of the legislative and executive branches. The GAO works with the personnel of affected agency when compiling its report, and typically allows the agency to review and comment on an early draft of its report. Once the formal GAO report is made, the President's Office of Management and Budget (OMB) puts into operation a set of procedures that require the agency to review and respond to the GAO's findings within a limited period, and to inform the OMB of any corrective action that is taken. Much of the time, the leadership of the executive branch considers the work of the GAO to be an important adjunct to its own supervisory procedures. In 1964 President Johnson told the heads of departments and major agencies:

> I want all reports made by the General Accounting Office and any Congressional Committee to be given prompt and thorough attention. Honest mistakes can be forgiven, but it is hard to forgive failures to examine and tighten agency procedures to guard against a recurrence of an error that is uncovered by the GAO or by a Congressional Committee. Look into them promptly. If the criticisms are justified, I will expect you to take corrective action so that the error is not repeated.[23]

At the higher levels at least, respect and cooperation more than conflict seem to characterize the executive's relations with the GAO.

SIGNIFICANT CONFLICTS

To a political scientist, the unusual instances of GAO involvement in the political process are the most interesting. We learn a lot when GAO becomes involved in intense conflict with the Administration, certain members of Congress or interest groups. Then we have an opportunity to see the test of authority in the crunch. What kinds of conflict center on the GAO? What does it take for an administrative agency to disregard the opinions of the GAO and still maintain the President's support? What issues divide the Congress in their support of the GAO? Who wins in an overt clash between the GAO and an administrative department? How are such conflicts decided? These are the questions to be answered. At this point, however, it is possible only to offer a short list of antagonisms that center on the GAO, and to probe more deeply into two instances for which there is a substantial public record. The antagonisms are expressed in the terms of certain partisans. Much of the upsets that focus on GAO are triggered by the threatened or actual goring of a favored ox. For each item on the list that follows, there are likely to be mirror images expressed by those with different perspectives.

(a) *The view of GAO as holding a policy bias that sets it against a program independent of the particular legal or financial case that the Office offers.* In recent years this view was expressed most forcefully by persons who *supported* the Labor Department in the Philadelphia Plan and *opposed* the Defense Department on weapons procurement. They trace a policy bias in the GAO to special relationships with the conservative chairman of congressional committees. They cite the role of John McClellan as chairman of the Senate Government Operations Committee (having jurisdiction over the GAO's statutory powers), and the occupation by southern or border-state members of eight out of the thirteen chairmanships of House Appropriations Subcommittees. Advocates of this position also find support in the review of the Philadelphia Plan by Senator Ervin's Subcommittee on the Separation of Powers rather than Ribicoff's Subcommittee on Executive Reorganization, and in the GAO's reluctance to follow the direction of various senators and congressmen in proposing alternatives to policies of the Defense Department.

(b) *The view of the GAO as being superficial in its review of government programs and careless in its legal research, and focusing on issues that are more distracting than illuminating to program administrators.* This view is expressed by administrators who find their lives complicated by the rulings or recommendations of the GAO. It is heard even in the Defense Department whose activities are the assignment of 1,200 GAO professionals. This view provides one example of the mirror-image nature of antagonisms towards the GAO. While certain members of the legislature feel the Office is reluctant to inquire into the activities of the Defense Department, certain officers in that Department felt that the GAO overreaches itself in DOD matters and produces undesirable complications for the Department's staff.

(c) *The view that GAO provides an illegitimate input into the policy-making process for those who have lost battles in the legislature.* We have seen this before in commenting on the allegation that GAO steps over the proper boundaries of auditing when it disallows certain expenditures. The proper action, according to this view, is for the GAO to inform Congress of a discrepancy in administrative operations, and let Congress take any corrective action that it desires.

In order to see some of these problems in operation, we consider two controversies that have left a substantial residue in the public documents. These controversies occurred: (1) when the GAO pursued information about the justification of major administrative programs, and was rebuffed by personnel claiming executive privilege; and (2) when the GAO ruled illegal certain key features of an Administration program.

1. *GAO inquiries and executive claims of privilege*

GAO versus executive disputes over the availability of information have occurred most prominently in research, development and procurement activities of the Defense Department. The reluctance of the Defense Department to share its information with GAO seems not to involve issues of security as much as issues of executive privilege. GAO investigators in the Defense Department are cleared for security and—pending these claims of privilege—are allowed to review otherwise secret details of military programs.

The Defense Department is especially concerned that inquiries of the GAO do not open alternative courses of action beside those already chosen by the Department. It wants GAO reviews limited to the adequacy of management procedures as applied to existing programs, or programs that have been included in the President's Budget. The Department would also allow GAO summaries of DOD policy analyses for Congressional review. Under certain conditions, the Department would permit GAO reviews of the planning *procedures* used when the Department 'establishes objectives, identifies alternatives and reaches conclusions and recommendations.' The Department would not release detailed information about alternatives to current policy. In the Department's official view, it is most desirable for Congress to review its recommendations directly, without independent analyses of policy alternatives by GAO. By making separate program assessments and recommendations the GAO would burden Congress with too much information, it would compromise the independence of its subsequent financial audit, and it would threaten the Defense Department with the administration of a program it did not want.

If the GAO did attempt to enter the program planning field, the Congress would then be presented with two sets of program proposals—those of the Administration and those of GAO. Because of the highly technical and complex nature of weapon systems, recommendations and alternatives would be very detailed. While the Congressional Committees and their staffs are made up of very able and energetic individuals, I can see no way for the Congress to find the time to study a myriad of program alternatives—for a great many programs—and reach decisions on each of them. A third agency, in addition to the Executive Branch and GAO would be required. The Congress can be much more effective by reviewing the program proposals of the Administration and evaluating the objective assumptions on which they are based. . . .

If the GAO did raise new alternatives or make recommendations, there is a distinct possibility that the Administration would find itself in the position of executing the GAO program. Just as it is difficult for an auditor to investigate a program objectively on which he has made a *positive* recommendation [italics added], it is equally difficult for an administrator to carry out a program when he is convinced some other course of action would be superior.[24]

The Department also prefers that GAO inquiries be coordinated by the military committees and the military subcommittees of the appropriations committees that normally consider the Department's programs. Here it shares GAO's preference (noted above) for working within the committee structure. 'If the GAO were required to respond to requests for investigations from the individual members of Congress, the result could be uncoordinated and could have an adverse impact on both GAO's work load and the work load of the Department.'[25] Perhaps the unrestrained response of GAO to legislator's requests for inquiries would expand the range of alternatives far beyond the customary zone established by the policy-planners of the Department and members of the military committees in Congress.

Despite the discouragement from the Defense Department (and other agencies), numerous legislators feel the need for 'their own' source of detailed information and program recommendations to consider along with those of the Administration. Senator Ted Stevens (R., Alaska) seemed to be speaking for many of his colleagues when he responded to the official spokesman of the Defense Department:

> If GAO is not to have what I think you really view as an invasion into the prerogatives of the Department of Defense, I think you should address yourself to the question of where in the Congress it should be, because as I view the mood up here, we want someone other than the Department of Defense to have the total program review capability.
>
> I don't think we have it yet. If it is not going to be GAO, it is going to be some other place which is an arm of the Congress.[26]

Senator Ribicoff joined in:

> I think you sense it, and I think there was an uneasy feeling during the entire debate on the Defense authorization, and I know that already every phase of those for or against the proposals had the feeling that these hearings were welcome and they would hope that this committee would develop a more effective GAO that all of us could use.[27]

As we have seen above, a number of legislators would have the GAO take a more active role in policy-making than is welcomed by the GAO. It was in response to an amendment proposed for the Military Procurement Authorization bill in 1969 that the Comptroller General defined as outside the 'scope of our competence to make independent studies and render judgments . . . (on) matters such as military strategy, threat assessments, and foreign policy.' Yet if the underlying studies were made available to the GAO, it could 'make useful summaries, highlight significant points, and develop questions, alternatives, and issues for consideration by the Congress in arriving at a position.'[28] On this issue, the position of the GAO seems to be somewhere between the Defense Department's wish that it confine itself to summaries of departmental analyses, and the wishes of certain legislators that the GAO undertake wide-ranging, independent systems analyses of policy alternatives.

The Defense Department reinforces its preferences about the analyses of GAO by control over the kinds of information needed to make program assessments. For the most part, the GAO does not have the capacity to make independent studies of policy alternatives; it is limited to summaries and reanalyses of the material compiled by the Administration. The Department has withheld all analytic information except that pertaining to the programs finally adopted by the Administration. Moreover, the Department releases to the GAO only certain types of internal reports pertaining to those programs. The GAO does not have 'ready access to uncensored files of the Department;' it is limited to the kinds of documents the Department is willing to release.[29] However, the Department's will is flexible, and subject to change in response to political pressure. When numerous legislators expressed an intense interest in a new tank: MBT-70, the Deputy Secretary granted the GAO complete access to all documentation in the Department's files. At the time, the Department insisted that this was a 'special one-time action and that it was an exception to the general guidelines.'[30] The Department explained its action by reference to the limited time available for GAO to make its analysis. It seems more likely, however, that the breadth of congressional interest and its insistence on administrative candor was a principal feature in the breach of executive privilege.

2. *The Philadelphia Plan*

A second variety of conflict has seen a ruling of the GAO outlaw an important item of Administration policy. It was an instance of the legislature's guardian of the Treasury saying that 'Money cannot be spent' for certain purposes, and the Administration responding with a 'Dammit yes.' Most of the time the adverse rulings of the GAO are accepted with little more than grumbling in the affected agency and among the clients and contractors who are affected by the decision. In the case of the Philadelphia Plan, however, the agency involved fought the decision through the highest levels of the Nixon Administration, and won a ruling from the Attorney General that set the executive branch squarely against the GAO.

The details of the Philadelphia Plan are numerous and complex, and have shifted between an original Plan and a revised version that was developed—still unsuccessfully—to satisfy the Comptroller General about its legality.[31] Only the basic dimensions of the Plan are relevant to our purpose: it consists of certain language written into government contracts (first attempted for a federal building project in Philadelphia) to require genuine efforts on the part of the contractor to employ members of minority groups. The issue gained its political importance from the virtually all-white nature of skilled workers in construction projects, the focus of militant and moderate black organizations against the alleged discriminatory practices of craft unions and contractors, and the widely perceived conservative record of the Nixon Administration on racial policies. Because of the 'southern strategy,' the Administration was said to be ignoring the needs of black Americans. The Philadelphia Plan was an important—some said the *most* important—move of the Administration in the direction of equal economic opportunity.

The clash with the GAO rested upon the Comptroller General's claim that the Plan ran afoul of the Civil Rights Act of 1964. In particular, section 703(j) which states that the Act does not require an employer to grant preferential treatment to any individual or group because of race, color, religion, sex, or national origin. The GAO found a further basis for its ruling in a memorandum authored in the Act's floor managers in 1964:

There is no requirement in title VII that an employer maintain a racial balance in his work force. On the contrary, any deliberate attempt to maintain a racial balance, whatever such a balance may be, would involve a violation of title VII because maintaining such a balance would require an employer to hire or to refuse to hire on the basis of race.[32]

The details of the squabble between the GAO and the Labor Department (author of the Philadelphia Plan) are too complicated to explore here. The issues include an allegation by the GAO that the Labor Department would 'obligate bidders, contractors or subcontractors to consider the race or national origin of their employees or prospective employees,'[33] and the response of the Administration that the Plan only requires contractors to take 'affirmative action' that will achieve reasonable goals of 'minority manpower utilization.' The debate included efforts by the antagonists—and their supporters among legislators, other government officials and interest groups—to draw distinctions between 'quotas' and 'goals;' to distinguish the responsibility of the contractor from the discriminatory actions of labor unions with which he must deal; and to identify the Civil Rights Act of 1964 and an Executive Order as sole or alternate bases of government policy for the employment practices of government contractors. In a memorandum to the Labor Department the Comptroller General recognized that the Attorney General had supported Labor's finding of legality for the Plan, but held to his earlier position 'until the authority (for the Plan) . . . is clearly and firmly established by the weight of judicial precedents or by additional statute.'[34] In this way, the Comptroller General invited action by Congress to clarify the legality of the plan, or a suit in federal court. Over the period of October–December 1969, the Ervin Subcommittee conducted hearings on the subject of the Philadelphia Plan, and the Senate accepted and later withdrew an amendment to an appropriations bill that would have approved the Comptroller General's position. Although the Comptroller General wrote to senators in behalf of the amendment that supported his ruling, the Senate's ultimate action satisfied him that Congress had expressed itself on the issue in question. After the Senate failed to enact a provision supporting GAO on the Philadelphia Plan, the Comptroller General wrote a memorandum to Congress indicating that he would take no further action on the Plan.

What is important for us in the hassle over the Philadelphia Plan are the following items. They indicate the kinds of political controversy that GAO may enter, and the problems that these controversies generate for the GAO and other actors:

1. the division of the legislature into a faction that supports, and a faction that opposes the actions of the GAO;
2. the potential for constitutional crisis as the rulings of GAO put in to doubt major items of the Administration's program;
3. the opportunity for certain legislators to use the powers of the GAO to win a battle in a war they seem to have lost earlier.

The Philadelphia Plan generated one of the few occasions when members of Congress publicly divided over their support of a GAO ruling. Their divisions appeared in a set of hearings conducted by the Subcommittee on Separation of Powers, and later during several days of debate and roll calls on the Senate floor. The alignments for and against the GAO reflected the curious mix of issue on a provision that would discipline government contractors *and* labor unions on a matter of equal employment opportunity. Supporters of the GAO at the Subcommittee hearings included Senators Ervin (D., N.C.), Fannin, (R., Ariz.), and Representative Pucinski (D., Ill.). Supporters of the Labor Department were Senators Javits (R., N.Y.), Brooke (R., Mass.) and Scott (R., Pa.). During the hearings, it is symptomatic that the witnesses in support of the Plan were liberal Republicans. It was an occasion for conservative Republicans to 'go fishing' (and thus to avoid their own identification with an employment rights program opposed by contractors) and for many liberal Democrats to show their reluctance to support the Republican Administration's prominent effort to attract otherwise Democratic black voters, with a program opposed by labor unions.

The authority of the GAO provided an opportunity for those who would—for partisan reasons—welcome an opportunity to embarrass the Administration. Nixon's appeal was weakest among the blacks, and the Plan stood as a major effort to attract some black support. Moreover, the Plan seems to have been promoted by high-ranking black officials in the Labor Department, which probably added to the Administration's inability to back down under pressure. A number of liberal Democrats were noticeably reticent in joining a campaign in behalf of the Plan. The ALF-CIO was a strong opponent of the Plan. Liberal Democrats could exploit the political neutrality of the GAO—not identified as being Democratic or Republican—and the nature of its opposition to the Administration's equal opportunity program. The fault, according to GAO, was procedural and not necessarily substantive. Democrats could support GAO and complicate the program of the Administration without taking a stand against equal opportunity.

Several roll call votes pertaining to the Philadelphia Plan were taken in the Senate. They allow us to gauge the kinds of pressures and cross-pressures that centered on the issue. It was a complicated issue. The only congressional factions that were relatively free from cross-pressures were liberal Republicans and conservative Democrats. Republicans like Javits, Brooke and Case could support their President and equal opportunity at the same time. They had to oppose the AFL-CIO, but this was not as difficult for them as it was for the liberal Democrats. Liberal northern Democrats showed twice the deviations from their group's voting tendency on the Plan as liberal Republicans.[35] Conservative Republicans could be forgiven a degree of confusion because they weren't used to seeing the Administration go directly against the combined intense views of management, labor, and the southern strategists. Some Republicans recalled a promise during the campaign that Nixon would relax bureaucratic intimidations over firms doing business with the government. Southern Democrats, alas, had an opportunity to vote against civil rights and the Republicans. In doing so, some of them may have felt uncomfortable in voting with labor.

A constitutional crisis threatened as the GAO ruling against the Administration on the Philadelphia Plan encountered an assertion of legality by the Attorney General. The GAO is used to having the final say on the legality of administrative actions, pending a contrary decision by the courts or by Congress. When the machinery functions smoothly, the Treasury stop payments on bills said by the GAO to have been contracted outside the intent of Congress. The Attorney General rested his defense of the Philadelphia Plan on an executive order rather than an Act of Congress, and thus made the executive-legislative conflict more sensitive. The Comptroller General avoided such inflammatory terms as 'usurpation,' but he left little doubt that the executive's basis for the Philadelphia Plan was ill-founded.

> Considering the fact that the sole authority claimed for the plan ordered by the Labor Department is the Executive order of the President, it is quite clear that the executive branch of the Government is asserting the power to use Government funds in the accomplishment of a program not authorized by congressional enactment, upon its own determination of authority and its own interpretation of pertinent statutes, and contrary to an opinion by the Comptroller General, to whom the Congress has given the authority to determine the legality of expenditures of appropriated funds, and whose actions with respect thereto were decreed by the Congress to be 'final and conclusive upon the executive branch of the Government.' We believe the actions of officials of the executive branch in this matter present such serious challenges to the authority vested in the General Accounting Office by the Congress as to present a substantial threat to the maintenance of effective legislative control of the expenditure of Government funds.[36]

The Comptroller General went on to predict a chaotic situation in federally-financed construction, with contractors risking their payment for work done under faulty contracts, and facing labor difficulties resulting from their efforts to comply with the plan.[37] It would be unfair to say the country was faced with a breakdown of government in the image of countries we think of as 'politically underdeveloped.' Yet we did come up against the threat of an uncompromising executive-legislative hiatus, and the loss of that rapport among protagonists that our constitutional framers recognized as essential to a healthy government.

For those legislators who opposed the extension of federal programs in the field of civil rights, the ruling of the GAO (even if it was aimed at the details and not the goals of the Philadelphia Plan) provided an opportunity to win a battle in an otherwise lost war. The trend of national policy had been in the direction of using federal powers to broaden the economic opportunities of blacks and other minority groups. The Philadelphia Plan appears consistent with this trend. Except for the GAO, conservative senators and congressmen would not have the opportunity to block the Administration. In this sense, the GAO was the functional equivalent of the filibuster or the control of key legislative committees by members who express a minority preference for policy. It is proper to ask if the creators of the GAO intend it to exercise such a dominant role in the design of major programs. As indicated above, however, the answer is academic. As the auditing function is defined and practiced in the national government, its outer boundaries are vague and flexible. The GAO is a substantial instrument that has important influences on the nature of programs that are implemented.

PROSPECTIVE PROBLEMS AND OPPORTUNITIES
OF THE GENERAL ACCOUNTING OFFICE

We saw that 'auditing' is a flexible concept that lends itself to expansion or contraction according to one's perspective. We also explored the political environment of the GAO. Rulings of the GAO affect the major institutions of the national government, and powerful actors see the GAO as an institution to be satisfied, evaded, or used in accomplishing their own ends. The GAO has important roles in the formulation and modification of major programs. It encounters controversy, plus the attempts to expand and limit its activities that are expected by-products of power. In this section, we assess the prospects of the GAO. We start by describing the activities that account for most of the GAO's resources. Then we reconsider some materials described above in order to gauge the trends of development. We identify some features that seem likely to continue, and may bring about a further expansion of the auditor's roles.

A number of signs point to an increasing role of the GAO in the evaluation of government programs. To be sure, the GAO continues in those areas that provided the bulk of its workload after its establishment as an independent unit in 1921: reviewing the legality of administrative expenditures, passing on the accounting procedures used by the departments, and reviewing programs for their efficiency. Its most recent *Annual Report* continues the practice of showing the 'financial savings' resulting from its operations. During fiscal 1971, the Office claimed measurable savings of almost $268 million due to its activities.

The kinds of issues that attract GAO's attention reveal its

sensitivity to issues of current importance. Recent *Annual Reports* show its concentration on military research and development and weapons procurement, plus expenditures of operations in Southeast Asia. Other topics of high priority include: the adoptions of systems analysis and the use of computer facilities by government departments; domestic programs developed in the middle- and late-1960s that involve innovative social technologies and complex relations with state and local authorities; and the burgeoning contractual arrangements between federal agencies and profit-making corporations, universities, non-profit corporations and social welfare organizations. GAO's work with the Philadelphia Plan and its pursuit of Defense Department information for its own program analyses are only two of the numerous actions the Office has taken in these fields that make it a relevant institution for those who design basic programs.

It is possible that certain factors external to the General Accounting Office have prompted the recent escalation in its activities. The division of party control between the legislative and executive branches may help the GAO take a more aggressive posture vis-à-vis the departments.[38] If the President's party also controlled Congress, the Comptroller General might not have found the encouragement from legislative leaders to go after a major civil rights effort as happened with the Philadelphia Plan. Also, the combination of legislative-executive party rivalry and the widespread disaffection with military policies may open the Department of Defense to unusually aggressive scrutiny of its procurement policies. Even if we acknowledge the importance of such special circumstances, however, there remain other factors that seem likely to encourage a continued prominence for the GAO, and its further involvement in controversial issues:

(1) Many congressmen feel themselves falling increasingly behind in their ability to analyze the Administration's requests for new programs and for the continued support of existing programs. This feeling is stimulated by the view that administrative departments are gathering impressive computer-based analytic capacity and lots of sophisticated personnel to operate the new technologies. Congressmen also perceive that the President is continuing to expand his own analytic capacities with an Executive Office that seems to grow in size and in the specialized units that it acquires.

(2) The GAO is the unit that is most likely to develop in

response to legislators' demands for help in analyzing departmental programs. The staffs of several committees may have approached the limits of their chairmen's preferences. Any further increases may have them approach the size of bureaucracies that congressmen seem *unwilling* to direct. Also, a number of committees seem unwilling to abandon the chairman's patronage as the principal staffing device, and to replace it with the search for highly qualified professionals who are assured—once hired—of reasonable freedom from arbitrary and partisan demands on their time. Aside from the Congressional Research Service (CRS), the GAO is the only existing unit with the basis of relevant skills and an established leadership that can give Congress sophisticated analysis that is independent of the Administration. The CRS has been small in size. As of 1970, under the label 'Legislative Reference Service,' the CRS employed approximately 300 professionals compared to GAO's 2,700, and its budget to fiscal 1970 was $4 million compared to GAO's $68.5 million. Some legislators felt the Legislative Reference Service concentrated on petty tasks, and was too beholden to serve the requests of individual legislators. It lacked the GAO's capacity and commitment to extensive field research into the operations of government programs, as well as GAO's insistence on controlling the allocation of its own resources. According to Senator Ribicoff: 'It is wasteful when (the Legislative Reference Service) is requested to prepare essays for high school and elementary school-children of Member's constituents. This now takes up 13 per cent of the LRS staff work. Perhaps, there should be reasonable limits on what individuals members could request. . . .'[39] This statement may exaggerate the portion of the Legislative Reference Service's resources that was allocated to petty tasks. The Director of the Service explained that much of its constituency service is routinized and takes up a small portion of its professional staff resources. Yet to the extent that Ribicoff's statement reflects the sentiments of important legislators, it points to a severe problem of status that will allow the GAO rather than the Legislative Reference Service-Congressional Research Service to receive the major benefits of increased congressional concern for sophisticated information. The Comptroller General told a House Subcommittee that:

The Legislative Reference Service, by its nature, is uniquely equipped to assist the committees by providing information and analyses of a background nature, bibliographies, etc., for use in evaluating new legislative proposals. The GAO, on the other hand, is perhaps better equipped to undertake longer-range studies of ongoing programs, to assess benefits and costs, the need for management improvement ...

Earlier in that same statement, the Comptroller General indicated that the GAO could 'assist committees . . . in analyzing information relating to alternatives considered by executive agencies and in reviewing the justification which prompted such agencies to propose specific research programs or other courses of action.'[40] Other officials have said in a patronizing manner that the work of the Legislative Reference Service tended to be 'academic.'

An extensive section of the Legislative Reorganization Act of 1970 changed the name of the Legislative Reference Service to the Congressional Research Service, and added to its powers. At the present time, however, any real competition between the GAO and the CRS seems questionable. The GAO enjoys not only a higher status in the eyes of many congressmen, but its leadership is expanding the skills that will provide the basis for more intensive program analysis. In recent years up to 50 per cent of new professional employees have come from outside the accountant category. Engineers, computer scientists, systems analysts, actuaries, statisticians, and economists are among the groups being recruited. There is an increasing willingness on the part of the GAO to employ outside contractors to supplement the skills available in its own staff. One study of Economic Opportunity Programs was conducted by GAO with the help of three research firms and nineteen individual consultants from various specialities.[41]

(3) With a continuation or escalation of GAO's involvement in program analysis, members of the executive branch may respond with additional assertions of executive privilege. Administrators will continue to snipe at the GAO for moving outside what—for the executive—is the preferably narrow auditor's role. Responsible persons in the executive branch state that GAO professionals aside from its auditors are inferior in quality. To many people in the executive branch, the GAO still fits the description that Harvey Mansfield wrote in 1939: 'arbitrary in many of the

decisions it makes with respect to the legality of expenditure, insensitive to the operating conditions that they interrupt with their rulings, and destructive not only of administrative efficiency and achievement but also of operating morale and of public confidence in the efficacy of governmental processes.'[42]

(4) The chronic tensions between the legislature's GAO and personnel of the executive branch may flare periodically as the substance of GAO's rulings provoke response from the highest levels of the Administration. It is one thing when an operating official must detour from his customary procedures because of the auditor's ruling, but another thing when a major program is rejected wholesale by the GAO. When this happens—as in the case of the Philadelphia Plan—the Administration may put up its back, important legislators may go over to the Administration's side, and the fray will attract the attention of interest groups.

It is unwise to predict whether the incipient constitutional crisis of the Philadelphia Plan will recur in other policy arenas. That will depend partly on the styles pursued by the antagonists, the administrators' calculation of gain or loss from an overt attack against a ruling of the GAO, the appreciation in the GAO and the executive branch of any threat to the political infrastructure that might result from an insistence on their preferred course of action, and perhaps on the happenstance of a Democratic Congress and a Republican President. Undoubtedly, a consideration of program substance as well as governmental procedure and constitutional theory will figure in any potential dispute. It may be difficult for an administrator *not* to push against a GAO ruling if it comes on an issue that matches the Philadelphia Plan in its apparent political importance to the President.

The resolution of legislative-executive conflict in the case of the Philadelphia Plan relied on a narrow vote in the Senate over the reconsideration of a resolution that had earlier endorsed the GAO's position, and the Comptroller General's forbearance in not asserting the status of his office into a more steadfast position against the Administration. There is no simple or tidy mechanism to guard against another, more protracted confrontation between the Comptroller General as spokesman for the legislature, and a Cabinet Member as spokesman for the executive. In future episodes of this sort we may also require a sense of appropriate

limits among a plurality of legislators, the Comptroller General
and/or his executive adversary.

Notes

* I wish to acknowledge the assistance of Rufus L. Edmisten, Chief
Counsel and Staff Director, Subcommittee on Separation of Powers,
Committee on the Judiciary, the United States Senate; Louis Fisher,
Analyst, Congressional Research Service; Lester S. Jayson, Director, Con-
gressional Research Service; Professor James Jones, University of Wisconsin
Law School (formerly of U.S. Department of Labor); Elmer B. Staats,
Comptroller General of the United States; Frederic H. Smith, Deputy
Director of the General Accounting Office; Carl W. Tiller, Special Adviser
on Budgetary Development, Office of Management and Budget, Executive
Office of the President. Of course, I am entirely responsible for the uses
made of their information and advice.

1. See Harvey C. Mansfield, *The Comptroller General: A Study in the
Law and Practice of Financial Administration* (Yale University Press, New
Haven, 1939); F. L. Normanton, *Accountability and Audit of Governments:
A Comparative Study* (Praeger, New York, 1966); and Robert E. Brown,
The GAO: Untapped Source of Congressional Power (University of Ten-
nessee Press, Knoxville, 1970).

2. Brown, p. v.

3. 'Priorities and Next Steps in the Carnegie Project on Accountability
and Independence,' a memo from Elmer B. Staats, May 1970.

4. Bruce L. R. Smith, 'Accountability and Independence in the Contract
State,' Department of Political Science, Columbia University, typescript,
p. 22.

5. Elmer B. Staats, 'New Problem of Accountability for Federal Pro-
grams,' in *Improving Management for More Effective Government: 50th
Anniversary Lectures of the United States General Accounting Office*
(U.S. Government Printing Office, Washington, 1971).

6. Ibid., pp. 88–9.

7. 'Priorities and Next Steps.'

8. See *Review of Economic Opportunity Programs*, a Report to the Congress by the Comptroller General, Joint Committee Print, 91st Congress,
1st Session, March 1969 (U.S. Government Printing Office, Washington,
1969) p. 6; also, James S. Coleman *et. al.*, *Equality of Educational Opportunity* (U.S. Government Printing Office, Washington, 1966).

9. *Capability of GAO to Analyze and Audit Defense Expenditures*, Hearings before the Subcommittee on Executive Reorganization of the Committee on Government Operations, U.S. Senate, 91st Cong., 1st Sess.,
Sept. 16–25, 1969 (U.S. Government Printing Office, Washington, 1969)
p. 166.

10. The Comptroller General of the United States, *Annual Report 1971*
(U.S. Government Printing Office, Washington, 1972) p. 18.

11. Smith, pp. 56 ff.

12. *The GAO Review* (U.S. Government Printing Office, Washington, Spring 1972) pp. 6 ff.

13. *Capability of GAO*, p. 165.

14. Ibid., p. 193.

15. *The Philadelphia Plan: Congressional Oversight of Administrative Agencies* (The Department of Labor), Hearings before the Subcommittee on Separation of Powers of the Committee on the Judiciary, U.S. Senate, 91st Cong., 1st Sess., Oct. 27, 28, 1969 (U.S. Government Printing Office, Washington, 1969) p. 219.

16. Statement of Elmer B. Staats before the Subcommittee on Science, Research and Development of the House Committee on Science and Astronautics, Dec. 4, 1969, mimeo, pp. 5–6.

17. 'A Report to Accompany a Bill to revise and restate certain functions and duties of the Comptroller General of the United States; to change the name of the General Accounting Office to Office of the Comptroller General of the United States, and for other purposes,' Committee on Government Operations, U.S. Senate, 91st Cong., 2nd Sess., mimeo, p. 3.

18. Woodrow Wilson, *Congressional Government: A Study in American Politics* (Meridan Edition, New York, 1956).

19. See Brown, p. vi, and Ralph K. Hvitt, 'The Outsider in the Senate: An Alternative Role,' *American Political Science Review*, LV (Sept. 1961) pp. 566–76.

20. 'A Bill to revise and restate certain functions and duties of the Comptroller General of the United States; to change the name of the General Accounting Office to Office of the Comptroller General of the United States, and for other purposes,' U.S. Senate, 91st Cong., 2nd Sess., mimeo. This Bill passed the Senate, in amended form, but was not acted upon in the House of Representatives.

21. Statement of Elmer B. Staats before the Subcommittee on Science, Research and Technology, p. 11.

22. *Annual Report*, 1971, pp. 1 ff.

23. Executive Office of the President, Bureau of the Budget Circular No. A-50, April 16, 1966.

24. *Capability of the GAO*, pp. 235–7.

25. Ibid., p. 236.

26. Ibid., p. 220.

27. Ibid., p. 220.

28. Ibid., pp. 192–3.

29. Ibid., pp. 242–3.

30. Ibid., pp. 243.

31. For a discussion of the development of numerous equal opportunity employment programs leading up to the Philadelphia Plan, written from the perspective of a participant in the Plan's development see James E. Jones., Jr., 'The Bugaboo of Employment Quotas,' *Wisconsin Law Review* (1970) pp. 341–403.

32. *The Philadelphia Plan*, p. 3.

33. Ibid., p. 133.

34. Ibid., p. 133.
35. A group of 14 liberal Republicans showed only 10 deviations from their group's tendencies on five roll calls on Philadelphia Plan amendments. The group included Senators Fong, Percy, Smith, Mathias, Brooke, Griffin, Case, Goddell, Javits, Hatfield, Packwood, Scott, Schweiker, Aiken. A group of 30 liberal northern Democrats showed 38 deviations from their group's tendencies on the same roll calls. This group included Senators Gravel, Cranston, Ribicoff, Inouye, Church, Bayh, Hartke, Hughes, Muskie, Tydings, Kennedy, Hart, McCarthy, Mondale, Symington, Eagleton, Burdick, Mansfield, Metcalf, McIntyre, Williams, Harris, Pastore, Pell, McGovern, Jackson, Magnuson, Nelson, Proxmire, and McGee. Deviations were defined by votes, pairs, and reports to CQ that went counter to the group's tendency on a vote, and no indication of preference.
36. *The Philadelphia Plan*, p. 147.
37. Ibid., p. 148.
38. Thanks to Bruce L. R. Smith for this suggestion.
39. *Capability of the GAO*, p. 167.
40. Statement of Elmer B. Staats before the Subcommittee on Science, Research and Technology, pp. 7, 13.
41. *Review of Economic Opportunity Programs*, pp. 3–4.
42. Mansfield, p. 10.

12 Independence and Accountability for Federal Contractors and Grantees

HARVEY C. MANSFIELD

On their face, independence and accountability appear to stand in an antithetical relationship, as in a zero-sum game: the more of one, the less of the other, and necessarily so. Such a relationship can be stated diagrammatically by a line of declining slope against two coordinates:

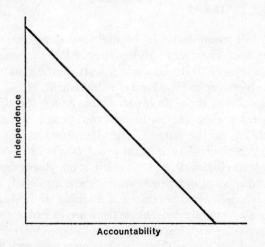

But observation and reflection warn us that the relation is too complex for expression in a single line. By performance and reputation, at least until lately, the Tennessee Valley Authority has had high marks for both qualities and the Post Office for neither. Evidently, there are different meanings included within the terms, as well as a range of degree in their presence or absence. If only differences of degree were involved, a diagram in matrix form with crude dichotomies might give a more realistic portrayal of the possibilities:

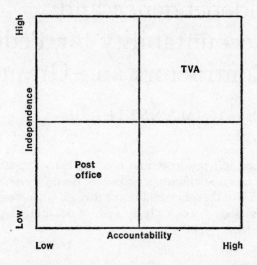

But the full complexity is beyond two-dimensional graphic representation. There are various sorts of independence, serving different purposes, and also various sorts of accountability, with differing objectives and methods of enforcement.

In approaching the main object of this paper, therefore, which is a general review of the means and prospects for exacting accountability on the part of federal contractors and grantees, who are not themselves governmental bodies, it seems an indispensable preliminary to start with some distinctions among sources and types of independence, for these are closely connected with the feasibility and propriety of auditing and other methods of securing accountability. Distinctions are in order, too, among types of activities with respect to which independence is exercised or prized, as well as with types of contractors and grantees— themselves an exceedingly heterogeneous category—and types of redress that acocuntability may bring about.

SOURCES OF INDEPENDENCE

It is convenient to speak separately of legal, fiscal, and political independence, though in operation these compartments are permeable. Possession of some of the second kind—fiscal—for instance, may be thought helpful in acquiring a measure of political independence too, or vice versa. But this is not necessarily the case, for the apparent emancipation from one master may be accompanied by enslavement to another. If the former is publicly accountable while the latter is not, abuses may be invited.

Legal independence is conferred by the terms of the contract or grant, read in the context of the network of applicable statutes and regulations that authorize, support, and limit the programs of the funding agency. This independence, being formal, may be real or only nominal. Its nature and latitude are influenced by a variety, and often a mixture, of motives. It may be broad because the contractor can be trusted or because he can be closely watched —making the risk minimal in either case—or because he is in a bargaining position to demand latitude, risky or otherwise; or because the goals and methods of the enterprise are in conflict and consequently ambiguous, or must be adaptable to unpredictable conditions and emergencies and so are too uncertain for specification in advance. 'When in trouble, delegate,' is a maxim that has guided a great many decisions to devolve unwelcome official responsibility onto outside parties by the route of contracts and grants.

Legal independence may be designed to assure freedom from hierarchical control over the selection of personnel, or the formulation and application of standards and criteria, or the review of particular decisions. This sort is important in protecting the professional integrity of advice, awards and denials, scientific research, investigative findings, and the like. It is a safeguard against censorship, a protection for academic freedom. Another sort may dispense, in the name of business efficiency, with various procedural restraints otherwise applicable to federal hiring, compensation, travel, procurement, and so on, after the manner of government-owned corporations as they operated before the Government Corporation Control Act of 1946. This type looms large in advanced engineering and technological development activities. It may be demanded also where a large volume of individually small transactions at retail must be handled in a hurry, as in the operation of commercial concessions on government property. For quite different reasons it may appear to be a necessity in many overseas operations, in large-scale lending and insurance transactions, and in covert activities at home as well as abroad. A third sort of legal independence is concerned with providing the contractor or grantee substantial autonomy in determining programs—intermediate goals, that is—as in the case of community service activities under OEO, where the end objectives are stated only in very general terms.

Fiscal independence is of two main varieties. One consists essentially in access to the public treasury coupled with relaxation of or exemption from various budgetary and other central controls customarily applied to appropriated funds. A classic historical case in extraordinary circumstances occurred when Lincoln in 1861 directed the Secretary of the Treasury to advance $2 million, without security and in direct violation of the Constitution and the statutes, to three private citizens of known loyalty in New York, to procure military supplies and provisions for the opening stages of the Civil War, at a time when the Treasury and War Departments were largely staffed with Southern sympathizers. In our day prosaic agencies like the Rural Electrification Administration or the Export-Import Bank, with 'backdoor financing'—a statutory right to borrow directly from the Treasury —have thereby some substantial fiscal independence; so do agencies, civil or military, with lump sum appropriations for purposes only broadly defined. Land-grant colleges and medical research centers that receive bloc grants for general support in amounts determined by some statutory formula of allocation are examples among grantees and contractors. Presumably formula grants, being less susceptible to alteration or individual treatment, confer greater fiscal independence than project grants, generically; but this depends upon how narrowly or specifically the conditions of eligibility are stipulated. Non-profit institutions that are given capital grants and allowed overhead percentages on project funds generous enough to permit the accumulation of reserves achieve fiscal independence in substance if not in form. Battelle Memorial Institute and Stanford Research Institute are examples that come to mind. In this category there must be hundreds of professional consulting firms, not all non-profit, commissioned to review and render evaluative reports on agency programs.

The second variety depends on an ability to generate revenues that can be intercepted and utilized directly, without going through the Treasury or becoming subject to appropriation control processes. This independence, to be sure, may be more in form than substance, particularly if the revenues defray only a portion of the costs, like postal receipts, and must be supplemented with appropriated funds. Budgeteers can then estimate the receipts and deduct these from the amounts that would otherwise have to be appropriated. A contractor's fiscal freedom may be illusory too, despite self-generated revenues, if these can be tightly controlled by the contracting agency. This is the case, for instance, with the municipalities and cooperatives that buy TVA power at wholesale and supply it to household consumers under retail rate schedules fixed in their contracts with TVA; or with the cafeterias operated in government buildings in Washington by GSI, Inc. under contracts with the General Services Administration. The giants in this category are the quasi-governmental Federal Reserve Banks, which receive and, after paying their own expenses and those of the Board of Governors, return to the Treasury annual sums reckoned in billions of dollars. In all these cases, vigilant supervision with an eye to the pocketbooks of the customers (or of the taxpayers, in the case of the Federal Reserve Banks) limits in crucial respects the apparent fiscal independence of the contractors.

A quite different situation prevails when that sort of vigilance cannot be counted on. A small example was contained in a press report (*New York Times*, Nov. 1, 1970, p. 73) of a directive to the Defense Concessions Committee, which administers the space rented to a score of commercial enterprises in the Pentagon building, to turn over to the Treasury a greater share of the rentals collected from the concessionnaires. The Committee had been found to be using the bulk of the rent receipts instead to finance an extensive welfare program—ranging from influenza shots to bowling tournaments—for Pentagon employees, who, after all, were the patrons of the concession shops. Much larger sums and more complicated interests are involved in the operations of the military post exchange stores in this country and abroad, which derive their revenues from sales to members and employees of the armed services, their families and friends. The characteristic risks here are patronage, embezzlement, and favoritism.

Political independence for a contractor or grantee consists in the possession of political support in some quarter not under the control of either the central budgetary authorities or the contracting agency, sufficiently potent to make the apparent obligations of the contract largely unenforceable in practice, or to win such a conceded degree of discretion for itself as to leave little in the way of obligation to be enforced. Several types of sources can be distinguished, invoking different moral claims. A small example will serve as an opener. In the name of philanthropy and of artistic and professional freedom of judgment the Smithsonian Institution—itself a shining example of independence—recently felt warranted in allowing a prospective munificent donor to obligate some hundreds of thousands of dollars of public funds in the private preparation, under his curator's direction, of his collection of paintings, then still his property but contracted to be given at a definite future date to the Smithsonian for display in the yet-to-be-constructed Hirshhorn Museum on the Mall in Washington. Much larger sums are involved in the discretion allowed, in the name of scientific freedom, to the manifold institutions selected, with the aid of a network of advisory committees and consultants, to be the recipients of grants and contracts for research in the physical and biological sciences. To take another sort of example, oligopoly in the maritime shipbuilding industry, strengthened by coalitions with operators and unions and favored by a friendly Maritime Administration and congressional committees, has produced subsidy contracts apparently immune to repeated criticisms that allege failure to protect the government's interests. The outdoor contractors who construct roads and public works for the Bureau of Public Roads and the Corps of Engineers are not independent of these agencies but enjoy a symbiotic relation with them that makes them together largely independent of central budgetary control. In principle, much the same can be said of the 'military-industrial complex,' where the plea of secrecy reinforces the political base for independence.

Of all the forms of political support for independence perhaps the strongest generically is that which interposes a state or local government body between the federal mission and funds and the contractor or grantee, particularly if the intermediary is an elected body. This is the case with the Soil Conservation Service district committees and the farmers' committees that pass on the eligibility of borrowers from the Farmers Home Administration. It has been substantially the situation of a good many local anti-poverty organizations. The Hunts Point Multi-Service Center Corporation in the heavily Puerto Rican section of the South Bronx may serve as an example. It was established under New York City auspices and funded chiefly with Model Cities allocations. Until the executive director of that organization ran in the 1970 Democratic congressional primary and lost, he appears, according to a subsequent press report (*New York Times*, Oct. 29, 1970, p. 37), to have deployed autonomously a $5 million annual budget for programs of health, job placement and related community services. Local autonomy is the watchword too for a good many recipients of grants and contracts to assist school boards in implementing desegregation plans. In short, from the standpoint of accountability, one form of independence puts the contractor beyond the effective control of the contracting agency; while another form binds the two in alliance in keeping central controls at a distance.

STANDARDS OF ACCOUNTABILITY

The problems of accountability depend upon, among other factors, what the contractor is to be held answerable for. At least four sorts of standards can be conveniently distinguished: fidelity, efficiency, policy (or function), and loyalty. The first two involve qualities dear to the hearts of central financial controllers. The third may produce whitewash, or an invitation to reconsider the whole enterprise. The fourth has to do with troublemakers.

Fidelity was the principal standard on which the accounting system of the Treasury was established in 1789, and which the Comptroller General inherited in 1921 when the offices of the Comptroller and Auditors of the Treasury were lifted out of that Department and consolidated as the General Accounting Office, an agency 'independent of the executive departments,' as the 1921 law put it and now recognized as an 'agency of Congress.' 'Accountable officers'—disbursing officers in the several departments, collectors of customs, postmasters, etc.—gave bond and were personally chargeable, under the law, for public funds coming into their hands. They were credited, when their periodic accounts were 'settled' by the Treasury auditors, for payments made in the discharge of government obligations, upon a proper showing that the payments were duly authorized according to applicable statutes and regulations, against an available appropriation.

Fidelity thus means more than honesty, the avoidance of embezzlement or other criminal conduct, yet less than the general standards of official performance are usually thought to demand. The central concern is for legality and regularity rather than morality or economy or effectiveness—a distinction akin to the difference between tax avoidance and tax evasion. This is a matter of 'living by the book,' of seeing that stipulated procedures are installed and followed, that required authorizations and clearances are obtained, records kept and limitations observed, including the Administrative Procedure Act as well as the statutes, appropriation riders, and regulations surrounding the handling of funds. For an ideal world, procedures and their restrictions no doubt should not only provide assurances of official fidelity in matters of money, property, time on the job, and so on, but also promote and sustain the accomplishment of the substantive policy ends of legislation and administration. In the real world, too much emphasis on fidelity may come at the expense of efficiency, let alone morality or legislative aims. It is then disparaged as bureaucratic red-tape, to escape some of which may be a leading motive for the resort to contracts or grants in the first place. There is consequently a built-in tension between fidelity and the other desiderata of accountability. The tension can be demonstrated historically in both directions. When an accountable officer suffered a disallowance because of a procedural irregularity, notwithstanding arguable equities in his favor, a multiplicity of devices—all the way to private relief bills in Congress—developed to let him off the hook; so that the batting average for recoveries was not high. On the other hand, the framers of the Budget and Accounting Act had no illusion that, because a given set of accounts was in order the expenditures they covered were necessarily prudent and sound.

The standards of fidelity are limited chiefly to financial and property transactions. But they have the advantage in comparison with other standards of being relatively objective, though not without room for argument over the sorts of issues that lawyers encounter in the construction of laws and regulations and accountants in the application of their professional principles. As applied to contractors and grantees, in contrast to regular departments, the fidelity standard alone would presumably be less revealing in most cases, since the terms of grants and contracts usually allow greater flexibility. But this is not always so. For instance, in the heated political disputes over federal and state audits of categorical grants for welfare in New York City—in a period when the welfare rolls were growing rapidly month by month—the charges of maladministration against the City rested in substantial degree on findings of payments to ineligibles or overpayments within a category. The city authorities apparently proceeded often on the assumption that if an applicant mother turned up and declared need, it did not matter much which of numerous categories were drawn upon, in what proportions, to validate the check she was given; the important thing was to fill the need for a family. The auditors looked at each category separately and were appalled at the irregularities and mingling they found, which invited and hid abuses, actual and potential.

Efficiency is a deceptively simple standard, apparently a matter of economy in the selection and employment of means to given ends—ends given by legislative or administrative policy-making. It is the essential criterion of cost-benefit analysis, the foundation of PPBS. But as soon as it is addressed to processes and results not so standardized as to be readily quantifiable its subjective nature emerges, and with that, controversy over its utility. A recent study by Frederick Mosher has traced the futile attempt to install PPBS in the State Department. Efficiency by financial measures has seldom been held in high regard in the military establishment, or in scientific laboratories; characteristically, it is congenial to engineers, cost accountants, and economic analysts, and irrelevant to those who rest their strategy on overkill. Subjective judgments in applying it as a test of performance for which a contractor should be accountable are partly a matter of the difficulty in finding and measuring standard and comparable units. But they result also from the ambiguity of the very definition of the term, which for some observers of a particular organization or operation will include among its ends long-run considerations and indirect benefits and costs that a short-run view might exclude as waste or irrelevance. If you start out by defining the object of a research contract as the discovery of a specified fragment of knowledge you may begrudge any charges beyond direct costs as extravagant. But if your definition embraces the training and maintenance of a research capability available for tasks beyond the immediate inquiry, overhead margins and capital outlays included in the contract may turn out to be efficient instruments after all. So too with outlays that bring participation and potential political support to a service or welfare enterprise. Apart from the difficulties of comparing incommensurables, judgments about efficiency may also turn upon whether the contractor or grantee is a single-purpose organization, a conglomerate, or a general purpose local government.

For all its ambiguity, efficiency has a continuing attraction for those who have a hand in allocating scarce resources, or in reviewing the yield of past allocations, for want of a better criterion; the alternatives are still more subjective. The ambiguity lends itself to another use. Outside critics of a project, whose real objectives are substantive but who do not choose to do battle on that ground, can cloak their animus in the guise of an attack on inefficiency simply by proceeding on a narrower definition of its ends than its defenders hold. Defense against such an attack inevitably links efficiency with other criteria.

At first blush it might seem unreasonable to make a contractor or grantee answerable for the function he is performing, and the policy that approves or authorizes it; let the principal—the funding agency—carry the burden of defending its agent. Political accountability does indeed rest on interests and obligations beyond fidelity and efficiency. For a number of reasons, however, it cannot always be safely shrugged off or disavowed on these grounds even if an attack is overtly leveled at the policy being pursued. One possibility is that the contractor is a more enthusiastic believer in what he is doing than the agency that authorized and funded it. If the latter is indifferent or timid the policy and the contractor may perish together unless his missionary zeal is persuasive; he is entitled to a civic as well as pecuniary interest in seeing the policy prevail. Another possibility is that the policy involves social costs to which neither the agency nor the contractor has been sufficiently attentive. Fashioning a response to criticism may then entail a reconsideration of the policy, to the general advantage of all concerned. An example here was the cessation of covert subsidies from the CIA to the National Student Association and other domestic organizations, following the disclosure of instances, and a policy review by a committee headed by the Attorney General.

A third possibility is that the attack strikes the contractor and the policy he embodies like a bolt of lightning, by chance and uncaring; he is only accidentally and symbolically the object of a blow aimed at ulterior goals, perhaps also symbolic. This was the situation of the Dow Chemical Co. on college campuses. Whatever the merits of particular cases, it is a political fact of life in our relatively open society that federal contractors and grantees will, from time to time as the currents of opinion, ambition, and controversy shift, be summoned in one quarter or another to justify their doings, and will find it imprudent to refuse to answer. Yet to answer at all is to acknowledge some sort of accountability.

There is a debatable gray area between activities that may be thought legitimate self-defense on the part of contractors and grantees, against attacks on their functions, and what may rather be thought self-serving lobbying to perpetuate lucrative deals. When accountability is extended to embrace the substantive desirability, scope, or emphasis of a given program, political sensitivities and perhaps partisan passions will be exposed. The intrinsic merit of criticisms will then be discounted or enhanced according to their source or sponsorship. To whose benefit will they redound?

It would be unrealistic to leave the standards of accountability without observing that from the point of view of a funding agency a measure of loyalty is an ingredient of what it expects from grantees and contractors. Too obsequious a loyalty, to be sure, displaces the recipient's independence. For this reason formula grants may afford more protection than discretionary projects. Too much loyalty may not be esteemed a virtue by outsiders, but a distaste for troublemakers includes a prejudice against those who bite hands that feed them.

FORMS OF REDRESS

What does it mean, to be held accountable, when, by any of the standards just reviewed, something is found to have gone amiss? What remedies may be applied, or sought? The ultimate goal is satisfactory performance. A favorable if not conclusive sign that things are going well is a situation in which a contractor or grantee, having acted *ultra vires*, comes forward promptly with a voluntary disclosure and request for ratification or dispensation, before being exposed in dereliction by others—the more so if the chance of exposure was slight.

Lacking this reassurance, a range of remedies can be considered. The mildest, no doubt, is an admonition: don't let it happen again. Publicizing the warning presumably gives it added force. If money has been misused and fidelity is the main standard, restitution is in order: get the money back—if possible. If the terms of a negotiated contract prove too generous, and statutory provision has been made, a price renegotiation proceeding may be invoked. If incompetence or malfeasance is shown, redress may take another tack: fire the man responsible, or terminate the contract. If the fault found is impersonal, a change in policy hereafter may serve the purpose, without recrimination. In addition to any of these steps, some reorganization and a tightening of the monitoring system may be in order.

AGENCIES, FORUMS AND PROCESSES

Accountability begins at home and for federal contractors and grantees moves upward and outward. It is conceivable in principle, though I can think of no actual instance, that such an instrumentality might so conduct and so advertise its affairs in all aspects for all to see that everyone would be continuously aware of at least as much as he wanted to know about them, without formal reporting or auditing arrangements. It would not be enough merely to make, or offer to make, any desired information available on request, for too much would then be left in obscurity for want of attention. In the absence of such a full familiarity, the function of rendering an accounting to outsiders is sometimes remedial, sometimes to flag an occasion for questioning, but usually to forestall doubts by giving the psychological reassurance either that all is well, or, if not, that someone else is duly told off to watch for trouble and will set any necessary steps in train. For these purposes someone on the outside must be kept informed and on the alert, at least occasionally or periodically, if not continuously.

The foundations of accountability are self-knowledge and a forthcoming disposition; both of these are susceptible of improvement by external stimuli. Evidently, an outfit that does not know what is going on within its own domain is in no position to answer for its conduct, as some welfare agencies in New York City learned when OEO programs and funds came their way and auditors presently followed. Records and procedures calculated to assure fidelity in transactions and to furnish the data for self-study and planning, for analyses of resources, programs, and performance are an indispensable minimum. And notwithstanding the Freedom-of-Information Act that Congress finally enacted, federal agencies have at least four grounds for claiming confidentiality for various aspects of their operations. It would be surprising if their contractors and grantees did not press corresponding claims as against public disclosure: (1) secrets touching national security; (2) trade secrets—information furnished by business firms with an understanding or pledge that it would not be accessible to their competitors, customers or suppliers; (3) privacy for personnel files of employees; and (4) privacy for internal and inter-agency communications and deliberations regarding positions and actions still tentative and not yet ripe for public discussion—in the interest of securing candid discussion and advice in executive councils. If it is nevertheless the policy of the contractor—and if he enjoys sufficient independence to make the option his—to publish frequent and reasonably full reports of his activities and to establish a reputation for responding to requests for further information, then all subsequent stages and forms of accountability dwindle in need and significance.

The main path of accountability no doubt leads ordinarily from the contractor directly to the funding agency. There if anywhere he should find both understanding and sympathy. If the relationships are at arms-length but marked by mutual trust and respect, then again subsequent proceedings elsewhere are apt to become formalities, since the whole range of questions—fidelity, efficiency, policy, and operational consequences—is open for examination at this stage. If on the other hand the relationships are too cosy, or contrariwise antagonistic, it is fair to ask in some other forum who has been had, and by whom. The answer may go one way at the bureau level and another way in the office of the Secretary or the general counsel or the management staff of the department.

In either event this path, though direct and always available, is not the only one. No doctrine of the exhaustion of administrative remedies shields the contractor from other inquisitorial bodies until the contracting agency is through with him. He may be hauled into court by prosecution of the Justice Department or at the suit of an injured third party if he has transgressed the criminal law or given a civil cause of action. The terms of his contract, the Treasury checks he cashes and the vouchers, payrolls and suporting papers he submits to justify payments are all open to the Comptroller General's post-audit examination and approval. Members and other agents of any of several congressional committees can reach through and around his contracting agency and summon him to testify. The Comptroller General is concerned with efficiency as well as fidelity: a congressional inquiry is unconfined. The contracting agency may try to run interference for him in either of these arenas, taking on a share of the responsibility if it does so. Other federal agencies, for instance the Equal Employment Opportunity Commission, or the Office of Federal Contract Compliance or the Wage and Labor Standards Administration, both in the Labor Department, the Internal Revenue Service, and so on, may monitor those aspects of his operations that fall within their jurisdictions. Finally, if he is a big fellow his contract may come to the attention of the Budget Bureau, and only in this case will the contact be necessarily indirect, through the contracting agency.

Among congressional committees, a minimum of three in either chamber—Appropriations, Legislative, and Government Operations—have overlapping jurisdictions to examine into his contract and performance, and, unlike most of the executive agencies noted, all have a subpoena power to compel the production of papers and the attendance of witnesses. No questions are off limits in a congressional inquiry, though the committees' interests are specialized and their time and staff are limited. Statistically speaking, it is highly improbable that any particular contractor, unless by his own seeking or unless he has already attracted notice in the Press, will be summoned to appear before a committee; or, if he is, that more than a fragment of his contractual operation comes under scrutiny by examiners knowledgeable in the premises.

What has been said about the contractor applies also, by and large, to the beneficiaries of federal grants, with two general reservations. Since the obligations the grantee assumes are not usually enforceable in the courts, as are contracts with penalty clauses, performance bonds, and so on, the remedies for failures of performance, if any, must be political and administrative.

And since the grantees are themselves often governmental units or eleemosynary institutions, or individuals selected by one of these, the available sanctions are likely to be subject to political constraints. Shutting off a grant may penalize the beneficiary more than the offending party. But the categories are so diverse that the differences among contractors and grantees, respectively, are greater than those between them. Some grants are said to aim merely at supplying federal funds to reinforce selected state or municipal functions, while other grants enlist state resources and agencies as aids in the performance of federal functions— assuming that such a distinction can any longer be drawn.

Finally, the ranks of official bodies empowered to bring contractors and grantees to account are supplemented by two sorts of unofficial guardians, or whistle-blowers. One comprises the news media, where there is a long tradition of doing well by doing good. The other is typified by a number of specialized pressure group associations, like the Sierra Club, Common Cause, or taxpayers' organizations, dedicated to ideological causes; lately another kind has emerged, the public service law firm, on the model of Nader's raiders. The legal standing of these self-appointed auditors to examine and challenge is often questionable, but they have nonetheless had an impact on behavior and on avowed standards.

PROBLEMS AND STANDARDS

Independence has virtues and attractions in the eyes of the planners, managers and operators of the federal government's programs such that over the past thirty years contracts and grants —which are organizational ways of harnessing the energies that independence inspires—have become standard methods of getting the government's work done. Because these forms relax the operation of hierarchical principles and erode the distinction between public and private—time-honored ways of assigning responsibility —their widespread use arouses concern for the preservation and improvement of means for assuring public accountability on the part of contractors and grantees. The problems of administering any federal system of accountability are complicated, as the problems of getting substantive programs carried out may be alleviated, by the vast multiplication of organizational units to be monitored, and their heterogeneous character.

Independence, however, is fundamental also to the design of our system of accountability—independence coupled with knowledgeability. As long ago as 1789, in the establishment of the Treasury Department, the framers of our government built in an administrative separation of powers for handling government funds, calculated to ensure that several distinct officers had the means of becoming familiar with the details of every transaction, at the same time that each had a step to take in order to complete it.

The heritage of these arrangements is such that in present-day circumstances our main reliance must be upon two resources, the contracting or fund-granting department or agency and the General Accounting Office. The one is best informed and has the chief responsibility for obtaining operating results; the other has a staff and mandate for continuous surveillance with a government-wide jurisdiction to maintain fidelity and promote efficiency. The rest have contingent and sporadic roles and disparate perspectives, frequently useful, sometimes essential, but seldom systematically reliable.

The contracting bureau may be too involved in the contractor's reputation for success to keep the detachment needed for impartial appraisal. The departmental secretary's staff may have the detachment but, with a wider span of activities to supervise and a higher turnover of personnel, lack the sustained attention. If the contractor or grantee is, or derives from, an elected local government, both bureau and department may be politically disarmed.

The GAO has all the political independence that could be wished. The statutory definition of its powers has been broadened but not greatly changed from those vested in the Comptroller of the Treasury before 1921. The great change arose from transferring the Office bodily out of the Treasury, and giving its head a fifteen-year term with a virtual guarantee against removal. The change in status has been reinforced by a vast improvement in the professional calibre and range of talent of its staff, and by a marked shift in outlook and emphasis, and consequent raising of sights. But like every police force, the GAO has finite resources; it cannot be everywhere all the time with equal attention and effectiveness. It too must have its own priorities, among which contractors and grantees will not always necessarily rank at the top. In the nature of things its priorities must be importantly influenced by the priorities of congressional committee chairmen, and particularly by those of the Appropriations, Government Operations and Judiciary committees. The number of organizations and the volume of transactions is so large that sampling and selection are inevitable.

There is then no single royal road to accountability, but instead some dozens or scores of paths more or less traveled, more or less tangled. In a relatively open society the strategy of the public interest depends on faith that sporadic abuses can be kept within tolerable limits by sample checks, while systematic abuses will attract the notice of someone who will alert one or another of the many potential policemen around, before things get out of control. There is, moreover, no sharp demarcation of the limits of accountability that the departments, the GAO, the Office of Budget and Management, the congressional committees and other guardians can severally enforce upon contractors and grantees. We are brought then to a concluding paradox: the more avenues there are for exacting accountability, the more difficult it seems to be to pinpoint responsibility for seeing that it is exacted. Who guards the guardians? At some point in the system, as Woodrow Wilson observed, someone must be trusted.

Index

Warner, D. C., xiii, 30, 198, 207ff., 214–28

Warren (Comptroller-General), 247

Weapon construction, 19. *See also* Military-industrial complex

Weapons market, 153ff., 254–5; and cost, 155–6; and size of systems, 156; and technology, 154ff.; competition in, 157ff.; contractors and subcontractors 160ff., 171; government involvement, 157ff.; time factor, 156–7

Weber, M., 1

Welfare, *see* Social welfare

Westinghouse, 160

Wilson, W., 297

Wolfle, D., xiii–xiv, 25, 109–48

World Bank, 49

World Wars, 6

Zoological gardens, 69